THE DIALECTICAL CONFLICT

of Religious and Secular Ideologies in the Middle East:

A Philosophical and Historical Analysis

DR. MAMOON AMIN ZAKI

outskirts press

The Dialectical Conflict of Religious and Secular Ideologies in the Middle East:
A Philosophical and Historical Analysis

v2.0

Outskirts Press, Inc.
http://www.outskirtspress.com

ISBN: 978-1-4787-9626-8

Library of Congress Control Number: 2018902773.

PRINTED IN THE UNITED STATES OF AMERICA

FOR

My late father, Muhammad Amin Zaki (Beg), the multilingual intellectual author who inculcated the love of knowledge in all of us, his children.

My late avid reader mother, (Hajjiya) Fawziah Muhammad Salih (Beg) al-Hurmuzi.

My late older sisters, Dr. Saniha Amin Zaki and Dr. Lam'an Amin Zaki, the medical professors who graduated hundreds of physicians scattered all over the world.

My precious family: my beloved wife, Hanan Aboud Jayid, and my dear children, Amin, Jasmine, and Miriam, and my granddaughters, Jenna and Ayyah.

They all enlighten my life and inspire me to keep contributing regardless of age.

Special Thanks

I am deeply thankful to my dear daughter attorney, Jasmine M. Zaki, whom I entrusted to edit this book in order to make it a family enterprise.

I am also thankful to my dear son, Amin M. Zaki, and my daughter, Miriam M. Zaki, who were instrumental in finding the right publisher for my book. And finally, to my wife Hanan, for her continuous support.

TABLE OF CONTENTS

ABSTRACT

This book explores the nature of two opposing ideologies in the Middle East: Islamic religiousness and secularism.

Utilizing Georg W. Hegel's dialectical conceptualization of the thesis, antithesis and synthesis, the author provides a historical exploration of the nature of the ideological conflict in the Middle East, which began in the nineteenth century and fully erupted after World War I. Since the collapse of the Islamic theocratic regime of the Ottoman Empire in 1918, two diametrically opposed ideologies, secular and religious, have been competing to overtake the Middle East.

One of the main objectives of this book is to illustrate that both secular and religious ideologies stem from the same two sources: awareness of social backwardness—characterized by rampant poverty and illiteracy, oppression of women, racial hostility, nomadism, religious fanaticism, and lack of education—and frustration with the Western imperialist power. Leaders who adhere to Islamic religion as an ideology, as well as those who choose secularism, are both convinced that they are providing the best means to serve their people in providing social advancement and countering the imperialist menace of the Great Powers.

The exploration of the regional social change typifies Hegel's perception of history and development: "Every historical process is something new under the sun; and nothing is ever precisely like anything before it." Any true law of historical change must conceive it as a progressive development in which every stage or "moment" is viewed both as a necessary consequence of its predecessor and radically different from it.

Hegel emphasizes the role of leaders as the power and force behind the movements of human history. Leaders, whom he describes as the instruments of dialectic change, possess two elements: ideas and passion for social change.

In the Middle East, leaders who typify Hegel's perception are: Kemal Ataturk, Gamal Abdel Nasser, Saddam Hussein, Ayatollah Al-Khomeini; Mohammed Morsi, and Recep Tayyip Erdogan. In later sections, we will delve more deeply into these leaders and their roles and influence as the instruments of dialectical change.

INTRODUCTION

The word "ideology" first made its appearance in France during the French Revolution, when A.L.C. de Tracy introduced "ideologies" as a short name for what he called the "science of ideas." Several other vague definitions were given for this term, and two of the most prominent philosophers in world thinking, G.W. Hegel and Karl Marx, used it in a pejorative way, describing ideology as "false consciousness." In modern usage, ideology is a set of beliefs and ideas that determine day-to-day, short- and long-range attitudes towards life.

This book provides an historical analysis of the dialectical nature of the ideological conflict that has been taking place in the Middle East since the end of World War I. The analysis typifies Georg W. Hegel's perception of the nature of events, as he asserts that history can be understood in terms of the movement of the dialectic, or a conflict of opposites. God is the author of the world and the idea is the plot.[1] The idea is in perpetual development and at constant war with itself, hence pushing forward the processes of historical changes.

History is a never-ending battlefield of ideas. The core of the dialectic theory is that at any point in time, an idea may be called a "thesis," which is the established manifestation of the pattern of the current historical period. A thesis, however, will not stay firm or unchanged forever. It will sooner or later give birth, phylogenetically, to an idea which stands in direct contradiction to that represented by its parent. There is a period of time where the offspring, or antithesis, will continue to co-exist with the thesis, despite the tension, disagreement

1 See Carl J. Friedrich (Editor), The Philosophy of Hegel (New York: The Modern Library 1954 Introduction).

and enmity that occur as a result of the conflicting ideas. This coexistence will likely result in dissidence, but it will be impossible to call one side the decisive victor and the other side vanquished. While the antithesis will be present, it will not completely annihilate the thesis. Furthermore, the struggle itself will transmute the antithesis so that it no longer is the purely antagonistic spirit it once was. The surviving remnants of the thesis and the battle-worn antithesis may combine in the "synthesis," which rises from the ashes of the conflict. This synthesis, once it has firmly established itself, becomes a new thesis. It will immediately conceive within itself its own antithesis. Thus, the dialectic is in continuous progression.[2] Hegel's theory provides a clear analytical framework to understand the nature of the present and the foreseeable future periods of the Middle East.

The term "Middle East" was invented in 1902 by the American naval historian Alfred Thayer Mahan to specify the area between Arabia and India, with the center—as perceived by Mahan—in the Gulf. However, today the term designates ethnic groups of Arabs, Turks, Persians and others, rather than a geographic area that extends from the Black Sea to equatorial Africa and from India to the Atlantic.

Since the collapse in the 1920s of the long-lasting thesis of the theocratic regime of the Ottoman Empire, two diametrically opposed ideologies, secular and religious, have been competing to overtake the region of the Middle East. Kemalism, Nasserism and Ba'athism are all aspects of secular ideologies (the thesis), while the movements of Al-Ikhwan al Muslimoon or the Muslim Brotherhood, and Khomeinism (the antithesis) are manifestations of religious ideologies. These ideologies will be described in more detail later.

Secularism is a belief system that rejects spiritual, ecclesiastic or religious beliefs in general. In politics, the term means that the state's leadership, power and authority, political institutions and services are controlled by worldly individuals who do not derive their plans, methods of rule and administration, and legislation from religion or religious sources. The religious ideology draws from religious texts and clergymen to apply its governing rule and administration of the public.

2 Georg W. Hegel, The Philosophy of History (New York 1956), translated by J. Sibree, p. 27.

They depend on their practical worldly experiences to implement their administration and legal duties.

The relationship between these two ideologies is of a dialectical nature. Each ideology gives birth to its opposite, or antithesis, thereby perpetuating the conflict.

The main objective of this book is to illustrate that both types of ideologies, the secular and religious, stem from the same sources: awareness of social backwardness, and frustration with the Western imperialist power. Leaders who adhere to Islamic religion as an ideology or those who choose secularism are both motivated to advance social progressiveness and oppose the imperialist menace of the Great Powers.

For almost thirteen centuries, the thesis of Islam dominated most aspects of Middle Eastern culture and was the pillar of several powerful empires, the last of which was the Ottoman Empire. [3] Islam was not only a religion but a way of life, a factual belief, an absolute truth, or briefly, an ideology that determined the social, economic, political, psychological and private lives of the people.

After the collapse of the Ottoman Empire, Islamic ideology, despite its overwhelming dominance, was seriously challenged by Kemalism, a secular ideology that represented the antithesis of Islam. It was forged by Mustafa Kemal Ataturk, an Ottoman military officer who later founded and became president of modern Turkey. Personifying the "progressive" late nineteenth century's Ottoman generation, which had been exposed to Western civilization, Kemal, a keen reader, was deeply influenced by the secularism of the Enlightenment and by the scientific positivism of Auguste Comte and Emile Durkheim, in which information is derived from sensory experiences and interpreted through reason and logic. Integrating European philosophers with ideas of the Turkish writers of the nineteenth century who preached social reform through modernization, Kemal set forth an ideology that he thought would extricate Turkey from the medieval legacy of Ottoman societal stagnation and propel it into the twentieth century along with the "civilized" European nations.

3 Muhammad Mahdi Shams al-Din, al-Ilmaniyah: Secularism: Critical Analysis (Beirut: State Institution for Studies and Publication, 1996), p. 126.

Kemalism precipitated substantial social change in Turkey, which was imitated by Iran and, to a lesser degree, other countries. Iran's Shah Mohammad Reza Pahlavi literally followed Kemal's secular ideology, and several prominent Arab thinkers perceived that Kemalism was the most effective ideological framework to attain independence from Western imperialism and achieve social progress.

In comparing the Ottoman theocracy with European modern societies, Mustafa Kemal believed that the main factor contributing to his country's lack of social progression was religion. He believed that religion was keeping the Turkish people illiterate, fatalistic and ignorant, while secularization and positive scientific thinking in Europe precipitated democracy, technological progress and advanced civilization. Thus, as president of the Republic of Turkey, Mustafa Kemal sought to remove all Islamic institutions and embarked on a profound plan of secularization, Westernization and social reform.[4]

Yet, Kemalism generated a fierce antithetical reaction—powerful Islamic movements in more than one country. The *ulema*, or religious scholars in Turkey, the *mullah*, clergy in Iran, and the movement of al-Ikhwan al Muslimoon (the Muslim Brotherhood) in Egypt, all strongly denounced Kemalism as an evil Western ideology aimed to destroy Islamic culture.[5]

Established in 1928, the Muslim Brotherhood grew into a highly organized ideological and semi-military organization that keenly opposed all ideas that contravened Islam, such as secularism, Kemalism, socialism or communism. The Brotherhood consistently attempted to establish branches in Islamic countries. Their main objective was to recreate an Islamic theocracy that would encompass all Muslims of the world.

However, during the 1950s and 1960s, the Middle East was overtaken by the leadership of Egypt's Gamal Abdel Nasser. Although other "progressive" movements such as Ba'athism and communism were also active, Nasser was the paramount political figure in the Middle East.

4 See Sydney N. Fisher, The Middle East: A History (New York: McGraw-Hill, Inc. 1990), Chapter 32.

5 Karen Armstrong, Islam: A Short History (New York: The Modern Library, 2002), pp. 155, 184-185.

Nasserism, with its pan-Arabism, socialism, anti-imperialism and anti-Zionism, fascinated the Middle East masses and galvanized them under Nasser's leadership. During the time that Nasser was the leader of Arab nationalism, religious movements went into ebb and Islam's political role in the Middle East was practically nonexistent.[6] The Muslim Brotherhood was not able to garner the support that Nasser did, and their role was minimal.

After Nasser's defeat by Israel in 1967 and his death in the 1970s, the Middle East witnessed an upsurge in no other ideology but Islam, the antithesis to Nasserism. The people felt that Islam was their only option to fill the ideological vacuity created by the failure of Nasserism and other ideologies.

Nasser's successor, Egyptian President Anwar el-Sadat, attempted to synthesize Islamic thought with Westernization, but in 1981 he was assassinated by Muslim zealots because of his rapprochement with Israel and his pro-United States policy. Sadat was perceived as the enemy of Islam who sold himself to the American-Zionist imperialist forces.

The religious ideology kept growing menacingly and eventually led to a destructive conflict with its antithesis—nationalism. The Iran-Iraq War (1980–1988) between Iran and Iraq represented the climax of the conflict between secular and religious ideologies in the Middle East. From 1968 to 2003, Iraq was ruled by the Ba'ath Party, bearing a socialist, pan-Arabist ideology, while Iran, after the downfall of Shah Mohammad Reza Pahlavi in 1979, was re-established into a full Islamic theocracy. In 1980, the two countries became entangled in a destructive war and the entire world was apprehensively awaiting its outcome. Had Iran won the war, the entire region would have fallen under its religious wave, but the Iraqi-Arab army was able to forestall the Iranian onslaught, thereby retaining the secular Ba'ath regime in Iraq. Yet despite its military setback, the Iranian regime remained and continues to represent proof of success for the ubiquitous Islamic movements in the Middle East.[7]

6 See Fisher: See Chapter 45.

7 Armstrong, pp. 173-175.

Competition between the two conflicting ideologies continued into the twenty-first century as a result of the United States' invasion of Iraq in March 2003. That invasion marked the end of the Ba'ath Party rule, which had lasted for more than three decades, and ushered Iraq into a new American-influenced era aspiring for democracy, modernization and prosperity. The new regime in Iraq would provide a model for other Middle Eastern countries. However, the majority of the Iraqis were and continue to be more prone to draw their constitution from the Holy Quran and Islamic *shari'ah* (holy code). Hence, the conflict between the religious and secular ideologies will continue unabated for the foreseeable future.

Studying the conflict between secular and religious ideologies in the Middle East will assist in understanding the nature of the upheavals which have erupted in that region for the last several decades and will probably continue to afflict it for several decades throughout the twenty-first century.

Chapter I

THE LAST PERIOD OF THE OTTOMAN THEOCRACY

HEGEL STATES THAT it is not a difficult matter for a student of politics to have an idea to establish a thesis of his own, nor is it hard to know when a war of ideas is actually in a society's mind.

To simplify his perception, Hegel puts his thoughts in a semi-mathematical equation. He states that if men set about to accomplish (X) they will also, without realizing it, put in motion forces that will lead to (Y), and (Y) will be in direct conflict with (X). Yet a synthesis of (X) and (Y) would continue for a certain period of time. During this period of synthesis, the old thesis (X) gradually fades away as (Y) emerges from the synthesis to become a new thesis. Thus the process of dialectic continues.[8] This logic will be utilized throughout the study to clearly illustrate the dialectical nature of the ideologies in the Middle East since the last period of the Ottoman theocracy, which is perceived in this chapter as (X), while its opposition, the secular Kemalist Republic of Turkey, is (Y).

The Islamic Ottoman state (X) came into being around the year 1300 under the leadership of Osman, son of Ertogrul Beg, a Turkish frontier warrior who possessed the land of Sogut as a fief. It was Osman's son, Orhan, who gathered the tribes into a nation under the banner of Islam, while his son Murad I embarked on expanding the state into an empire. After several centuries, the Islamic state was brought to an end with the abolition of the theocratic sultanate (X) and the proclamation

8 Georg W. F. Hegel, Philosophy of History (New York) Dover 1956, translated by J. Sibree, p. 27.

of a secularist Turkish republic (Y) in October 1924.

At the time of its greatest splendor, during the fifteenth to seventeenth centuries, the Ottoman Empire extended from the Crimea to the Sudan, from Iraq to Bosnia, from Caucasus to the Maghrib.[9] Within its confines it embraced numerous nations, creeds, languages and traditions.

It was neither race nor language but religious allegiance which determined the status of groups and the individuals within the society. The Shari'ah, the sacred law of Islam, provided the foundation of the entire social infrastructure of the Ottoman state. Its Muslim majority, regardless of ethnicity, were first-class citizens, while other creeds were treated according to the Holy Quran's perception of *Ahl al-Kitab*, people of the scripture who were allowed to live under their own religious law subject to their acceptance of the status of *dhimmi*, or protected subject. This status involved the payment of a slightly higher rate of taxes and poll tax not levied on the Muslims. Religious communities comprised of Greek Orthodox, Catholics or Jews were established and given the name of "millet," an autonomous self-governing religious community, each organized under its own laws and headed by a religious leader. The ecclesiastic dignitaries and the wealthier class formed within each millet, and the elite were endowed with autonomous control over communal affairs. The Muslims also constituted a millet, but it was one which wielded supreme power in the state.[10]

The Ottoman Empire was established as a despotic militaristic and absolute theocratic state. The sultan possessed supreme spiritual and political authority. The tendency to keep the sultans in absolute power was probably intensified by the institution of the janissary (the new military system), which was formed about the year 1355 by Sultan Orkhan and blessed by Sheikh Bakdash, a mystic cleric who headed the sophist Bakdashi order. The janissary had carried the Islamic flag to victory in landmark battles and had become a great striking force, and the spearhead of the Ottoman army.

9 Lord Eversley, The Turkish Empire, Its Growth and Decay (London: T. Fisher Unwin Ltd., 1917), p. 148.

10 Abu Khaldun, Sati al-Husary, Muhadarat Fi Nushu' al-fikrah al-qawmigya (Lectures on the Incipience of Nationalistic Ideas) Beirut: Dar. al Ilm Lil, Malayin 1964, pp. 194-195.

The growth of the Ottoman Empire had continued almost unchecked from the time Sultan Mehmet the Conqueror captured Constantinople in 1453, until 1683, when King John Sobieski of Poland compelled the Ottomans to cease the siege of Vienna. The victory over the Turks in Vienna, however, marked the zenith of the Ottoman Islamic expansionism. From that time onward it declined, and after 1800, it quickly began to disintegrate.[11]

The sultans of the nineteenth century were weak figures who lacked the strength to meet the vicissitudes befalling the empire. To cope with the corruption, inefficiency, incompetence, harem indulgence[12] and the vested interest and indolence of the court, great willpower was required—willpower that most of those sultans lacked.

They also lacked comprehension of the legal policies and norms of their country and the importance of training and education, because each one of them came to the throne after decades of confinement, having been denied the opportunity to learn the craft of statesmanship or develop an effective personality. Often the sultan's mother or a wife dominated the government, although these women also lacked experience to conduct the functions of the state.[13]

Early in the nineteenth century, under diplomatic and economic pressures by the European countries, several attempts were made to change the nature of the Ottoman state and inject into its ailing system some of the democratic European practices. The *hatt-i humayun* (Imperial Words) of the 1850s is often described as the Magna Carta of the Ottomans. The hatt-i humayun endorsed a previous reform decree, called the imperial words of order; however, the new decree was more specific in its details and more extensive in scope.[14] The hatt-i humayun and Tanzimat were concerned with the amelioration of the conditions of minorities, enforcement of justice, modernization of the legal

11 William Miller, The Ottoman Empire 1801–1913 (Cambridge: The University Press 1913), pp. 212-229.

12 Ali al-Wardi, Lamahat Ijtima'iyah min Tarikh al-Iraq al-Hadith (Glimpses from the Modern History of Iraq) Vol. II (Baghdad: al-Irshad Press 1971, pp. 66-68.

13 Miller, pp. 212-229.

14 Sir Edward Shepherd Creasy, History of the Ottoman Empire (London, Richard Bentley & Son, 1877), pp. 531-543.

system and improvement of the social and economic infrastructures.[15]

Social change was accelerated greatly by the Crimean War (1854–1856). England, France and Scandinavia were allied with the Ottoman Empire during this war and were determined to preserve it against destruction by Russia.[16]

The presence in Istanbul of large numbers of British, French and Italian troops, as well as government officials, merchants, journalists and tourists, had a marked sociological effect upon the Muslims. Contacts between East and West had never been so widespread, and the money spent by the Western allies in Turkey gave many Ottoman people the financial means to satisfy their desire for European travel, books and ideas. A European education became the fashion and every young man of a good, ambitious family was sent to Paris, Geneva, London or other cities to acquire as much Western culture as possible.[17] Hence, the seed of the secular antithesis (Y) of the long-lasting thesis of the Islamic theocracy was planted in the womb of the Ottoman Empire.

The last three decades of the Ottoman rule witnessed a vigorous dialectical conflict between the religious and secular ideologies as the Ottoman youth became indoctrinated into the European culture.

THE REIGN OF SULTAN ABDUL HAMID II

On August 31, 1876, Abdul Hamid, a shrewd and conservative prince, was declared sultan of the Ottoman Empire after his brother, Sultan Murad, became mentally ill and was pronounced unfit to rule. Before and upon his enthronement, Abdul Hamid enjoyed a reputation as a devout, liberal-minded and progressive prince. Both European powers and some of his subjects had occasion to test him during the first year of his reign. The powers were outspoken in their insistence on reform in the provinces' administration. When Abdul Hamid assumed the throne as the caliphate of the Muslim world, two political parties were forming.

A group of men in Turkey found that studying Western political

15 Ibid.
16 Al-Wardi, pp. 66-68.
17 Lord Eversley, p. 270.

constitutions and practices would greatly benefit their country. One of the leaders of this newly forming political party was Midhat Pasha, a highly educated lawyer and extremely competent official who had begun to develop in the 1860s as a provincial governor in European Ottoman territories and then later in Baghdad.[18] The party was distinctly liberal, progressive and Western in its desire for constitutional government, fiscal reform, economic progress, separation of religion and state, and industrial and commercial development.

The other party, under the leadership of Damad Jalal and Redif Pasha, was conservative, corrupt and composed of self-serving, ruthless and narrow-minded religious men.[19]

Meanwhile, since the Crimean War (1854–1856), the Ottoman society had been witnessing social change. In the spring of 1854, a large Russian army crossed the Danube River into Turkish territory. The Ottoman sultan, Abdulmecid I, called for help from his allies, Britain and France, and Russia was defeated.[20] The war inadvertently led to significant alteration in the Ottoman beliefs. Due to intermingling with the British and French, the youthful Muslim soldiers were exposed for the first time to the European modern concepts of democracy, human rights, constitutional government and women's rights. As a result, French-style liberalism and urbanity became the fashion.

After dramatic successes in initiating deep reform in different parts of the empire, Midhat returned in 1872 to Istanbul, where he drew a new law of the provinces. However, Midhat's most unforgettable feat was his long and difficult, yet ultimately successful, effort to establish a new constitution and a representative parliament (later labeled "Midhat's Parliament"). On December 23, 1876, after being appointed grand vizier, he announced that a constitution would be promulgated and a representative parliament would be established. The new constitution created a bicameral legislature: a senate appointed by the sultan, and a chamber of deputies elected in rates of one deputy per 50,000 citizens, and declared all Ottomans of whatever creed to be

18 Ibid, pp. 311-312.
19 Ibid, pp. 43-59.
20 Sydney Nettleton Fisher, The Middle East: A History (New York: McGraw-Hill, Inc. 1990), pp. 294-295.

equal before the law.[21]

Abdul Hamid began his reign by appearing to live up to his reputation, revealing at the same time a talent for subterfuge. He named Midhat grand vizier and granted the constitution that was announced by Midhat on December 23, 1876.[22] This date coincided with the assembling of representatives from European powers conferring to draw plans promoting better government for Abdul Hamid's empire. Therefore, naming Midhat the grand vizier and announcing the new constitution was an astute move by Abdul Hamid, for it not only gave his subjects the deceptive appearance of his good intentions, but also gave him the advantage of preempting the European powers' attempt to reform the government. Abdul Hamid's euphoria, however, was short-lived. His inclinations towards democracy became less pronounced after consolidating his position on the throne. It is very difficult to determine whether Abdul Hamid's acquiescence to grant a constitution was an appeasement to the opposition and a means to satisfy the European powers, or a demonstration of initial sincerity which later changed as a result of fear and distrust.

In his widely published book entitled *The Ottoman Centuries*, Lord Kinross asserts that Abdul Hamid was not a blind reactionary. He still drew upon the West, as the forebears of Tanzimat had done, in his pursuit of modernization, not only in the field of technology, but in judicial and particularly educational reform. He expanded and brought to fruition many changes that previous reformers had planned but only partially achieved. However, the relentless pressure for quick social change by foreign powers in collaboration with the domestic reform group rendered Abdul Hamid paranoid with suspicion.[23] The shrewd sultan became convinced that the European Christian countries were overtly pressuring for reform while their covert aims were to dethrone him in order to eliminate his centralized Islamic authority as caliph of the entire Muslim world.

The constitution was originally the work of Midhat himself and

21 Miller, p. 476.

22 Al-Wardi, Vol. III, p. 14.

23 Lord Kinross, The Ottoman Centuries: The Rise and Fall of the Turkish Empire (London: Jonathan Cape 1977), pp. 513-574.

was imbued with his liberal ideas. One of his deepest beliefs was that a check on the autocratic powers of the sultan was indispensable to the welfare of the empire and, indeed, to its existence. Another was that the equality of treatment among subjects of various races was a necessary prelude to the enlistment of popular support for the constitutional government. This belief may have been based on an imperfect assessment by Midhat of the forces at work. Possibly he believed these forces to be a product of tyranny and misgovernment and failed to realize that they were, in fact, nationalistic aspirations. Or, more likely, Midhat fell prey to the European Great Powers, who were plotting to destroy the Ottoman Empire once and for all, while using the reform demands as a disguise for their real goals. In any case, the remedy Midhat sought to apply through establishing a coherent democracy was due more to his sense of justice than to his powers of discernment. In the form in which it was issued (after modification by the sultan), the constitution did not ensure real equality, but it paid due homage to equality as a principle of the government. Its main virtue, however, was that it provided for some restrictions—though not enough to satisfy Midhat's desires—on the previously unchecked behavior of the sultan.[24] Promulgation of the constitution was a great achievement by the reformist.

After cajoling both foreign and domestic powers and securing his position at the throne, the sultan was now prepared to deal with his adversaries. In February 1877, only a few months after the announcement of the constitution, Abdul Hamid abruptly dismissed Midhat Pasha and exiled him to Europe. Early in March, after having inaugurated the new parliament in a grand speech from the throne, Abdul Hamid seized upon the fears of the masses resulting from the pretext of Russia's declaration of war to decree suspension of the constitution; it remained "suspended" for thirty-one years.[25] Midhat Pasha and several of his compatriots were assassinated. Henceforth, with the constitution suspended and the opposition eliminated, Abdul Hamid was free to rule in the name of Islamic code, thereby ushering in an era of deeply traditional and theocratic rule.

24 Niyazi Berkes, The Development of Secularism in Turkey (Montreal: McGill University Press 1964), pp. 223-250.

25 Antonius, p. 64.

The foundation of Abdul Hamid's rule rested upon a group of sycophant religious men who maintained control through espionage and repression. A system developed in which the sultan employed spies for his political ends and protection. This system of employed spies became a powerful oligarchy of corrupt hoodlums against whom no one, however eminent or innocent, was safe, except, perhaps, by expedient bribery. A stifling system of censorship succeeded in eliminating any kind of literary enterprise.

The courts of justice became the subservient instruments of the palace clique and could generally be counted upon to find the required judicial grounds for imposing a preordained penalty.[26]

The two dangers most deeply feared by the sultan were attempts on his life and constitutional amendment. His spies were devoted almost exclusively to uncovering elements involved in these two endeavors. Severe punishments were inflicted based merely on suspicion of participation in either of the above matters.

To mitigate dissention and avoid a possible explosion of violent protest, the sultan embarked on substantial economic and social reform, constructing various educational institutions and universities, and developing local and international means of transportation and communication. Yet, in spite of all these constructive attempts, revolutionary movements against the sultan's tyrannical, corrupt and reactionary regime were rampant, especially among the educated youth. Further aggravating the situation was the development and growing Westernization of certain portions of the empire, and the consequent effects of contemporary democratic and secular ideas on the minds of the Turkish youth.[27] They began to question and dispute the religious authority of the sultan and the very nature of the empire's theocracy. Hence, the movement of the Young Turks was born in the very schools that the sultan himself had established. Dissention threatened to become unmanageable, and domestic and international demands for basic changes grew stronger.

The progressive movement of the national Young Turks was

26 Al-Wardi, Vol. III, p. 20.

27 Berkes, pp. 302-304.

conceived and born in the schools that the sultan himself had established. It was this same movement that later in 1909 ended the tyranny and propelled the Middle East into a synthesis period, combining (X) and (Y) as a symbolic monarchy that kept the traditional throne of the sultan-caliph, while the real power was forcefully overtaken by the opposition. This period lasted for a few years before yielding to the new thesis of the secular "Kemalist" Turk Republic. General Mustafa Kemal Pasha, who was profoundly influenced by the progressive philosophies of the Enlightenment era, became president of the newly born Turkish republic, and immediately embarked on a strenuous endeavor to remove all aspects of religious influence from the government and all curricula. Thus the thesis of the secular state was born and rigorously established amid the Middle East after almost fourteen centuries of religious theocratic reign (since the Umayyad Islamic Empire, which ruled during the seventh to eighth century A.D.).

BIRTH OF TURKISH NATIONALISM

In 1889, a group of students at the Imperial Military Medical School in Istanbul, deeply influenced by European culture, formed a clandestine revolutionary organization called the Young Turks to overthrow Abdul Hamid II, the then sultan of the Ottoman Empire who bore the title of caliph (spiritual leader of Islam) for many of the world's Muslims.

At the beginning of the Young Turks movement, an Albanian student, Ibrahim Temo, led a new organization known as the Committee of Union and Progress (CUP), whose main goal was total social reform. The organization was patterned after that of the Italian Carbonari in Italy, by which Temo was influenced, and the goals of which were to defeat tyranny and establish a constitutional government.

The CUP movement spread to the military academy, the naval academy, the veterinary school, the civil college and the artillery and engineering school, most of which were established by Abdul Hamid. The CUP espoused nationalistic ideas and reform, as suggested in the anti-sultan fiery writings of such men as Murat Beg and Ahmed Riza.[28]

In spite of the sultan's notorious spies and secret police, the CUP continued growing and gathered new members from various schools and of social prominence. CUP members, who escaped the sultan's oppression by moving to Europe, made connections with other Ottoman dissidents, among them the well-known writer Ahmed Riza, who in conjunction with Halil Ganem and other exiles, established a widely circulated monthly paper, *Meshvret* ("deliberation" or "consultation"). At the same time, Murat Beg, a teacher of history, fled to Paris and published an anti-Hamidian journal, *Mizan* ("scale" or "balance"). These two papers readily found their way to the Empire and gathered a considerable following. Eventually there arose anti-Hamidian societies in Paris, Macedonia and Salonika.

In 1907, all of these groups joined in a congress of Ottoman liberals and merged into the CUP. They set up a permanent committee in the CUP to implement the programs adopted by the congress to oppose the Ottoman authority in every way possible and plan a military uprising at a suitable time.

The CUP found the Freemason Lodge of Salonika to be well-suited for its purposes. Indeed, the CUP utilized the Freemasons' various lodges and meeting places, absorbed many of its non-Muslim members, and made good use of the organizational techniques developed by the Freemasons. It is quite likely that the work of the CUP was accelerated to an appreciable extent by the contacts with Salonika Freemasonry.[29] At this historical period, the religious (X) and the secular (Y) were in full conformation within the social structure of the Ottoman Empire.

Unlike their obedient military predecessors who were indoctrinated with religious and mystic beliefs, the young officers trained in the Ottoman military academies began to feel excited by the new revolutionary ideas. They found intolerable the social, religious and economic backwardness of their country and the scorn in which it was held by other countries. In 1906, dissatisfaction and unrest grew among the officers of the Third Army Corps stationed in Salonika. Among

28 Ernest Edmondson Ramsaur, Jr., The Young Turks: Prelude to the Revolution of 1908 (Princeton, IV. J. Princeton Univ. Press 1957), pp. 14-20.

29 Al-Wardi, Vol. III, p. 130.

them was a young man named Mustafa Kemal, later to be the founder of the Turkish Republic. Already as a young man he had exhibited the singleness of purpose and drive that was to prove so distinctive later in his life. While serving in Damascus, he organized a revolutionary cell called the "Fatherland and Freedom Society." In 1907, he was transferred to Salonika, his birth place, and presided over a conference merging the different societies into the single entity that joined the CUP. The CUP was headquartered in Salonika and began its struggle against Sultan Abdul Hamid.[30]

Of even more importance than Mustafa Kemal was the real leader of the Salonika officers, General Enver Pasha. General Enver was an extremely ambitious military officer who held the position of deputy commander in chief. When Abdul Hamid ordered an investigation of the Third Army Corps in 1908, Enver and another officer prominent in the council of the CUP captured the general sent by the sultan and shot him to death. By now the unrest in the Third Army Corps had spread to the Second Army Corps at Edizine. Faced by so serious a revolt and with the CUP openly demanding a constitutional government, the sultan resorted to threats and bribery. However, such efforts no longer had any effect, and his only course was to capitulate to the rebels' demands. Finally, bowing to European and popular pressures, on July 23, 1908, Sultan Abdul Hamid announced that the constitution was restored and ordered elections to be held for members of the Chamber of Deputies, later called the Grand National Assembly.[31] He also gradually started initiating other aspects of social reform in order to avoid sudden shocks to his conservative society.

Despite these reform attempts by the sultan, revolutionary reaction against the tyrannical regime continued to be rampant, especially among the Young Turks and in the Arab provinces, where the vast majority of the Ottoman population resided. Educated Arabs were questioning the very authenticity of the sultan's claim to the Muslim caliphate.[32] They believed that they should be ruled by Arab leadership

30 Charles Swallow, The Sick Man of Europe: Ottoman Empire to Turkish Republic 1789–1923 (London: E. Benn 1973), p. 4.

31 Sir Edwin Pears, The Life of Abdul Hamid (London: Constable 1917), pp. 292-294.

32 Antonius, p. 26.

and not by a Turk. Added to this was the growing Westernization of certain portions of the Empire and an increase in democratic ideas from educated Turkish youth.[33] Thus the secular antithesis (Y) of the Ottoman theocracy was growing quickly in the womb of the empire.

A tremendous euphoria prevailed throughout the Ottoman Empire, with Christians, Jews, Muslims and ethnic minorities expressing feelings of brotherhood toward each other and anticipating an era of freedom for all. Enver Pasha, the leader of the revolution, exclaimed in a statement from Macedonia:

> Arbitrary government has disappeared. Henceforth we are all brothers. There is no longer Bulgar, Greek, Arabs, Romans, Jews, Christians or Muslims. Under the same blue sky we are all equal, we glory in being Ottoman.[34]

This euphoria, however, was short-lived. The new trend immediately created its opposite reaction among a large segment of the populace. Soon after the restoration of the Ottoman constitution, a religious organization, the Muhammadan Society, was established in Istanbul. This society, although disguised under a religious façade, was also a political movement whose main objective was to destroy the constitution and bring the country back to the sacred law of Islam.[35]

Preaching concern about the fate of religion, "the anti-constitution" movement spread among certain soldiers and some politicians, with the claim that the constitution was an innovation of the infidels that contravened the Laws of Shari'ah and therefore it should be abolished. Within one short year after restoration of the constitution, the antithesis was created, expressed by a religious counter-revolution that struck Istanbul on April 13, 1909. Soldiers and dervishes demonstrated in the streets, firing guns and carrying signs praising the sacred law of Islam,[36] with cries of "Down with the constitution, down with the committee (CUP), long live the Shari'ah."

33 Berkes, pp. 302-304.
34 Miller, p. 476.
35 Al-Wardi, Vol. III, p. 140.
36 Kinross, pp. 576-577.

Sultan Abdul Hamid supported the counter-revolution and gave it his blessing as the religious upheaval spread throughout most parts of Turkey. However, on April 16, 1909, just three days after the demonstrations began, Mahmud Shawkat Pasha, commander of the Third Army Corps and ardent supporter of secularism and the constitution, marched on Istanbul, severely crushing the religious revolution and preserving the constitution.

Subsequently, in an executive session held on April 27, 1909, the pro-CUP parliament decided to depose Abdul Hamid. In the same decision, the parliament proclaimed Muhammed Rashad (Abdul Hamid's brother) sultan under the title of Muhammed V, Caliph of the Muslim world.[37] Hence a short period of synthesis began, during which the caliphate office, along with the highest religious office and the head of Islamic code, was retained, while real power was practiced by members of the CUP.

After Abdul Hamid was deposed in 1909, the CUP held a party congress in Salonika and established a central committee, which remained active until the end of World War I. During that period, the CUP ruled the party and the government from its headquarters in Salonika. The reins of government fell into the hands of a triumvirate of members of the Young Turks: Tal'at Pasha, Enver Pasha and Jemal Pasha,[38] with Sultan Muhammad Rashad acting only as a figurehead. When the war erupted in Europe, the great majority of the Ottomans, including Sultan Muhammad V, opposed the decision to become involved; they desired neutrality and believed that therein lay the best interests of the Empire, already torn and impoverished by wars and upheavals.

By 1914, a glory-seeking group of army leaders dominated the CUP and had come under the spell of German military influence. Guided by the ever-ambitious Enver Pasha, head of the CUP, and supported by Baron von Wangenheim, the German ambassador, the Ottoman sultan was coerced to sign a secret alliance with Germany in August 1914. By November 7, the Ottoman Empire was a full participant in

37 Al-Wardi, Vol. III, p. 145.
38 Kinross, pp. 595-596.

the war.[39] At the urging of Shaykh al-Islam, Enver shrewdly utilized the diminishing authority of Khayri Efendi and issued a *fatwa* (religious decree) declaring *jihad* (holy war) and exhorting all Muslims to join in this holy war against the infidel allies, the enemies of Islam. Although the civil authority of Shaykh al-Islam had been substantially reduced after the downfall of Sultan Abdul Hamid, the Muslim masses retained their profound respect for that religious office.

Germany's failure on the Western front in the summer of 1918 and the subsequent collapse of Germany meant the end of warfare in the Middle East, because without Germany's assistance, the archaic Ottoman Empire could not maintain effective resistance against the Allies. Shortages of every sort developed, war profiteers appeared, physical suffering among the masses became rampant, diseases and famine spread everywhere, and the already dire standard of living deteriorated even further as inflation raised the prices of all essential commodities. About 2.5 million Ottoman Muslims, approximately 18 percent of the total Ottoman Muslim population, perished between 1914 and 1918.[40] On October 30, 1918, the new Ottoman government signed an armistice with the allies, ending the war.

The war also engendered some positive results. Greeks, Arabs and other subject nationalities began to aspire for freedom and national sovereignty. Furthermore, the Middle East witnessed the presence of numerous British, French, Italian and German soldiers—and their modern equipment—for the first time. Western culture and technology had a profound impact on the native people. A new age of the Middle East was born, characterized by the fading away of the long-standing thesis of the Islamic era, X, and the birth of its secular antithesis, Y, in Turkey, Iran and some other parts of the Middle East.

39 Al-Wardi, Vol. IV, p. 18.
40 Fisher, pp. 388-389.

Chapter 2

The Birth of the Kemalist Turkish Secular Republic

After the downfall of Sultan Abdul Hamid in 1909, until the mid-1920s, the Turkish people were overtaken by tumultuous instability. Between 1911 and 1922, there were five wars between the Ottomans and the ethnic minorities under their rule, and only twenty-two months of peace.[41]

The synthetical period of post-WWI, which lasted for a decade, witnessed a typical Hegelian antagonistic coexistence between the moribund X and the vigorously growing Y. The nationalist movement (Y), led by Mustafa Kemal, was gradually undermining the sultan's theocratic authority (X). This period typifies the following Hegelian description:

> The offspring of the antithesis continues to stay with the thesis despite tension and disagreement and enmity that occurs.[42]

On April 11, 1920, in an attempt to assert his authority, Sultan Abdul Mejid I dissolved the Ottoman parliament, while on the same day, Shaykh al-Islam, as chief clerk of state, published a fatwa declaring that the nationalist forces were infidels and that it was incumbent on

41 Fisher, p. 403.

42 G.W. Hegel, Philosophy of History (New York, 1956) translated by J. Sibree, p. 9.

the believers to kill them.[43] The nationalists swiftly reacted by pressing the *mufti* (religious judge) of Ankara to announce a fatwa declaring that the sultan was under the control of foreign infidels (meaning the Western allies), that it was the duty of the faithful to reject him and his domination, and that the fatwa issued at the behest of the enemy's state lacked validity.[44] Hence the synthesis period kept seething while the Ottoman thesis was fading away.

The formation of an orderly new state was accomplished on January 30, 1921, when the Grand National Assembly (GNA) (formerly known as the Chamber of Deputies) passed ten fundamental articles as amendments to the Ottoman constitution of 1876. These articles designated the assembly as a permanent institution to be elected every two years. This development marked the incipience of the first fully secular state in the Middle East and the elimination of religious authorities from the newly born Turkish government. The Grand National Assembly was to serve as an interim government until April 20, 1924, when a new constitution was promulgated. Meanwhile, a second assembly was elected, granting Kemal and his entourage at the opening of Lausanne Conference full support in their committed stand for complete economic independence from foreign powers.

In 1922, Kemal established his people's party (Halk Firkasi) and in 1923, the name of the party was changed to the Republican People's Party (RPP) or Cimhuriyat Halk Firkasi (CHF). The CHF ideology was, in fact, a reflection of Kamal's, which will be discussed later.

On November 1, 1922, the GNA passed a law deposing Sultan Mehmed VI and voiding all laws of his government. The Nationalists took control in Istanbul on November 5, and the sultan fled aboard a British cruiser for Malta.[45] In the autumn of 1923, a new law school was inaugurated to teach lawyers and judges the fundamentals of Western laws. Then in 1926, the Grand National Assembly promulgated the new civil code and debt law based on Swiss law, while the new penal code was designed after Italian law, and the new commercial code was

43 Mango, p. 275.
44 Ibid.
45 Palmer, p. 71.

derived from the German code.[46]

When Sultan Mehmed VI left Istanbul, the Grand National Assembly declared the caliphate vacant and elected to the office Abdul Majid,[47] who was known for his pro-nationalist attitude. This period marked the end of the short transmission era which exemplified Hegel's perception of the synthesis (X and Y) that will give birth to a new thesis.

After the downfall of Sultan Abdul Hamid II, the fading spiritual authority of the sultan-caliph coexisted with the growing current of secular-nationalism until the old (Y) metamorphosed into a new thesis (X), which was the Republic of Turkey. The synthesis period came to an expected end in March 1924, when Kemal proposed that the caliphate should be abolished and the GNA approved his proposal. Caliph Sultan Abdul Hamid left Turkey accompanied by his family. This date marked the extrication of Turkey from the archaic medieval system and its propulsion into the modern twentieth century.[48] With the new codes of Western and secular nature firmly established, the old regime of the Ottomans seemed to have faded into the past for good.

On April 20, 1924, the Ottoman constitution was replaced by the widely accepted constitution of the Republic. The new constitution upheld sovereignty in the Turkish nation, represented by the Grand National Assembly. It declared that all Turks, regardless of religion, ethnicity or gender, were equal before the law and forbade special privileges for groups and individuals.[49] Freedom of speech, press and travel were guaranteed. The seat of government was Ankara and the language was Turkish. Other measures were also taken: a unified educational system was established, and the ministry and its application of Muslim canon law, the administration of pious foundations, and the office of Shaykh al-Islam were all abolished.[50]

Article 1 of the constitution states the Turkish state is a republic.[51] It

46 Fisher, p. 405.
47 Fisher, p. 404.
48 Palmer, p. 77.
49 Fisher, p. 404.
50 William Cleveland, A History of the Modern Middle East (USA: West View Press, 2009), pp. 180-181.
51 Fisher, p. 405.

is noteworthy that Kemal had the option to declare himself a constitutional king similar to the European kingdoms without any objections. Yet, Kemal chose republicanism because it was a more advanced and democratic Western system. He was convinced that the republic would better suit Turkey and expedite its political modernization. The Turkish republic was unprecedented in the Islamic world.[52]

The new government was based on democracy. In 1924–1925, the country witnessed the first experiment of a two-party system—the Progressive Republican Party and Kemal's Republican People's Party. This period lasted for nine months, followed by two decades of a one-party government controlled by Kemal and an elite constituency of his cohorts.[53]

Initially, the GNA was elected for a four-year term by universal male suffrage—women were not enfranchised until 1934. The president of the republic was elected by the GNA from its membership for a similar term. The president appointed the prime minister, who selected his cabinets from the deputies with the approval of the president and consent of the GNA. All aspects of government functions were in the hands of the Republican People's Party. Candidates for election of deputies from the various districts to the Grand National Assembly were nominated by the RPP. It also decided who could run for the various offices. Overtly all these democratic practices were impressive, but the final decisions were made by Mustafa Kemal, who assumed dictatorial powers. He determined the country's polity, selected higher official bureaucrats and imposed his decisions on the RPP as well as the entire nation. Yet, by and large, Kemal skillfully galvanized the people in the GNA by good oration and convincing arguments.[54] This was a far cry from the rule of the Ottoman sultan, who proclaimed himself the shadow of God on Earth. Kemal was convivial and convinced the masses that he knew what was best for them. He possessed a brilliant mind, was incorruptible, and proved that he was sacrificing his own interests because his paramount ambition was to serve the Turkish people. Thus he established his legitimacy and gained popularity amongst the intelligentsia.

52 Palmer, p. 77.
53 Mango, pp. 418-419.
54 Fisher, p. 405.

Reform permeated every aspect of life in Turkey in the 1920s and 1930s. At the onset, changes were rather sudden and uncoordinated. Sensing the need for a better plan for reform, Kemal outlined a well-organized blueprint for social reform termed "Kemalism," which was strictly based on six principles. They were: Republicanism, secularism, populism, nationalism, statism and continuous reform.[55] These six principles constituted the RPP campaign platform for the election of 1935. After the election was won, they became the foundation of the ideology of the newly born Turkish nation and were incorporated into the constitution in 1937.

The following is a detailed discussion of the six principles of Kemalism.

SECULARISM

The most important reform decision was the secularization of the state and society. Islamic religion permeated all aspects of life in Turkey, and Kemal and his cohorts, as a result of close contact with Western culture, were strongly convinced that religion was hampering society's progress and leading to notable differences between the West and East. Hence, Kemal began to enforce his secular plan throughout the country.

The Muslim calendar for legal, official and everyday use was expunged and replaced by the western Gregorian calendar. Throughout the country the Muslim "Hijri" year of 1342 became 1926. The Muslim calendar was kept only for calculating Ramadan, the month of fasting, and all other religious holidays.[56]

In 1925, Sufi orders were dissolved, Sufi practices were banned, and holy shrines were closed. Perhaps most surprising of all was the law that upset most adult males, forbidding them to wear the fez (the traditional Turkish cap).[57] Kemal told his people that henceforth they were to wear

55 Cleveland, pp. 180-183.

56 Ibid, p. 437.

57 See Fahmi Huwaidi "al-ilminiyun yastabdiloon salaf bi salaf" (The Secularists Exchange Past by Past) al-khalij, No. 2753, 4/11/1986.

European-style clothes, beginning with European hats. Headgear had been a distinguished mark of ranks, profession and religion throughout the history of Turkey and most of the rest of the Middle Eastern countries. The turbans, fez and bonnets were a display of gender, rank and profession—civil or military. In particular, Kemal considered the fez as an eminent symbol of the Middle East. Hence, he viewed changing of the fez to Western hats as a major step towards modernization.

The fez had evolved out of the red, soft cap of Mediterranean sailors and derived its name from Fez, one of the main cities of Morocco. Imposed by edict, the fez had been taken to heart by the Ottoman Muslim middle class, although it was worn by a good number of Ottoman Christians as well. However, because the Christians' mentality was closer to that of the Europeans', many of them wore the rimmed European hat, known in Turkey as the shapka. For the majority of Ottomans, the shapka was the distinguished mark of the infidel.[58]

In World War I, Enver Pasha dealt with the problem by introducing a sloping rimless topi, which became known as the *enverye*. To deter all possible negative reactions, Mustafa Kemal rejected the euphemism and called the new head cover a shapka. He wanted to incorporate the hat as part of the "civilized dress,"[59] the Ottoman dress of the civilized people. Kemal was convinced that all civilized people should have the same way of life; that culture and civilization were synonymous. So, too, were orientalism (*sharkilik*) and backwardness. In several newspapers, Kemal was photographed wearing a Western hat, and he ordered the armed forces to wear Western-style military caps.

Women's veils were discouraged but never outlawed. Most women wore long head scarves which they drew across their faces in the presence of a male stranger. The government of the republic banned the head scarf in official premises, including schools under civil service regulations. In perorations exhorted on several occasions, Kemal asserted, "Friends, our women have minds like men's. Veils, head scarves and others are imposed on women as a result of male selfishness, as symbols of scruples and purity. Now you can teach women morals and

58 Mango, p. 436.
59 Ibid, pp. 436-437.

stop being selfish. Let them show their faces to the world and see it with their eyes. Don't be afraid, changes are essential."[60]

Kemal was determined to create a new environment that established greater equality between genders. He was an ardent believer of emancipation of women and encouraged Turkish women to imitate the stylish behavior of European women. Defying the disapproval of the religious and traditional men, a substantially progressive step was initiated by adoption of universal education, which qualified women to enter public life. By 1933, there were thirteen female judges in Turkey. In 1934, women were enfranchised and allowed to run as candidates for the GNA; the 1935 election resulted in seventeen female delegates elected to the GNA.[61]

In addition to changing clothing styles and encouraging women's liberation, Kemal targeted the Muslim Brotherhood. In a speech, he referred to the shrines of Muslim saints, saying "it is a disgrace for a civilized society to appeal for help from the dead."[62]

While Western law had a profound effect on elevating the low status of women, one of the reforms was the official banning of polygamy. Yet, it had little actual effect because, in the twentieth century, not many men could afford to marry more than one wife due to the high cost of living. More consequential were equal rights of divorce, joint custody of children, and equality in both inheritance and courtroom testimony.[63] These new measures, however, while effective in the cities, were mostly ignored in the countryside.

POPULISM

During the Ottoman Empire, the capitulations (fifteenth-century trade agreements with Christian states) and the millet system (separate legal court under which certain communities were allowed to rule themselves under their own system) gave special privileges to foreigners and numerous religious minorities. These systems were abolished

60 Palmer, p. 82. Also see Bernard Lewis, The Emergence of Modern Turkey (Oxford University Press, 1961), p. 263.

61 Mango, p. 435.

62 Ibid, p. 437.

63 Fisher, p. 407.

by Mustafa Kemal as he stated his principles of "populism." Populism was put into practice to increase interaction between the state and the people. Article 69 of the constitution states that all Turks are equal before the law and that all privileges of whatever description claimed by groups, classes, families and individuals are to be abolished and forbidden. To win the support of the poor and peasant classes, and to revamp domestic production, in 1925 the Grand National Assembly abolished the religious tithe upon lands, and eased taxes on agriculture.

To eliminate another religious characteristic of the Ottoman theocracy, Kemal coerced the Grand National Assembly to pass a decision replacing the Arabic alphabet, which was the language of the Quran, with Latin characters. From 1929 onward, all public signs, newspapers, books, etc. were published in the new script. Eventually, the old education system faded away, while the new generations were exposed only to the new pedagogical system.

The second phase of populism was universal education. Primary education in government-supervised schools became free and obligatory. Schools were built by the thousands. Each village was required to establish a primary school, while secondary schools were constructed in towns to prepare students for vocations and higher education. Graduates of high schools were admitted to Ankara University and the University of Istanbul. As a result, literacy in Turkey increased 80 percent.[64] Between 1923 and 1940, the number of schools in the country doubled, the number of teachers increased by 133 percent, and the number of students increased by nearly 300 percent.[65] By the end of 1929, a million children and illiterate adults (about one in sixteen of the total population) had learned how to read due to this rigorous education discipline and the new alphabet.

STATISM

This principle of Kemalism dealt with modernizing the economy and making Turkey independent from foreign influence. Kemal fervently desired to develop the economic sources of his country and

64 Ibid.
65 Cleveland, p. 183.

initiate industrialization with the least dependence on foreign aid. Kemal and his cohorts rallied against European colonialism, which had given Germany, Great Britain, France and Italy a powerful grip on the pre-war Ottoman Empire.

Kemal was aware that agriculture was the main economic resource of his nation, so in an effort to enhance and increase agriculture outputs, he established a European-style model farm near Ankara, in which he publicly demonstrated the latest farming techniques. The farm was originally founded in 1889, and in 1929, then-dormant plots of land were substantially expanded, loans to small farmers were increased and credit cooperatives were established.

Liquidation of foreign economic concessions became a dominant principle of Kemalism.[66] Concentrating on revamping the domestic economy, Kemal successfully embarked on an economic system based on exports and imports, with the least-controlled trade measures.

Kemal was gradually moving towards reestablishing Turkey's economy on a John Keynesian foundation. To further enhance the Turkish economy, Kemal endeavored to expedite industrial progress along with agriculture. He noticed that private industry was lagging because of lack of know-how and the propensity of those who owned capital to invest in the traditional projects of real estate enterprises and buildings. Hence, he turned to state enterprises and incorporated a five-year economic plan. The five-year plan was masterminded by a very competent financier, Celal Bayar, who was strongly backed by Mustafa Kemal. He noticed that government investments in tobacco, cigarettes and alcohol, acquisition and operations of railroads, harbor facilities, electric utilities and coastal steamers were highly successful. Numerous factories were built to manufacture textiles, paper, glass, sugar and steel. All were operated as part of state enterprise in cooperation with the private sector.

Due to the 1920s to 1930s depression, Turkey's exports suffered and the government began to impose more restrictions on imports. Nazi Germany, after its economic revival by Adolf Hitler, took advantage of the weak moment and proposed a lucrative trade agreement

66 Palmer, p. 98.

with Turkey. The Turks happily accepted and, in 1936, over 50 percent of Turkey's exports went to Germany. In further efforts to push Turkey's economic relations away from the Islamic world and closer to the West, Kemal entered into trade agreements with numerous allies, especially the United States.

In Turkey, this policy of predominately state-owned enterprise managed by the government (statism) generated a nationwide debate. Some perceived it as an obvious movement towards communism, while others thought it was a kind of autocracy akin to those adopted by Hitler and Mussolini. Kemal was compared with the two notorious dictators. Still a third group expressed full support of statism, asserting that it would develop the country without creating a wide gap between the haves and the have-nots, or creating industrial tycoons such as the Rockefellers, Henry Ford, JP Morgan and others who wielded incredible power in their societies.[67]

NATIONALISM

The fourth principle in the Kemalist program was the changing of Turkish identity from religion to nationalism. The growth of nationalism in the nineteenth century was effective in the Ottoman Empire in diverse ways. Before the turn of the century, Greeks, Arabs, Serbs, Armenians, Bulgarians and others were seeking independence.

After Kemal assumed presidency, Kemalist principles were all mixed with nationalism. None was more outstanding than the new history written in the Latin alphabet for elementary and secondary schools. Though the books undermined the history of the Ottoman Islamic Empire, they established for the Turks highly exaggerated glories and a significant past. Sumerians and Hittites were claimed as Turks; indeed, all people who came from Central Asia were described as Turks. Even Adam, the first man, was proclaimed a Turk, since the word in the Turkish language for man is "adam." Therefore, all people were proclaimed to be originally Turks.[68]A large number of Turks reveled in the pride they derived from those concepts, which were also utilized

67 Fisher, pp. 409-410.
68 Fisher, p. 408.

to justify the ethnocentric movement of "Toranism" or Turkish ethnic superiority.[69]

One of the indelible aspects of Kemal's legacy was his effort to extricate the Turkish language from Arabic. After adopting the new alphabet, the drive to free the Turkish language from Arabic vocabulary and replace it with Turkish words made great progress. The newly resurrected old Turkish words written in Latin scripts gave the Turks a feeling of national pride, even though the Turkish language is still extensively permeated with Arabic vocabulary.

The task of rewriting the history of Turkey was entrusted by Mustafa Kemal in 1930, to a committee of the nationalist Turkish Hearths (an organization formed to combat the ideas of Islamism and to convince Turkish people to accept the ideals of Turkish nationalism). Turkish historians worked with President Kemal in Ankara, where they had their own office. In 1930, they wrote a book intended for people fifteen to eighteen years old, entitled, *Outline of Turkish History* (Turk Tarihinin Ana Hatlari). Mustafa Kemal dictated and drafted parts of it. Maps were also provided showing how, in prehistoric times, the ancient Turks had left their original habitat in central Asia and spread civilization to other parts of the world. The children were required to memorize the difficult names of the Hittite and Mongol kings, while they were indoctrinated that Islam and the Ottoman Empire were a period of aberration.[70]

CONTINUING REFORM

The sixth principle of Kemalism was the drive for reform, which, for Kemal, was synonymous with Westernization. To Kemal, reform meant opposition to blind conservatism and adherence to old traditions. He was aware that change is a continuous task and once it stops, society becomes stagnant.

In an effort to promote women's liberation, Kemal compelled wives of cabinet ministers to learn Western dance such as the tango, waltz, etc., and opened the way for women to assume such previously taboo

69 Mango, p. 494.
70 Ibid, p. 507.

careers as actresses, public officials, doctors, lawyers and politicians.[71]

All aspects of Islamic-Ottoman culture were to be replaced by European styles and practices. Western classical and popular music were encouraged, while traditional art and music were undermined. Poetry and literature became diversified in subjects and included romance, politics and the meaning of democracy. The old religious opposition to painting and sculpture was abandoned, and young artists were encouraged to contribute.

In the 1930s, Ottoman-style architecture was replaced by the Bauhaus style, inspired by German architects who trained young Turkish architects. During the same period, Kemal introduced Western sports such as soccer, tennis, and field and track.

One of the most significant aspects of reform was the change of the Turkish approach to life and destiny. Previously, if some unpleasant circumstance or unfortunate event took place, it was passively attributed to the will of God and fate. Through relentless theoretical and practical training, the young Turks began to accept the scientific explanation of diseases, the effectiveness of modern medicine, planning for the future and taking control of their own destinies instead of succumbing to superstition.[72]

Kemal was a competent military commander, a shrewd politician and a leader of reform. He was deeply influenced by the French Enlightenment principles of secularism and separation of church from the state. He was an ardent believer in social equality for all components of his society and was a liberator of women. He was able to surmount solidified archaic traditions, extricate his country from the medieval Ottoman theocracy and propel it into the twentieth century.

His socio-political system became a paragon that inspired other

71 Fisher, p. 410.

72 No doubt, the modern Republic of Turkey of 1939 was entirely different from the medieval Ottoman Empire of 1919. Within two decades the mentality of a nation, at least the segment of the Arabian intelligentsia, was altered from adhering to the archaic beliefs of religious and superstitious metaphysics to the scientific pragmatism of the twentieth century. The dialectical conflict between the two systems, which led to the downfall of the theocratic thoughts of the old regime and the rising of the modern and practical new one, is attributable to the planning and implementation of one leader—Mustafa Kemal Ataturk—whose last name means the father of the Turks. Kemal clearly typifies Georg W. Hegel's perception of the leader who is the instrument of dialectic and possesses two elements: the ideas and the passion for social change.

Middle Eastern leaders such as Shah Reza of Iran, King Faisal I of Iraq, as well as the pioneer intellectual elites such as Taha Hussein, Abbas al-Aqqad, Sati al-Husari, Salama Moussa, and other liberal writers who spearheaded the Arab Renaissance, to call for reform, modernization and equal rights for women.

THE INFLUENCE OF KEMALISM IN THE MIDDLE EAST

The social changes rendered by Kemal generated two kinds of reactions in the Middle East: one positive, the other negative. Shah Reza Pahlavi of Iran openly expressed his admiration of Kemal and boldly adopted his policies. The shah substantially undermined the role of the powerful *mullah* (a Muslim learned in Islamic theology and sacred law; clergy) in his government, adopted modern scientific curricula for Iranian schools, liberated women from religious restraints and embarked on profound social reforms.

To a lesser degree, King Faisal I of Iraq and King Fouad of Egypt were also influenced by Kemalism. While they were both constitutional monarchs, they allowed suffrage, enhanced women's status and ensured that religion played a minimal role in their government. Several Arab scholars preached Kemalism as the only path to independence and social progress.

Kemalism also generated its own antithesis. In Turkey, the religious element rebelled against Kemal's Republican People's Party. The Muslim Brotherhood movement in Egypt and a coalition of mullahs in Iran both vehemently rejected Kemalism as the ideology of the infidel Western stooges who were attempting to undermine the name of God, subject the Muslim world to Western imperialism and corrupt the traditional Islamic family.

Believers in Islamic ideology aspired to establish a government and a society modeled after the theocracy established by Prophet Mohammad and pursued by the Rashidun caliphs in the seventh century. Thus, a new dialectical conflict between religious and secular ideologies began with full vigor in the Middle Eastern countries.

KEMALISM AND THE MONARCHY OF IRAQ (1921–1958)

An early country that was gradually influenced by Kemalist secular modernizing ideology was the Kingdom of Iraq under the leadership of King Faisal the First, his followers and his offspring. With his royal background and acumen, King Faisal was able to gradually modernize his kingdom to follow the example of the Western systems without antagonizing the influential clergy.

When the monarchy of Iraq was proclaimed and Prince Faisal—son of Hussein, the sherif and prince of holy Mecca—was enthroned its king in 1921, there was a wide gap between the mentality of the leadership and the Iraqi masses. After being ruled for several centuries by the theocratic Ottoman Empire, the Iraqi populace continued to identify themselves as Muslim-Ottomans long after the collapse of the archaic empire. They supported King Faisal ardently because of his religious background as a descendant of the Hashimite family of Prophet Mohammed. The Iraqis expected King Faisal to establish the state system along the lines of the Ottoman Islamic theocratic state.[73]

However, King Faisal and his entourage, most of whom were comrades of Mustafa Kemal Ataturk in the Ottoman army, were impressed by Kemal's ideology. They eschewed religion and espoused the Kemalist Western progressive doctrine of nationalism. They considered Iraq as an Arab state and part of the entire Arab nation.

While the new monarchical system was predetermined by Arab tradition, the form of the Cabinet, parliament and administration was designed along the lines of the British system of government. Therefore, numerous medieval socio-political institutions that prevailed for centuries were either eliminated or substituted by modern ones. The populace of Iraq, who remained Ottomans in their feelings, values and attitudes, witnessed the following abrupt changes in their society.

1. The title of the sultan-caliph was changed from *Amir al-Mu'minin* (meaning "prince of the believers," and assumed by the Ottoman sultans) to *Malik* (meaning "king").

73 Ali al-Wardi, Social Glimpses of Modern Iraqi History, op. cit., p. 359.

2. The caliphate had been a combination of a spiritual, political and military position. Sultan Abdul Hamid was even called "The Shadow of God." By contrast, Faisal proclaimed himself a secular king whose duties were defined by a constitution. He possessed no spiritual authority.
3. Throughout the history of the theocratic Ottoman system, the office of Shaykh al-Islam, meaning leader of the Muslims, played an extremely important role in the social and political lives of the Islamic code and the authoritative exponent of the sacred Islamic law (*al-Shari'ah al-Islamiyah*). In certain cases the shaykh, as the interpreter of the code, could demand the obedience of the sultan himself. If the sultan was deemed mentally unqualified or if he deviated from his religious obligations, a sanction in the form of a fatwa, a religious decree by the Shaykh al-Islam, was necessary in the eyes of the Muslims to legalize the dethroning of the sultan. Such fatwas were issued when four earlier sultans were deposed.[74] In the new Iraqi regime, the position of Shaykh al-Islam or any similar religious office was never established.
4. The office of *Sadr al-Azam*, grand vizier, was changed in Iraq to *rais al-wizara*, meaning prime minister.
5. The Ottoman sultans had a part of their courts devoted to their harem (women of the sultan), following the Islamic concept of *ma malakat al-ayman*, meaning the slaves a person owns. The keeper of the sultan's slaves was entitled *harem aghase*, the chief eunuch. The eunuchs were men who were emasculated in childhood to be assigned as harem keepers. The harem keeper enjoyed high status in the courts, and at times his influence equaled that of a grand vizier. Sometimes the slaves and/or wives in the harem interfered in the policy of the empire and affected the decisions of the sultan.[75] But in a departure from this custom, King Faisal followed a monogamous course and married only one wife, Huzaymah. By eliminating the harem

74 Ibid.

75 Yusef al-Hakim, souria wa al-ahd al uthmani (Syria and the Ottoman Era) (Beirut: The Catholic Press, 1966), p. 31.

institution, King Faisal set an example of monogamy for his close followers and successors. The harem/eunuch institution was never reestablished in Iraq. (In some Arab and Islamic countries, the harem custom and polygamy were practiced until late in the twentieth century.)

6. Modern, secular education was one of the first concerns of the new leadership. Indeed, King Faisal considered education to be the panacea for all social ills. Hence, with the government's encouragement, in one year (1921–1922), enrollment in elementary schools increased 75 percent. More details of educational progress will be presented in due course.
7. The quality of health care was another priority of the government of Iraq. The new leadership, in cooperation with the League of Nations, initiated a health care plan fashioned along modern concepts. A more detailed comparative study of the development of health care will be presented in due course.

Before studying details of the socio-political development in Iraq, a brief discussion is necessary of the origin, nature and structure of the government.

In 1920, a nationwide religious revolution by Islamic forces against the British Mandate erupted in Iraq, but it was brutally squashed by the British army. After quelling the unrest, the British authority endeavored to establish a provisional government (October 1920)[76] under the leadership of Sayyid Abdul Rahman al-Gaylani, *Naqueeb Al Ashraf Baghdad*, the representative of the prominent people of Baghdad. Its function was to make preliminary preparations prior to the accession of King Faisal. Although the national government of Iraq was established in 1921, its constitutional organization was not completed until 1924, when the Organic Law was drawn and submitted to the constitutional assembly for approval.[77]

76 Al-Hasani, Abdul Razzaq, tarikh al-Iraq al-siasi al-hadith (Modern Political History of Iraq), op. cit., p. 205.

77 Muhammad M. Al-Adhami, al-majlis al-ta'sisi al-Iraq (The Parliament of Iraq) (Baghdad: Al Sadoon Press, 1976), pp. 5-7.

THE ADMINISTRATIVE SYSTEM

After the establishment of the national regime, the administrative system was organized. In 1927, a law was passed dividing Iraq into fourteen administrative divisions called *liwa*, each governed by a *mutasarrif*, a governor. The mutasarrif, who represented the central government and directed the officers of the liwa, was responsible to the minister of interior and assisted by an administrative council.

THE CONSTITUTION

Article 22 of the League of Nations covenant with Britain stated, with regard to the Ottoman territories placed under the mandate, that their existence as independent nations could be provisionally recognized subject only to the rendering of administrative advice and assistance. The advice was to be rendered by a mandatory power until such time as they were able to stand alone. The original draft was later replaced by the treaty of alliance, which indicated the need for a constitution for Iraq. Faisal declared at his accession that he would promulgate a constitution.

The main provisions of the constitution were included in Article 3 of the Anglo-Iraqi treaty of October 10, 1922, in which it was stipulated:

> His majesty, the King of Iraq, agrees to frame an organic law for presentation to the constitutional assembly of Iraq, and to give effect the said law, which shall contain nothing contrary to the provisions of the present reality and shall take account of the rights, wishes, and interests of all the population inhabiting Iraq. This organic law shall ensure to all, complete freedom of conscience and free exercise of all forms of worship, subject only to maintenance of public order and morals. It shall provide that no discrimination of any kind shall be made between the inhabitants of Iraq on grounds of race, religion, or language, and shall secure that the rights of each community to maintain its own schools for the education of its own members in its

> own language, while conforming to such government of Iraq may impose, shall not be denied or impaired. I shall prescribe the constitutional procedure whether legislative or executive, by which decision will be taken on all matters of importance, including those involving questions of fiscal, financial, and military policy.[78]

The above-mentioned article lays the foundation of not only a bill of rights for Iraq, but also the fundamental principles of the framework of its government. For this reason, Article 3 of the treaty of 1922 is an important landmark in the monarchical constitutional history of Iraq.[79]

The drafting of the Organic Law as well as discussions on its provisions were referred to British and Iraqi committees. The British committee included Major W.G. Young, M.E. Drower, and Sir Percy Cox, the high commissioner. The British committee utilized the constitution of Austria, New Zealand, and some small kingdoms to draft the constitution of Iraq.[80]

King Faisal referred this first draft to an Iraqi committee, constituted of three of his highly qualified followers, to examine it. After some disputes about the extent of the powers of the king, the two committees reached a compromise and outlined a new draft of the Organic Law that was somewhat satisfactory to both sides. In the autumn of 1923, the deliberations culminated in the final draft of the Organic Law, which later became the basis for the constitution of Iraq.

Distribution of the rights, delegation, and authority of people and the government are paraphrased in the following selected articles:[81]

Part I: The Rights of the People

Articles 5 to 18 of Chapter 1 in the constitution define the rights of the people, such as safeguarding personal freedom, equality before

78 Government of Great Britain and Iraq: Treaty of Alliance signed in Baghdad, October 10, 1922.
79 Majid Khadduri, Independent Iraq: A Study in Iraqi Politics Since 1932, op. cit., pp. 1-14.
80 Al-Hasani, op. cit., p. 205.
81 Government of Iraq, the Constitution of Iraq (Arabic) (Baghdad: Dar al-Salam Press, 1925).

the law among people, safeguarding domiciles and private property, among others.

Part II: The King

Articles 19 to 26 outline the limits of the powers and authorities of the king. These powers are exercised by means of royal decrees, which are issued upon requests by the prime minister or the responsible minister and after obtaining their signatures.

Part III: The Parliament

Legislative power in Iraq is shared by the parliament and the king. The parliament is bicameral and is comprised of a senate and a chamber of deputies. The king may open the parliament personally, with an address, or he may deputize the prime minister or any minister to address the chamber and deliver the opening speech from the throne.

In 1928, deputies numbered eighty-seven, and of these, the Baghdad liwa (province) had thirteen, including one Christian and two Jews; the Mosul liwa had twelve, including one Christian and one Jew; and the Basra liwa had eight, including one Christian and one Jew.[82] Christians and Jews were included in the parliament in accordance with Article 37 of the constitution, which required that non-Muslim minorities be represented.[83]

Part IV: The Cabinet

Article 46 states that ministers are appointed by the king. Their number may not be less than six nor more than nine. Any person appointed to the cabinet must also be a member of parliament. If a cabinet member is not already a member of one of the two houses, he may not retain his position for a period of more than six months without obtaining an appointment as a senator or becoming elected as deputy. This system duplicates the parliament-cabinet system of Great

82 Ibid.

83 Government of Iraq, the Constitution of Iraq, op. cit., p. 5.

Britain.[84] Should the chamber of deputies pass a vote of no confidence in the cabinet, the cabinet must resign. If the vote of no confidence is directed toward one minister, that minister must resign.

On May 21, 1925, the day the constitution was promulgated, King Faisal selected a cabinet which comprised a prime minister and six ministers. Among the minorities included, according to the constitution, was one Jew and one Shi'ite.

King Faisal and his entourage prepared a progressive secular constitution comparable with the democratic modern countries of Europe. Most of its provisions were derived from the principles of the liberal enlightenment era, which stopped medieval religious prejudice, promoted the concepts of human rights, and stipulated that religious and ethnic minorities must be represented.

INTERNAL DEVELOPMENT

The aspects of change included: integration of tribal, religious and ethnic social components, and development of education, health and some economic details.

In 1921, with its tribal population, anti-British sentiment, sectarian divisions and inadequate means of communication relative to its size, Iraq was a particularly difficult country to administer through the usual lines of bureaucratic routine. The predominantly Muslim population numbered three million, not counting the Bedouin nomads.[85]

The Christian minorities, made up of six distinct sects, amounted to some one hundred twenty thousand, and the Jewish comprised approximately eighty thousand people, most of whom resided in Baghdad. The Assyrians, who played a violent role in the early 1930s, formed another distinct non-Arab group of about thirty-five thousand concentrated in the northern region of Mosul, and belonging to the Nestorian church. These and other minorities, plus a large tribal and nomadic population, created political and administrative problems that delayed

84 Peter Sluglett, Britain in Iraq 1914–1932 (London: The Middle East Centre, 1976), p. 1.

85 Hashim Jawad, muqaddimah fi kian al-Iraq al-ijtima'I (Introduction About the Social System of Iraq) (Baghdad: al-Ma'arif Press, 1946), pp. 27-29.

progress and unification and even threatened to thwart it.[86]

The tribes caused the most serious difficulty. Tribes have always been a problem in the establishment of the orderly modern governments in the Middle East, but in Iraq, the problem was rendered more complex due to a variety of local factors such as land, water and religion. Several tribal groups, mostly residing in the middle parts of the country, belonged to the Shi'ite sect in closer solidarity with the Shi'ite ulema (religious wise men) in Najaf and Karbala (two holy Shi'ite cities) than with the predominantly Sunni government in Baghdad. Disputes over the ownership of land and water rights frequently arose between them and the government. Aggravated by intrigues on the part of politicians in Baghdad and by the tribesmen's dislike of bureaucracy and its requirements, disputes frequently developed into armed conflict.[87]

The Kurds, who predominantly live in the mountainous northern parts of Iraq, have caused difficulties throughout the various stages of modern Iraq. Their deep attachment to their own language and customs have made it more natural for them to seek union with fellow Kurds in neighboring Turkey and Iran than to be a small minority in an Arab state.

The Assyrians, another minority, were for the most part immigrants from southeastern Anatolia who had fled Turkish persecution during World War I, sought refuge in Iraq, and became the protégés of the British military command. They had absolutely nothing in common with the other social components of Iraq, and they were determined to live in isolation.

Throughout the decades of the 1920s and 1930s, the Kurds and Assyrians fought arduously to realize their dreams of establishing homelands in the northern part of Iraq. Ultimately, however, both minorities were subdued, and their leaders recognized the futility of pursuing resistance against the central government backed by Great Britain.

Endeavoring to solve all of these problems, the ruling elite of the newly established government of Iraq were rather successful in most aspects of their plan. After quelling the violent resistance movements,

86 Peter Shafett, op. cit., p. 1.

87 Abdul Jalil al-Tahir, al-asha'r al-Iraqiyah (The Tribes of Iraq) (Beirut: Dar Lebanon Press, 1972), pp. 6-15.

the government resorted to a policy of tolerance and understanding, acknowledging the rights of the minorities to maintain cultural values, communal identity and freedom. The minorities received wise and generous concessions from the government.[88] The result was a series of special enactments and measures arrived at in agreement with the leaders of each minority, which have proven workable.

In addition to the inclusion of Christians and Jewish representatives in parliament, two cabinet ministers, two senators out of twenty and fourteen representatives out of eighty-eight were Kurds. Fourteen percent of the armed forces, and 33 percent of the railway employees were Kurds.

Twenty-five schools were established in Kurdish territory, five of which were earmarked for Christians. In these five schools, both Kaldian—a language used strictly by a Christian faction—and Arabic were employed. The language of instruction in the rest of the twenty schools was Kurdish. An unknown number of qualified teachers belonging to Jewish, Christians, Kurds and other minorities were employed throughout Iraq.[89]

After securing relative calmness in most parts of the country, the government turned its efforts to developing other aspects of life.

EDUCATION

In 1921, only 1 percent of the population of Iraq was literate. Education was largely provided by very archaic religious centers (*Katateeb*), taught by the mullahs, semi-illiterate religious men. From the beginning of their first efforts and self-determination, the Iraqi leadership regarded education as a cure for all of their social ills. Under the Ottomans, education was taught in the Turkish language, thus alienating the Arabs. Also, among the wealthy, education was thought to be needed only by the poor, because it was necessary for them to find employment either with the government or the wealthy. Since the wealthy would inherit money and possessions, they reasoned that it was totally unnecessary that their children become educated. Additionally,

88 George Antonius, The Arab Awakening (London: Hamish Hamilton, 1938), p. 367.
89 Al-Hasani, Vol. 3, op. cit., pp. 129-133.

the wealthy perceived the act of educating their children as beneath their dignity.[90]

However, in 1921, Arabic replaced Turkish as the language of school education in Iraq, which provided a natural stimulus and positive psychological effect upon the people. Large numbers of students immediately enrolled. The new curricula were predominantly secular and included historical and cultural studies of the powerful illustrious position the Arabs historically had occupied, and the profound scientific contribution they had rendered to human knowledge.[91] Religious classes received much less emphasis.

Over a ten-year period, the educational system evolved from a rather simple and basic one to a relatively sophisticated one, based along the lines of the British system. The results were as follows:

1. The percentage of the Iraq annual budget devoted to education between 1920 and 1930 was increased from 130,360 Iraqi dinar, which constituted 2.3 percent, to 270,438, which is 6.1 percent, an almost 400 percent increase.
2. Between 1920 and 1930, the number of elementary schools and number of students increased from 84 schools with 6,743 students to 291 schools with 30,880 students—an almost 400 percent increase in number of schools and almost 500 percent increase in the number of students.
3. In 1923, there were no secondary schools and therefore no secondary-school students. In 1923, four secondary schools were built, which accommodated 233 students. By 1930, the number of secondary schools grew to 15, with 1,863 students, an increase of almost 400 percent in the number of schools, and an increase of 800 percent in the number of students. The numbers of schools and students continued to steadily increase as the government kept earmarking more funds for education.[92]

90 Ibid., pp. 85, 86.
91 Ibid., p. 55.
92 Jawad, op. cit., p. 106.

GROWTH OF THE MIDDLE CLASS

The direct consequence of the progress of education in Iraq was the continuous growth of the size of the middle class.

The main feature of the Iraqi social class system is that it did not have an aristocratic class according to the traditional European concept of social classes. When King Faisal was enthroned, he and his entourage did not own lands. The ruling class, most of whom were ex-Ottoman military officers and some civilians, were receiving salaries from the government. The Iraqi society was divided into the typical three classes: the rich upper class, the professional middle class, and the lower class. The upper class included the sheikhs of tribes who owned vast acreage of land and used their own related tribesmen as peasants to cultivate the land in a relationship almost akin to the serf system. The upper class also contained the urban owners of agricultural lands who hired their peasants, provided them with food, shelter and some income, plus the wealthy businessmen who practiced local and internal commerce. The middle class included professionals, like engineers, doctors, lawyers, professors and college graduate government employees, military officers, etc. The lower class were the destitute peasants, household, government and commercial servants.

These details are a close description of the Iraqi society, which means the country was very close to an oligarchy ruled by a political elite, while its economy was managed by a small wealthy class. The country pursued a free market economy as the constitution secured legal private property and local and international entrepreneurship.

After World War II, when the government succeeded in extricating 50 percent of the oil income of Iraq from the rapacious Great Britain, the newly earned copious income led to the creation of a nationwide range of carrier opportunities for the qualified segment of the society. Engineers, physicians, technicians, educators, etc. were needed to run the numerous modern facilities created by the government to develop the country.

Hence, Iraq witnessed an obvious range of upper mobility and large numbers of youths whose parents were destitute. Lower-class citizens climbed the socio-economic ladder to join the prosperous middle class.[93]

PROGRESS OF THE HEALTH SERVICE

Iraqis of the Ottoman era were prone to attribute their bodily ills to providence. They thought that if these ills appeared as a result of providential design, they should disappear, if at all, by the same manner.[94] At times, however, they tried to alleviate their ailments by consulting a quack or a primitive medical man. In the early and mid-twenties, quacks had enormous influence in Iraq; they were popular because they spoke the language of the people, knew their habits and prejudices, and usually had their consulting room in the bazaar—that is, in the place most accessible to the public.

The new regime, in cooperation with the British authority, seriously endeavored to enhance the system of health service in Iraq. Between 1921 and 1931, twenty-eight hospitals and ninety-six dispensaries were built. Wider distribution of hospitals (1,250 beds in all) and low-cost medication increased popular appreciation for modern medical treatments. By 1930, medical institutions were providing the best possible services at the lowest possible cost.[95]

As part of the educational program of the new state, a school of pharmacy and royal medical college were established. In 1931, as a result of training in hospitals and in the school of pharmacy, there were 129 registered pharmacists in Iraq. The curriculum of the medical college was based on average British qualifications, and instruction was given in English. The first group of doctors, who graduated from the college in 1932, were obligated to enter government service for five years, practicing medicine in rural areas, and in return their medical education was free.[96]

The work of the health service provided during the 1920s and early 1930s, which shows about a 500 percent increase in the number of

93 Zaki, Mamoon Amin, izdihar al-Iraq taht al-hukm al-malaki (Iraq's Prosperity Under the Royal Regime) (London: Dar al-Hikma, 2nd ed. 2013), pp. 308, 309.
94 Al-Wardi, op. cit., pp. 269-273.
95 Foster, op. cit., p. 264.
96 Ibid.

outpatients, is clearly indicative of the rapid yielding of an educated people to modern, scientific treatment.[97]

As a result of these efforts, a new generation of health propagandists emerged in schools, where hygiene became a regular subject of instruction. As early as 1925, all school populations were medically inspected on a regular schedule and students submitted to inoculations whenever necessary. A weekly health bulletin was published in the official gazette by the government illustrating various medical statistics throughout Iraq—deaths, cures, causes, and so on.[98]

To push Iraq's scientific endeavors beyond the local benefits, the government signed agreements to several international health conventions:[99]

1. The Hague Opium Convention of 1925
2. The International Agreement of Brussels for treatment of venereal diseases of merchant seamen of 1924, 1928
3. An Agreement at Beirut Conference of Near Eastern States for Regulation of Pilgrim Traffic from these states to Mecca, 1929
4. The Dangerous Drug Convention in Geneva of 1925, 1930
5. The International Sanitary Convention of 1926, 1931.

King Faisal and his entourage were guiding Iraq toward a future of modernization and scientific knowledge, while the quacks and religious charlatans were retreating, especially in Baghdad and some other large cities.

97 Ibid.
98 Official Gazette of Iraq, No. 311, June 25, 1925, p. 3.
99 Foster, op. cit., p. 266.

Chapter 3

REZA SHAH'S KEMALIST IRAN[100]

HISTORICAL BACKGROUND

IRAN IS ONE of the largest Islamic countries in the world, with a population of approximately 78 million, and an area equal to about one-fifth of the continental United States.

Its history goes back more than 2,500 years.[101] From its inception, the state was theocratically organized under the religion of Zoroastrianism. The Islamic era began in 636, when the second Rashideen Caliph Umar Ibn al-Khattab defeated the Persians in the Battle of Qadisiyyah.[102]

The Persian sovereigns based their legitimacy on divine rights, which allowed no criticism or opposition of any kind.

The king had a large hierarchy of subordinate officials and feudal lords. The state belonged to the family of the king, and the hereditary nobility owned a large number of villages and considered their inhabitants as private property.[103]

Early in the sixteenth century, Ismael Shah Safavi converted from Sunniesm to Shi'ism and turned Persia into a full-fledged Shi'ite Islamic

100 The names Iran and Persia are used interchangeably.

101 Bahman Nirumand, Iran: The New Imperialism in Action (New York: Monthly Review Press, 1960), p. 17.

102 Karen Armstrong, Islam: A Short History (New York: The Modern Library, 2002), p. 27.

103 Nirumand, op. cit., pp. 17-18.

theocracy.[104]

In 1794, the Qajar family overtook power in Persia after deposing Shah Lotf Ali Khan, the last of the Zand dynasty; they made Tehran the capital and remained in power until 1925.

Under the weak and uncaring Qajar king, who kept exchanging Persian sovereignty for foreign economic favors, Persia fell under the hegemony of the great powers.

Exports from Russia to Persia were rivaled by England in political, military and finance influence. The flood of manufactured goods from Western Europe and Russia inundated the country, and Persians of the nineteenth century were fascinated by European technology and science, even though their own domestic production was negatively affected.

Also, popular European literature such as Victor Hugo's *Three Musketeers*, *The Count of Monte Cristo* and the like was translated and infiltrated the country, and was positively received by the intelligentsia.[105]

Concurring with the modernization plans of the Ottoman Empire such as the Tanzimat reforms, the Hatt-i Humayun edict (imperial reform edict) and other aspects of modernization began to penetrate traditional Persian society, and the educated elite began to regard their country as backward and felt alienated from their own culture.

With the founding of the first university in Tehran in 1852, which was staffed mostly by European teachers, and the establishment of foreign schools with European curricula (French and English), Westernization was institutionalized. With the Westernization trends, which were encouraged by Europe, Persian demands for European goods increased.[106]

However, the increasing influence of the Great Powers agitated resentment among the majority of the population. Similar to the last period of the Ottoman Empire, Iran at the end of the nineteenth century was seething with overt and covert religious-political resentment and demanded reform and independence from British colonialism. The unrest came to a head when, in 1890, the shah granted a fifty-year

104 Armstrong, op. cit., p. 21.
105 Nirumand, op. cit., p. 21.
106 Ibid, p. 20.

concession to a British company to produce, sell and export the entire crop of Iranian tobacco. The deal secured the shah an income of fifteen thousand sterling pounds, while the rest of the revenue went to the British company. The deal precipitated a vehement popular protest against the exploitation of an important national industry by a despotic ruler and a foreign company.[107] A prominent religious leader named Mirza Shirazi hastened to promulgate a fatwa forbidding any sort of use of tobacco and labeling it as abhorrent behavior.

The popular response in support of the fatwa was so ardent and unanimous that it amazed the international community as riots, strikes and demonstrations overtook the entire country. The violent upheaval prompted the British plenipotentiary in Iran to report to his government stating, "We are witnessing a revolution here." (This event is historically known as the Constitutional Revolution. The aims of the revolution were to rid the country of foreign influence and transfer the absolute political system to a constitutional monarchy.) Finally the shah was compelled to call for an assembly meeting and the tobacco deal was canceled. Subsequently, the relentless popular demand enabled the assembly to prevail on the shah and coerced him to promulgate a constitution in 1906. The shah was forced to comply, and a constitutional assembly was chosen by means of wide popular election, and met for the first time in 1906.

The first section of the constitution deals exclusively with the formation and legislative procedure of the Persian parliament, which was composed of two separate chambers as follows.

THE NATIONAL ASSEMBLY OR THE MAJLIS – AND THE SENATE, OR UPPER CHAMBER[108]

In its early stages, parliamentarianism in Iran was hampered due to the population's lack of understanding of liberalism and a constitutional state, and the violent intervention of British and Russians in the operations of the weak Iranian government. Also, the unruly tribal princes and local tyrants defied the weak central government and ruled

107 William Cleveland and Martin Bunton, A History of the Modern Middle East (United States: West View Press, 2009), pp. 115-116.

108 Nimurand, op. cit., p. 24.

their own territories. Furthermore, Persia was in a dire social condition. The Qajar dynasty, which had ruled for more than a century, was on a steep decline; the state was bankrupt and under control of the Great Powers, and extreme corruption was rampant.

Utilizing the widespread resentment, the ardent patriot Reza Khan, a semi-literate trooper and later an officer of the elite cavalry the Cossack Brigade, marched on Tehran in 1921. He overthrew the government, and in a subsequent cabinet meeting took over the War Ministry.[109]

In that same year, Soviet Russia canceled all the Russo-Persian treaties, pacifying the people and stabilizing the north of the country, which was seething at the notion of imperial influence in Iran.

Hence Reza Khan became powerful enough to subdue the Persian feudal lords and bolster his authority. He inspired confidence and hope among the vast majority of the people, as he promised to enhance social and economic conditions and achieve national independence from foreign powers. In 1923, he became prime minister; in 1925, the parliament bestowed on him substantial military authority; and in October 1925, the Qajar monarchy was deposed.

Upon the downfall of the Qajar dynasty, Persia was facing a historical turning point—whether to remain a kingdom or to become a republic. Reza Khan, an ardent student of Mustafa Kemal Ataturk and a strong believer in Western modernization, suggested the country's system be turned into a republic, and he aspired to be elected its first president, similar to the Republic of Turkey and its first president, Kemal. Yet, the Iranian people had a very vague understanding of republicanism. In 1924, at the time Reza was prepared to announce the birth of the republic of Persia, Kemal had abolished the caliphate in Turkey and proclaimed his rigorous plans of secularism, which caused a severe shock in the entire Islamic world. The Iranian political elite were taken by surprise, while the ulema, or religious leaders, were terrified. The ulema raised such a powerful storm of protest that Reza was forced to meet with them in Qum, the Iranian holy city. The process of republicanism was aborted, and in 1925, Reza Khan, with the support

109 Ibid, p. 24.

of the majlis (parliament) and the ulema, was proclaimed shah. The throne was vested in the male members of the Pahlavi family born of Iranian mothers.[110]

In spite of the protestation by the ulema, Reza Shah embarked on deep and far-reaching reform plans. In fact, these plans exemplify the spread of the Kemalist secular new thesis to other parts of the Middle East. At the same time, Kemalism constituted an antithesis of the Iranian long-standing Shi'ite theocratic thesis established by Shah Ismael Safavi in the early sixteenth century.

Shah Reza's first modernization steps were to forbid women to wear veils, which even Kemal did not do, and men were similarly forbidden to wear turbans or national traditional costume. He reduced the number of religious holidays, substantially limited the influence of the recalcitrant clergy, ordered the Western use of surnames, undermined the Islamic law and introduced a new legal code modeled after the Napoleonic code.[111] Hence began the dialectical conflict between the religious and secular ideologies in Iran.

The problems facing Reza Shah in Iran were similar to those confronting Kemal in Turkey, only much more complicated. The two most urgent issues were the reestablishment of a recognized central government and reform of the economy. The first matter was, by and large, achieved by Shah Reza and his army, while the second was entrusted to an American economic expert, Dr. Arthur C. Millspaugh.[112]

With vast power and the strong support of Shah Reza, Dr. Millspaugh was able to balance the budget by restructuring the tax system and implementing the collection of taxes. State enterprises were initiated, and economic conditions began to steadily improve.[113]

One agreement between Shah Reza and Dr. Millspaugh was that the budget of war would always take precedence because the military should be the source of power in the state. By 1932, Shah Reza had personally led his army to quell rebellions in several parts of his kingdom and subdued the nomadic tribes, including the suppression of the

110 Milton D. Graham, Iran (New Haven: Human Relations, Area files 1957), p. 24.
111 Nimurand, op. cit., p. 25.
112 Fisher, op. cit., p. 465.
113 Ibid.

Qashqai confederation of nomadic tribes in 1929 and 1932.

One of the spectacular achievements was his successful cooperation with the powerful Anglo-Persian Oil Company (APOC) to end the semi-independent rule of Sheikh Khaz'al of the oil-rich province of Mohammarah, whose ambitions were not confined to expansion of his influence in Iran, but included his aspiration to become king of the newly born Iraq.[114] The extension of Reza's authority over that vital southern territory increased the revenues of the central government of Iran and consolidated Dr. Millspaugh's economic policies.

According to the constitution of 1906, which was still in effect, the power of the state was vested in the shah, the senate and the assembly, which by 1926 was controlled by Reza's staunch followers. The senate positions were appointive, but Reza never made any appointments to it. The assembly nominated prime ministers who had been selected by the shah.[115]

A remarkable work by the indefatigable shah was his assiduous campaign to inspire an enthusiastic work ethic among ministry personnel. Quite often he would suddenly enter a government office early in the morning to ascertain that the officials were punctual and at their duties. Shah Reza's imposing presence and despotic behaviors were imitative of Kemal Ataturk.

Although Iran had a constitution guaranteeing a representative form of government, legitimacy in the Western sense was hardly practiced.[116] Its majlis (parliament) was created by and approved by Shah Reza. There was little, if any, interest in forming organizations representing different opinions. Very little opportunity for political growth or improvement existed, except for the elite, who constituted the government and competed among themselves for prestige, power and economic benefits.

Reza Shah was determined to modernize Persia even though his power continued to rest on traditional foundations of despotic power

114 Abdul Razzaq Ahmed al-Nisairi, Nuri al-Said wa dawruh fi al-Siyasah al-Iraqiyah (Nuri al-Said: And His Role in Iraq's Politics) (Baghdad: Times Publishers, 1987), pp. 96-97.

115 Fisher op. cit., p. 466.

116 Legitimacy is defined by Professor Harold Laski as the mutual respect between the people and their government.

and landlords. Public veneration given to religious leaders had proven a stumbling block to Iranian government reform plans. Reza Shah rejected the most anachronistic disciplines of Islam. Following Kemal Ataturk's path, Reza embarked on efforts to curtail the authority of the religious institution and its leaders and relegate them to less influential positions in the nation's culture.

He destroyed the Quranic village schools, replaced the religious law with imported civil codes, replaced the *mujtahids* (interpreters of Shari'ah law) with civil judges and opened his country to European intellectualism.

Sufis were forbidden to appear on the streets or along the roads of the countryside. He even banned the very revered ritual of mourning the commemoration of the assassination of Imam Hussein Ibn Ali, during the Shi'ite holy month of Muharram. The clergy were utterly helpless before the shah's formidable force. Shah Reza was determined to free Iran from religious restrictions by the end of the 1930s.[117]

As part of his modernization program, Reza, like Kemal Ataturk, decreed European dress for Iranians, which for women meant rejecting the veil and the notorious chador—the long black robe.

To implement his women's liberation policy, the shah in 1928 urged his wife, the queen and mother of his crown prince, to visit the holy city of Qum defiantly unveiled. A religious leader in the mosque reproached the queen in his sermon for unveiling her face. Shah Reza took advantage of this event to teach all clergy a lesson. Upon hearing what the Qum religious leader dared to say about the queen, Reza stormed the mosque with armored cars, entered it without removing his boots, which was against religious requirements, and savagely whipped the offending preacher publicly.

At another site, the mosque of Khor Shad, a large number of people barricaded themselves within the mosque in protest to protect their religious men. When the shah was informed that the police and the army had killed four thousand people, he astonishingly questioned, "The mosque accommodates ten thousand people—why were the remaining

117 E.A. Bayne, Persian Kingship in Transition (New York: American Universities Field Staff, Inc. 1968), p. 46.

six thousand not killed?"

Some people wrote letters to the highly regarded Shi'ite clergy in the holy city of Najaf in Iraq to plead to the shah to have mercy towards the religious men and to respect the desires of those women who chose to keep their veils, but he considered such suggestions to be inconsistent with his modernization plans and answered, "Those who prefer to die because they cannot stand our reform programs, it is better for them to commit suicide so that the country would be relieved from them."[118]

Confiscation of many religious properties and endowments took place, the incomes from which were rechanneled to support modern schools, hospitals, state industry and other state enterprises, similar to Ataturk's statism. No longer were religious leaders completely independent, and most of their schools were closed. Much of the ulema's livelihood subsequently came from the state, and their influence was substantially diminished.

Secularization of the law was expedited. A mixture of Shari'ah and French judicial principles was enacted into the law codes of 1925–1928. Religious law was limited in scope and authority, and by 1931, religious courts exercised jurisdiction only over domestic relations, personal status and marital acts. Theological students previously exempted from military duties were subjected to compulsory enlistment. Education became a public responsibility under the supervision and regulation of the central government.[119]

By 1935, Reza Shah had passed orders forbidding people from wearing turbans, and a severe anti-clergy campaign was waged all over the country. Subsequently one hundred thousand men discarded their religious outfits. The shah aimed to eradicate the religious segment from society by resorting to two methods: encouraging cooperation with rewards and deterring rebellion by persecution. Those who opted to abandon their religious attire were rewarded and employed in suitable government jobs, while those who resisted were subjected to dire consequences. Hence, flock after flock of clergymen were forced to

118 Musa al-Mawsawi, Iran fi rubu'qarn (Iran in a Quarter of a Century) (Tehran 1978), p. 178.
119 Fisher, op. cit., p. 466.

abandon their turbans and vests and wear civilian clothes.[120]

In 1935, Tehran University was expanded to include an indigenous secular institution of higher learning, and in 1937, female students were admitted. By 1940, about 10 percent of the population was receiving an elementary education.

Intellectual life also began to change as poets, novelists and journalists attempted, like Turkey, to extricate their country from Arabic-Islamic culture by emphasizing the glories of the pre-Islamic empires of Persia, such as the Sassanid dynasty.

Following Ataturk's steps, Reza did everything possible to spread the Persian language and to eliminate the Arabic and Turkish vocabularies that were used in various regions of Iran.[121]

ECONOMIC REFORM

In 1921, when Reza Shah came to power, Iran's dire economic conditions were clear. There were no more than two thousand miles of roads in the western region of the country, and people were living in squalor.

Hence, Reza, who was deeply impressed by Kemal Ataturk's economic reform and progress, embarked, as his first step of economic improvement, on enhancing the country's communication and transportation sectors, and endeavored to bring the remote parts of Iran under the control of the central government in Tehran. By 1939, the net road system had been expanded to seventeen thousand miles.

In view of Iran's role in the world's economy during World War II, the paramount achievement of Reza Shah was the construction of the Trans-Iranian Railway from Bandar Shahpur on the Arabian Gulf to Bandar Shah on the Caspian Sea. Completed in 1938, the railway was fundamental in supplying Russia with essential commodities during the war. Financed totally by Iran, the road became an economic artery for connecting the commercial northern part of Iran with the agricultural territories of the southern region. It also proved a powerful means to extend the military authority of the central government into

120 Mawsawi, op. cit., p. 178.
121 Cleveland, op. cit., p. 189.

the lands occupied by tribes and nomads.[122]

As a result of the enactment of conscription in 1925, the Iranian army was augmented in size and strength. Between 1921, when Reza seized power, and 1930, the number of troops increased from 4,000 to 100,000. Modern military training schools were established to train troops inside Iran instead of sending troops to European military academies. Between 25 to 40 percent of government revenues were earmarked for military purposes. Military and police trucks used the newly built highways to facilitate vehicle movement to previously remote areas of Iran. A modern air force and a small navy were established, thereby increasing security and allowing easier transportation of people and goods, which precipitated economic growth.

Following Ataturk's example of statism, Iran's government increased its involvement in economic endeavors. In 1927, Iran was able to set its own tariffs, and duties were increased to raise more resources and promote industry. New clothing factories and sugar refineries were built. However, Iran had an agricultural economy, and most of the labor forces were engaged in farming. Thorough economic reforms were undertaken, which led to better irrigation and improved agricultural results. Yet, due to a shortage of technicians and plant managers, industrial development under Reza proved unsatisfactory.[123]

The world economic depression of the 1930s negatively affected Iran's capabilities for foreign trade, which prompted Shah Reza to put most foreign trade under the government's management. State monopolies were established to control production of essential commodities such as sugar, tea and some food supplies, which helped to finance the building of the Trans-Iranian Railway.[124]

Reza sought to renegotiate the notorious 1901 agreement with Britain that was formed when oil was discovered in Persia. The Qajar Shah Muzzafer al-Din, the fifth Qajar king of Persia, conceded 84 percent of the country's oil sources to Britain, while receiving only 16 percent of the company's lucrative annual profits.[125] Because of this

122 Cleveland, op. cit., p. 190.
123 Fisher, op. cit., p. 191.
124 Graham, op. cit., pp. 204-209.
125 Cleveland, op. cit., p. 190.

agreement, the Anglo-Iranian Oil Company (AIOC), previously named Anglo-Persian Oil Company, was the most powerful economic institution in Iran. It controlled the prices and possessed the authority to shut off or open the oil pipelines at will. The company was virtually a state within a state, as its power was derived from being the largest industrial employer in the country with more than 30,000 citizens working for it. These conditions kept the budget and finance of Iran totally under the mercy of the British. In 1933, after marathon negotiations, the parties reached an agreement which increased Iran's revenue to receive 20 percent dividends, more than £671,250. Although the increase was not large enough, this agreement by Reza Shah was considered one of his paramount economic and diplomatic successes against the formidable imperial power of Great Britain and the AIOC.[126]

Shah Reza Pahlavi's historical importance is evidenced by his ability to reform certain aspects of the Iranian society and usher it into the twentieth century in two short decades. He played a paramount role in confronting the deeply rooted power of the clergy and spread the modern secular thesis of Kemalism in Iran and the Middle East.

FOREIGN POLICY

Reza Shah's foreign policy was no less bold than his domestic affairs. He diligently sought to maintain friendly relations with his neighbors. In 1934, he was lavishly received by Kemal Ataturk in Ankara. One of his major diplomatic achievements was the signing of the Sa'ad-Abad Pact in 1937 with Turkey, Iraq and Afghanistan, which outlined the terms of non-aggression and friendly relations between the signatories, with the objective of uniting these countries against the European menace.[127]

Shah Reza's progressive domestic and foreign affairs plans were steadily advancing. Frustrated with the continued British control of Persia's oil and its hegemony in the south and the Russian sphere of influence in the north, Reza Shah established commercial relations with

126 Fisher, op. cit., p. 469.

127 Law No. 18, March 10, 1938, promulgating notification of Sa'ad-Abad Pact. Official Gazette of Iraq, No. 1619, 22 March 1938.

Germany. However, when World War II erupted, the Allies became very leery of the Persia-Germany rapprochement due to Persia's strategic geographic location and the tremendous demand for oil, which was needed for war equipment. Persia's strategic and economic importance to the Allies is discussed in detail in Winston Churchill's war memoirs.[128]

On August 25, 1941, the British and Soviet Union armies invaded Iran in what was code-named Operation Countenance, under the pretext of having to stop the advancement of the Germans. The Iranian army was too weak to undertake a serious resistance to the invaders.

A few weeks after the British and Russian armies had marched in, on September 17, 1941, Shah Reza was forced to abdicate and was exiled to South Africa.[129] Subsequently, the Trans-Iranian Railway connecting the south of Iran with the Russian borders was confiscated, expanded and used for dispatching American and British weapons to Russia.

128 Winston S. Churchill, The Second World War (London: Cassel, 1950) Vol. 3, p. 423.
129 Mawsawi, op. cit., p. 183.

Chapter 4

SHAH MOHAMMAD REZA PURSUES HIS FATHER'S KEMALIST THESIS

IN 1941, AFTER Shah Reza Pahlavi was forced by the Great Powers to resign, his throne was bequeathed to his son, Mohammad Reza Shah (1919–1980). At twenty-two years old, inexperienced and weak, the new ruler was overwhelmed by the complicated domestic and foreign affairs to which his government was subjected during the first period of his reign.

Mohammad Reza was raised to succeed his father, but the nature of his modern secular upbringing distanced him from the vast traditional majority of the Iranian people. After spending his early teenage years at the exclusive Le Roy School in Switzerland, he came back to his country to receive political and military training under the supervision of his father, who inculcated the principles of Kemalism in his son's mind.[130]

While World War II raged on, a treaty of alliance was signed by Great Britain and the Soviet Union that stipulated that Allied forces would withdraw from Iran within six months after the war. At the Tehran Conference in 1943, U.S. President Roosevelt, USSR President Joseph Stalin and Great Britain Prime Minister Winston Churchill signed a statement that their governments would preserve the independence, sovereignty and territorial integrity of Iran.

130 Cleveland, op. cit., p. 288.

After the armistice ending the war, Iranians were waiting for March 1946, when all foreign (infidel) troops would leave the country. Their high hopes were dashed, however, when the Soviet Union decided to create two autonomous entities in north Iran, Kurdistan and Azerbaijan, which were administered by the Russian Red Army.[131]

By the end of the war, Iran's economy was utterly ruined. Its currency became almost worthless as it depreciated 600 percent. At the Yalta Conference, the Allies agreed to extend aid to reconstruct the Iranian economy, but the aid was inadequate and slow. Hence, before being able to develop his country, the young shah was faced with two voluminous dilemmas: foreign occupation and a devastated economy.[132]

Before Reza Shah's abdication, the country had a constitutional government, the *majlis*, but it had been largely produced and approved by Reza Shah. There was hardly any political awareness or mature public opinion. Political participation was primarily limited to the elite or members of the government, who vied among themselves for prestige, power and emoluments. After Reza Shah's abdication, the first period of Mohammad Reza's reign witnessed some measures of political progress.

A new government, headed by liberal politician Zika Al-Mulk Faruqi, bestowed some new freedoms such as the ability to form political parties, and reduced restrictions on the mass media. Yet, the vast majority of the population remained uneducated in modern concepts of political life. Despite the government's efforts to educate its people, 70 to 80 percent achieved little progress in political awareness. The peasants remained largely unaware of any roles in political life. Their only involvement with politics occurred during elections of the Majlis, when they exercised voting for their landlords, the only candidates they knew. Also, the shah's educational programs in rural areas had induced some farmers to assume a pro-shah attitude.

The city dwellers had gradually developed a deeper interest in politics and the importance of political participation. They were particularly susceptible to emotional oratory and demagogy. In the 1950s and 1960s, the middle class was still small and its reaction to events was

131 Fisher, op. cit., p. 513.

132 Nirumand, op. cit., p. 24.

unclear, yet the mere fact that it was growing meant it would eventually have a more influential role in the political processes.

The growing upper middle class experienced more political progress. Its members were apparently affected by the shah's secular Westernization programs. They became better educated, had higher aspirations and a more profound perception of the political needs of the country, and a better understanding of how to attain them. This class comprised businessmen of high status, professional men, and upper bureaucrats; i.e., people of higher education whose interests were related to the stability of the government. They also comprised the groups of educated people who were seeking reform of public affairs.

The sudden relative freedom to form political parties led to the appearance of a multitude of politically immature power-seeking groups loosely calling themselves parties, none of which (except the Tudeh, an Iranian Communist party formed in 1941) had organization, programs or cohesion. The Pahlavi dynasty was only able to control the almost chaotic situations because of the military missions based in the country since 1942, which provided the regime with military, economic and political backing.[133]

THE TUDEH PARTY

Among the organized political groups, the Tudeh party was the largest and, for a certain period, the best-ordered party in Iran. The Tudeh was founded in 1942 after the downfall of Reza Shah, and though outlawed since 1949, it remained a well-structured entity. Although based on Marxism, its platform included principles of liberalism with strong emphasis on trade unions and working conditions. Hence, it was able to attract the working class, the intelligentsia and some moderate religious groups.[134]

The Tudeh created the "Freedom Front" in 1943. This organization was an aggregation of newspapers and press that preached the principles of liberalism and progress according to the Communist ideology. The Freedom Front, which for a certain period controlled 50 percent of

133 Halliday, op. cit., p. 24.
134 Cleveland, op. cit., p. 289.

the country's newspapers, was the Tudeh's main means of propaganda and communication, and conveyed, both at home and abroad, that large portions of Iran were pro-Russia and pro-Communism.

THE NATIONAL WILL PARTY

The other party that demonstrated organization and order, and exerted some popular influence, was the National Will Party (NWP) of Sayyid Zia el-Din. After a period of exile, Zia el-Din returned home and established his party on the cell system (a pyramidal system based on assigning members of the party to a hierarchically structured cell from the foundation which is constituted of the rank and file upward to the top leadership position) and well-established discipline. The party had both liberal and conservative members, and was united by its pro-West and ardently anti-Tudeh stance. The NWP gained enough popularity to compete with the Tudeh Party, which aroused the ire of Prime Minister Ahmad Qanam, who was a Tudeh sympathizer and an advocate of understanding with the Soviet Union. Sayyid was accused of fascism and pro-Western intrigues, and was arrested. The NWP began to deteriorate, but it had been instrumental in supporting the rise of Reza Shah.[135]

THE NATIONAL FRONT PARTY

Probably the most influential opposition leader in Iran's modern history was Dr. Mohammed Mossadeq (1882–1967), an author, administrator, lawyer (Ph.D. in law), renowned philanthropist and politician who introduced progressive modern plans such as social security and land reform. He was an ardent patriot who sacrificed his political career and privileged life to reform and free his country from foreign control. He was the founder of the National Front Party, which was comprised of diversified patriotic groups who supported Dr. Mossadeq's calls for independence and political reform.

Early in the 1950s, dissatisfaction against the AIOC was rampant in Iran, and loud calls were made in the majlis to rectify the injustices

135 Graham, op. cit., p. 87.

practiced by the AIOC against Iranian interests. Prime Minister General Ali Razmarah was reluctant to listen to the national demands to confront the company. He was assassinated on March 7, 1951.[136]

Mr. Hussein Ala' became prime minister for forty days, after which Dr. Mossadeq, chairman of the oil committee, was democratically elected prime minister on April 29, 1951. The following day, a law was passed to nationalize the oil industry of Iran and evict the AIOC. Since 1908, when AIOC had discovered oil in Iran and signed a concession with the Qajar shah, Iran had received a trivial £350 million annually—while the AIOC was reaping enormous profits. Hence, upon announcement of the nationalization of the oil industry, Mossadeq and seventeen parliament representatives declared that Iran "is emancipated from England's enslavement and imperial control." The mass media was teeming with cheerful patriotic slogans such as: "The people are their own masters," "Democracy is achieved," "Rule of the people by the people," and the like.[137]

Mossadeq's popularity reached its zenith in 1952 as he induced the *majlis* to grant him emergency powers to purge corrupt military officers and bureaucrats. He formed a special parliamentary committee that placed the armed forces under the control of the government and replaced the despotic rule of the monarch with constitutional law, and he introduced land reform to redistribute the wealth and land of the privileged classes.[138]

To appreciate why Dr. Mossadeq and his National Front organization were so popular, it must be understood that Iran had suffered for decades from the unjust agreements signed since the beginning of the twentieth century. Its economic resources were by and large controlled by the Great Powers. The relations between Europe and Iran were characterized by Europe's lack of respect for Iranian culture, and economic and imperial abuse. Virtually all of Iran resented the dominant presence of all foreigners, whether they were Soviet engineers, British oil experts or U.S. military advisors. That is why most of the patriotic popular movements supported Mossadeq's bold campaign against the

136 Fisher, op. cit., p. 517.
137 Mawsawi, op. cit., pp. 88-89.
138 Cleveland, op. cit., p. 202.

foreign imperial influences in Iran. Between 1951 and 1953, Mossadeq was able to mobilize most Iranians to replace the despotic royal regime with a Western-style democratic system in an attempt to achieve national sovereignty.

THE FADA'IYAN-E ISLAM PARTY

Another movement that caused havoc, riots, assassinations and severe headaches to Shah Mohammad Reza was the party of Fada'iyan-e Islam. Founded in 1945 by a tweny-five-year old Shi'ite religious fundamentalist, Navvab Safavi (born Mojtaba Mir-Lowhi), who studied theology in Iraq's Shi'ite holy city of Najaf, the party spread among young religious men and gained substantial political influence when it enlisted the support of the well-known cleric activist Ayatollah Abu al-Qassim al-Kashani.

For ten years, this party caused much trouble to the shah's government, as Navvab Safavi carried out several armed attacks, including in 1951 the assassination of the notoriously tough Prime Minister General Ali Razmarah and several others, but was impervious to punishment because the government feared arousing religious frenzy. The party was invariably opposed to the government's secular programs and kept causing turbulence until the shah was able to quell it after the SAVAK (Organization of Intelligence and National Security) rounded up and executed its leadership, including Navvab Safavi, in 1955.[139]

THE SHAH TRIES TO REGAIN CONTROL

Facing these inimical domestic forces and the abhorred presence of the Soviet Union and Britain in the north and south of his country, the shah began to use despotic authority and turned to the United States for help, as the U.S. had supported a military mission in Iran since 1942. The U.S. extended military and economic aid as well as political backing. The USSR, unwilling to confront the U.S., began in March 1946 to pull out from the northern territories it had occupied during the war, thereby giving the shah an opportunity to extend his control there.

139 Mawsawi, op. cit., p. 110.

The Tudeh Party, with the help of the Soviets, had grown very strong during the war, and many thought that it would soon control Iran, especially after Ahmad Qavam, who was pro-USSR and a supporter of Tudeh, was elected by the majlis as prime minister. However, the Tudeh Party was weakened and its power began to shrink.[140]

Political instability and resentment continued, especially by and among the religious people who were suspicious of the secular inclination of the young shah and the growing foreign influence. They applied an infamous folklore proverb saying, "a snake does not give birth but to a snake," in reference to his father's anti-religious policies. For example, the Iranian clergy recalled an event when Mohammed Reza was still a crown prince in 1939, when he was about to enter a very sacred Shi'ite shrine in Baghdad, Iraq, the mosque of Musa Al-Kadhim. He was reminded by the attendant, with the Quranic verse, to "take off your sandals while thou are inside the sacred pit." The young shah replied that he had no desire to take his shoes off to make pilgrimage to "tons of useless gold and silver." On another occasion, he was audaciously rude towards a very respectable Iraqi religious leader and politician, Mr. Al-Sadr, when he pointed towards Al-Sadr's turban and long beard and scoffed, "My father had eliminated the last of these reactionary aspects," which almost precipitated a political and diplomatic crisis between Iran and Iraq.

Following Shah Mohammad Reza's assumption of the throne in 1941, after his father's ejection and until the end of the 1940s, Iranian popular resentment against the foreign influences was growing fast. By 1951, the shah was faced with a complicated crisis. He was trying to avoid confrontation with the Great Powers, which had extensive interests in his country's oil, but he also had to consider the profuse popular demands to retrieve the country's oil industry for the benefit of Iran.

In spite of American financial and military support, political conditions were unstable. Between 1945 and 1951, Iran had already witnessed six prime ministers, some of whom stayed only for a month or two. In 1951, after Dr. Mohammed Mossadeq nationalized the oil industry, he became a national hero. When the oil well of Abadan, one

140 Halliday, op. cit., p. 24.

of the largest in the world, stopped production for a while after the British engineers and technicians left, Dr. Mossadeq became even more popular when he defiantly utilized Iranian experts to resume production, thereby refuting Great Britain's arrogant claim that Iran did not have the knowledge to operate its oil industry.[141]

While Mossadeq was able to mobilize most Iranians to replace the despotic royal regime with a Western-style democratic system in an attempt to achieve national sovereignty, Shah Mohammad Reza Pahlavi was more cautious. He was aware that Iran was too weak to oppose the Western oil companies that were supported by their powerful governments. He followed a more practical policy of assuaging them. The AIOC, the British government and the United States all came to support Shah Mohammad Reza against Mossadeq. Iran's main revenue came from exporting its oil, and the Great Powers decided to use that dependence on oil exportation to overthrow Mossadeq's government.

It is noteworthy that the historical period of Iran from 1945 to 1954 remarkably typifies Hegelian phenomena, as the nature of conflict was based largely on creeds. There were three main, separate, contradicting ideological umbrellas that encompassed and were found in most social classes:

- Mossadeq and his secular Western-Liberal National Front were supported by the middle class intelligentsia, the upper middle class, as well as a portion of his downtrodden proletariat who were impressed by his calls for reform. The National Front was also supported by the Tudeh Communist Party. The National Front reached the zenith of its influence when in 1952, it won 60 percent of the majlis votes, and Mossadeq assumed the positions of prime minister and minister of defense.[142]
- Shah Mohammad Reza's despotic, secular Kemalist ideology, which he pursued after his father's departure, encompassed some merchants of the bazaar, some elements of the middle class, and some farmers and peasants who were exposed to the

141 Mawsawi, op. cit., p. 12.
142 Cleveland, op. cit., p. 292.

shah's educational campaigns, which he implemented in rural areas. He gained the support of the people by means of his propaganda.

- The Fada'iyan-e Islam Party and the clergy: This fanatic Shi'ite movement and its believers invariably attempted to change Iran into an Islamic theocracy based on the Shari'ah. This movement gained the support of the clergy and religious believers in general, ranging from the highest to the lowest classes. The Shi'ite creed, which is based on glorifying the *imams* (descendants of the household of Caliph Ali Ben Abi Talib) and religious men of the past, had for centuries appealed to the spiritual needs of a large segment of the Iranian people.[143]

These diverse ideologies were vying to control the political arena of Iran. Upon Mossadeq's announcement of nationalization, the entire British Empire was severely shocked, and the government of Great Britain imposed a boycott against the Iran oil industry. Mossadeq attempted in vain to use all available sources to ease the economic suffocation that befell the Iranian people because of the boycott. Mossadeq was still a very popular reformer, but without adequate revenues to implement development programs, inflation, unemployment and the cost of living substantially rose, which provoked resentment among the workers and the poor. And, because of the powerful status of the National Front and its alliance with the Tudeh, the West was alarmed that Iran, with all its economic and strategic importance, was going to fall under the influence of the Soviet Union. Thus, a plot was drawn between the West and the shah to bring down Mohammed Mossadeq once and for all.

However, the plot was unveiled, and in the middle of September 1953, Shah Mohammad Reza and his Prime Minister Fazlollah Zahedi fled the country because of fear of retribution,[144] but they came back after a few days. Immediately, a police and military force attacked Mossadeq's house and arrested him. This coup against

143 Munadhamat al-iilam al-Islami (Organization of Islamic Information, Khat al-Imam al Komeini (Imama Khomeini's Line) pp. 9-12.

144 Cleveland, op. cit., p. 292.

Mossadeq was well planned and coordinated by the United States Central Intelligence Agency (CIA). A new cabinet was formed under the ardent royalist supporter General Zahedi, and President Dwight D. Eisenhower sent US$45 million to the shah's government on an emergency basis.[145]

After bolstering his position, the shah began to retaliate with utmost harshness against the groups that opposed him during the Mossadeq era. With the assistance of U.S. and Israeli advisors, the shah's newly established SAVAK began to brutalize the shah's opponents. The National Front was disbanded and its leaders, including Mossadeq, were imprisoned. SAVAK concentrated its effort to eradicate the Tudeh Party. The Tudeh's underground headquarters were uncovered, hundreds of its members were tortured in jails and a large number of its leaders were chained and drowned in a remote lake.

After destroying the Tudeh, the shah turned to confront the powerful and dangerous religious movement Fada'iyan-e Islam, whose youthful leader, Navvab Safavi, was supported by a number of young men willing to sacrifice their lives for the sake of Islam and who had taken an oath to kill any ruler or higher official figure who did not follow the Islamic rules.

One such target of Fada'iyan Islam was Ahmad Khisrawi, a renowned scholar and prolific author who ridiculed the imams and all religions, including Islam and the Quran, and described himself as the savior of humanity from religious superstition. In an attempt to eliminate this influential secular reformer, Navvab Safavi shot but missed Ahmad Khisrawi. Khisrawi was not hurt, but he took Safavi to court. While the court was prosecuting Safavi, another member of the Fada'iyan-e Islam party, Hussein Imami, stormed into the court and fatally shot Khisrawi. To avoid religious upheaval by the clergy, Imami received a light punishment, and subsequently the court released both Safavi and Imami.

Several other assassinations of highly ranked officials were perpetrated by the Fada'iyan-e Islam Party, and after each of these violent events, they sent the shah threats that if he did not abandon his secular

145 Fisher, op. cit., p. 521.

programs and strictly follow Islamic laws, the "next bullet" would be his.[146]

Supported by such prominent religious leaders as Ayatollah Al-Kashani, the group kept growing stronger and continued preaching fanatic Islamic conservatism and anti-Western ideas. Eventually they assassinated the loyal royalist, pro-West Prime Minister Hussein Fatimi.

The shah decided to rid Iran of this terrorist group and ordered SAVAK to arrest the leaders of the Fada'iyan-e Islam Party. Five of its leaders and members were executed, including Navvab Safavi, which marked the end of the party.

To appease the omnipresent religious group and clergy, Shah Mohammad Reza kept contact with the acknowledged leader of the Iranian Shi'ites, the eminent mujtahid (religious interpreter) Ayatollah Hossein Kazemeyni Boroujerdi, who was the unrivaled spokesman of the clergy. The shah and Boroujerdi kept a close but precarious relationship of mutual respect until 1958, when the government introduced a program that redistributed land to peasants as they were too poorly paid to be able to purchase it themselves. By the mid-1960s, the government enlarged the programs to affect nearly 14,000 villages—25 percent of the rural settlements. Boroujerdi, with the endorsement of many landlords, opposed the move as being against the Islamic law that allowed unlimited ownership of private property. The clergy's opposition to the shah's reform programs ended all possibility of reconciliation between the regime and the religious groups.[147]

After he was able to marginalize the clergy, the shah felt powerful enough to pursue his father's Kemalist secular ideology to modernize Iran. However, in 1963, Grand Ayatollah Imam Abu al-Qasim al-Khoei attacked the shah's secular program and declared him a non-Muslim and a non-legitimate ruler due to his close relationship with the West and Israel. Al-Khoei's declaration, however, was inconsequential, as the shah stayed in power due to the loyalty of the SAVAK and the army. Thus, the conflict between religious and secular ideology continued in Iran.

146 Mawsawi, op. cit., p. 100.
147 Bayne, op. cit., p. 48.

THE GOVERNMENT OF SHAH MOHAMMAD REZA

The main features of the Iranian state under Shah Mohammad Reza were secular nationalism, capitalism, the White Revolution (development of capitalism), a monarchical form of dictatorship, and dependence on the advanced capitalist countries.[148]

SECULAR NATIONALISM

The first foundation of the shah's monarchical system was to purvey an ideology that would secure broad popular support. Like his father and Mustafa Kemal Ataturk of the Republic of Turkey, Mohammad Reza Shah endeavored to eliminate the archaic Islamic identity that had united the Iranian people for centuries and replace it with secular national pride that would become the basis of vigorous social solidarity of the Iranian people. He emphasized the greatness of Iran's ancient history and stressed the fact that it was the monarchs who brought it about. The exaggeration of a specifically Iranian "national mythology" was promoted and encouraged by Reza Shah and pursued by his son, the second Pahlavi shah.

Noticeably absent in Shah Mohammad Reza's ideology was any reference to Islam. For centuries the national unity of the Persian people had been based on Islamic dogmas and led by the ulema (religious scholars). Since 1921, however, those who were outspoken in their support of Islamic policy were condemned, and Shah Mohammad Reza severely clashed with religious leaders as he attempted to replace religious social foundations with secularized laws, education and secular nationalism as a means of social solidarity.[149]

In his determined effort to promote legitimacy of his rule, the shah resorted to avid emphasis on the Pahlavi dynasty as the heir to the pre-Islamic Achaemenid and Sasanian dynasties. His father had already designated for the monarchy the ancient Persian royal title Shahan Shah, or King of Kings, to which Mohammad Reza Shah added Aryamehr, "light of the Aryans." In emphasizing the achievements of

148 Halliday, op. cit., p. 62.
149 Bayne, op. cit., pp. 46-47.

the pre-Islamic Persian empires, the shah virtually ignored Iran's glorious Islamic past and offered no substantial proof connecting his origin to the ancient Persian civilizations. His statement was utterly areligious and accentuated secular nationalism.

To accentuate the inveterate Persian-Iranian nationalism worldwide, the shah in 1971 gave an extremely extravagant celebration, to which he invited most dignitaries of the world; it cost $100 million to commemorate 2,500 continuous years of the Iranian monarchy.[150]

CAPITALISM

A very fundamental component of the Iranian state is capitalism; i.e., it guarantees the conditions to produce, reproduce and expand the capitalist ownership of private property and private enterprise. The main characteristic of modern Iranian capitalism is substantial growth of the Iranian capitalist class; i.e., a bourgeoisie that developed through economic expansion. The government welcomed the development of the bourgeoisie because by the 1960s, the power of the pre-capitalist feudal lords was eliminated.

The Iranian state was an institution that provided for growth and establishment of a prosperous middle class which, in return, supported the government. The main components of the middle class were the upper stratum of state employees, the capitalist land owners, and those engaged in finance, trade and industry.

The social change represented a major departure from the pre-capitalist class of feudalist lords and highly ranked clergy who dominated the country's economic system.[151]

The above-mentioned components formed the Iranian bourgeoisie, whose interests were defended by the Pahlavi state. Each owed its conditions to the support and intervention of the state. The state employees achieved their high positions by having developed from a small group of administrative personnel in the 1920s. The armed forces and the higher echelon of the civil service were channels for recruiting new members of the bourgeoisie, and they were entirely dependent on state

150 Fisher, op. cit., p. 525.
151 Halliday, op. cit., p. 4.

policy for retention of their positions and privileges, especially after oil revenues began to soar in the world market. This social segment increased greatly in numbers and wealth. Both urban and rural land owners benefited greatly from the state policy of developing the countryside along capitalist lines. Those who agreed to follow the capitalist development style retained ownership of their property, while those who lost their land to development were compensated and encouraged to pursue industrial and trade projects.

THE WHITE REVOLUTION (DEVELOPMENT OF CAPITALISM)

The third feature of the Pahlavi Iran was the development of capitalism, or the White Revolution (meaning reform without violence). The main purpose of the White Revolution was to continue to pursue economic and social development. After the oil crisis caused by Mohammed Mossadeq was settled in 1953, the shah embarked on a five-year development plan, to be financed by oil revenues. The plans began in 1954 and included building dams on water sources to irrigate arid lands, developing hydroelectric power plants and draining swamp areas to prepare new arable lands.

Because the vast majority of the Iranians were peasants and the national interests would be served by improving their capabilities, the government began to provide financial loans to enhance agricultural, industrial and social services and electric power production.[152] Additional steps of the development plans of the White Revolution were launched in 1963. They concentrated on reformation of the land system, nationalization of forest lands and sale of state-owned industrial enterprise to encourage the private sector.

The shah concentrated not only on land reform but also on the establishment of literacy corps to combat illiteracy among the peasants. However, in order to educate the peasants as part of his modernization plan, the shah saw that because the mullahs (clergy) had great influence over the village dwellers, their influence must be undermined. By 1963, mullahs were put under village arrest and the unruly Ayatollah

152 Fisher, op. cit., p. 523.

Ruhollah Al-Imam Al-Khomeini was exiled. With the national wealth steadily growing as a result of the increase of oil production, the government could afford to recruit 8,000 members of the corps, administered by the army, to serve in the villages as well as urban areas.[153]

The shah's reform program was dynamic and kept improving the status of the rural peasants who moved to the cities. The program had led to major movements in the educational institutions and facilitated the process of urbanization. In twenty years the population of the capital had tripled, and that of the provincial cities nearly doubled. Between the 1960s and 1970s, enrollment in elementary schools grew from 1.6 billion to over four million, and university enrollment increased almost sevenfold to 154,215. During the same period, the number of hospitals, health clinics and trained physicians rose also.

A noteworthy point is that in, 1948 Tehran had about fifteen major mosques. However, by 1965, with three times the population (estimated at 2.5 million), there were only twenty major places of public worship. Apparently education and urbanization had effectively spread secularism, and religious influence had decreased.[154]

The shah changed the name of the White Revolution to the Shah-People Revolution, which triggered an acceleration of social reform. The election that the shah had promised to hold came in 1963, which included both the majlis and the senates. A new political party was established by Ali Mansur strictly to support the shah's reform programs. As expected, Mansur controlled the majlis, which was dominated by agrarian reformers and city dwellers.

The shah's obsession with Kemalism pushed him to espouse a secular Western model of social and legal reform to enhance the status of women and religious minorities. He appointed thirty members of the senate and, in spite of its recalcitrant clergy, made the revolutionary decision to include two women senators, and he elected six women representatives to the majlis. For the first time in Islam's history, women voted in large numbers, and their votes were counted.

Other major progressive decrees regarding family protection laws

153 Bayne, op. cit., p. 51.
154 Ibid.

and marriage, restricting polygamy, and expanding education, employment and enfranchisement were passed by the majlis, granting women great legal equality.[155]

The shah kept expanding his legal reform and enhancing the status of religious minorities as he canceled the requirement of obtaining approval of the religious judges to pass laws, and cancelled the "jiziyah" tax imposed by Islamic laws on Jews and Christians. He also substantially promoted the political, legal and social status of the Baha'is. Baha'ism is a rather new faith established during the early decades of the nineteenth century by Russian and British governments in Iran to undermine the influence of Islam. In his memoirs, which have been translated to several languages, Maxim Gorky, the famous Russian writer who was once a Russian counselor in Tehran, admits that he inspired the monk Mohammad Baha' to establish the Baha'is religious movement in Iran to serve the Russian interests there.

Baha'ism recognizes and pays respect to all religious prophets, including Abraham, Moses, Jesus, Buddha, Krishna, and Mohammad. The religious book of the Baha' is the "Aqdas," which means the holy book. Even though Baha'ism is not included in the Quranic concept of the people of the scripture, or "Ahl al-Dhimmah," people protected by Islam, the Baha'is enjoyed a period of prosperity under the Pahlavi dynasty. Shah Mohammad Reza, due to his secular, extensive education, and as part of democratization of his country, extended special attention to the Baha'is. Perceiving them as a peaceful group who were loyal to him, he assigned several of them to higher military and administrative positions of his government. Even the shah's private physician and close friend was a Baha'i—Dr. General Ayadi.[156] Additionally, to demonstrate his modern tolerance of non-Muslim minorities, in 1966, the shah approved to his cabinet seven men with Baha'i family backgrounds.

The clergy were keenly disgruntled with the shah's favoritism toward the Baha'is, and the ayatollahs accused him of practicing syncretism, as they perceived Baha'ism to be in conflict with Islam. Yet, the

155 Fisher, op. cit., p. 525.
156 Mawsawi, op. cit., p. 184.

shah defiantly kept pressing secularism, and Kemalism kept marching on in Iran under the Pahlavi dynasty.

MONARCHICAL DICTATORSHIP

The fourth major feature of the Iranian state is it is considered a dictatorship kingdom. In diversified political systems, the state rests on a combination of coercion and consent. The domination of either of these two aspects of influence determines whether the rule is dictatorial or democratic. In the industrialized, advanced democratic countries, consent is the dominant feature of their governments. In Iran, after the downfall of the tyrannical Reza Shah in 1941, the intelligentsia was optimistic that their country was heading towards a brighter, more democratic future. At the beginning of his reign, the young, highly educated new Shah Mohammad Reza Pahlavi, contrary to his father, was a constitutional king who possessed no power; his decisions were restricted by the constitution. He was a representative figure and his signature was only a form of procedure.[157] Iran witnessed a short period of lenient policies allowing freedom of mass media and opinion, and the new shah seemed to be gradually steering Iran towards a true modern democracy. The mullahs were disgruntled with his secular, pro-West inclinations, while the liberal movement and the Tudeh resented the Great Powers' domination of Iran's policy and economy. The protests by political forces alarmed the shah, and he gradually resorted to strong confrontation of the opposition.

After he was able, with the help of the American CIA, to squash the violent upheaval led by Dr. Mohammad Mossadeq and the National Front in 1953, the shah emerged as the most powerful entity in Iran, and he moved into the political situation as a full-fledged despotic ruler.

To justify his tyrannical policy, the shah stated that political turbulence leads to dire economic consequences because entrepreneurs would not venture to invest in a politically unstable country for fear of loss. To reinforce his argument, he asserted that in the advanced democratic countries, political stability led to the growth of a thriving

157 Graham, op. cit., p. 90.

bourgeoisie and flourishing economy, whereas in the developing countries only a powerful centralized government or a dictatorship is able to attain stability and encourage investments.

In order to bestow legitimacy to his regime, the shah allowed the formation of a two-party system: the government Melliyeen, later changed to the Novin Party, and the so-called opposition, the Mordon Party. Each party nominated candidates for the majlis, but no candidate was suggested without the approval of the SAVAK. The majlis to which they were elected was powerless, and even the prime minister was appointed by the shah. Any representative of the "opposition" Mordon Party who dared to utter a serious criticism of the government was dismissed. The party system was without influence and totally under the shah's control.[158]

The intelligentsia never believed that the system was really an authentic two-party system such as the United States. Yet the shah, accentuating his legitimacy, declared in one of his speeches, "If I were a dictator rather than a constitutional monarch, then I might be tempted to sponsor a single dominant party such as Hitler organized or as you find in a communist country."[159]

In 1975, the shah decided to end this pretense. He abolished the two-party system and replaced it with a new single party called Rastakhiz, or the National Resurgence Party. The Iranians were coerced to join.

The shah justified his decision of changing the system to one party by emphasizing that the country needed discipline in administration and industry in order to achieve social stability. He stated in one of his speeches:[160]

> We must straighten out Iranian ranks. To do so, we divide them into two categories: those who believe in the monarchy and the constitution, and the Sixth Bahman Revolution (i.e., the date on which the White Revolution was announced in 1963) and those who do not... a person who does not enter

158 Halliday, op. cit., p. 46.
159 Ibid, pp. 47-48.
160 Ibid, p. 62.

> the new political party, does not believe in the principles which I referred to, will only have two choices. He is either an individual who belongs to an illegal organization, or is related to the outlawed Tudeh Party, or in other words is a traitor. Such an individual belongs in an Iranian prison, or if he desires he can leave the country tomorrow, without even paying exit fees; he can go anywhere because he is not Iranian, he has no nation, and his activities are illegal and punishable according to the law.

Individuals, groups or organizations who dared to criticize the regime were crushed by SAVAK. The usually unruly religious leaders were restricted or controlled by the state agents. Their sermons were monitored by the government's secret police in the mosques. The intelligentsia had no choice but to follow the regime since all employment in the sector and high-level educational appointments were granted on the condition of cooperation.

Whereas the previous two-party system had only the façade of an active political system, the new single-party system became a mass organization. By 1977, it was claimed that five million Iranians had joined the party, and local cells were established all over the country. Iran had a small but thriving bourgeoisie, the military was loyal to the regime, SAVAK ensured stability and control of the society, and the shah enjoyed absolute power. Hence, Iran could be accurately described as a capitalist totalitarian monarchy.

DEPENDENCE ON THE ADVANCED CAPITALIST COUNTRIES

The fifth and last feature of Shah Mohammad Reza's government is that it largely depended on the support provided by the U.S. and the advanced capitalist world. Since 1946, Iran had been closely connected in political and military matters with the U.S. Had it not been for the U.S. military and political support during the decades following World War II, especially during Mossadeq's crisis, the Iranian monarchy and its capitalist system would have been overthrown.[161]

Friendly relations with the United States were pursued by most Iranian prime ministers, and in return they received all the support they needed from the United States. An American mission to train the Iranian army was instituted, and a large quantity of military equipment was rented to Iran according to a mutual defense agreement.

During and after World War II, dependency between the United States and Iran intensified. The capitalist monarchy of Iran needed the support of the United States to confront the menace of the neighboring great power, the Communist Soviet Union, with which it shared 37,860 miles of border. In return, the United States had a deep interest in Iran's strategic and economic importance, especially Iran's huge wealth of oil.

By the 1940s, America's oil revenue and production were not sufficient to meet its domestic and military needs. The first alarming reports of American experts on the oil requirements of the U.S., and whether those requirements could be met by the reserves of the American continent, were published during World War II. According to the report submitted to President Roosevelt by the director of the commission of experts:

The future of the Great Powers, oil, no longer lies on the American continent. The center of gravity of the world's petroleum outputs is shifting more and more from the area of the Gulf of Mexico and the Caribbean (Venezuela) to the area around the Persian Gulf. This trend will continue in the future, leading to the ultimate rearrangement.

Thus, the Middle East region, which contains 63 percent of oil reserves, became of vital importance to the American national interest. The threat of an oil shortage forced the United States to bolster its presence in the Middle East region. Iran, which has 12 percent of the world's oil reserve, in third place behind Kuwait and Saudi Arabia, gradually came to the attention of the United States. During the first few years after the war, military interest dominated the relations between the two countries. In 1947, Iran received its first financial aid payment, according to an agreement signed that year between the two countries. Other funds

161 Nirumand, op. cit., p. 39.

totaling $16 million were to bear interest at the rate of 2.5 percent and were payable over twelve years. By 1966, nonmilitary aid—grants for technical aid, loans from the World Bank, and outright gifts from the United States—totaled more than $550 million.[162]

These huge funds made it possible for the shah to execute his White Revolution, as well as other economic plans, and augment the military arsenal needed to bolster his country's position in the region. Iran's capitalist development was a result of the cooperation between the Iranian state and foreign interests, at both state and private enterprise levels. Iran's continuous importation of skilled personnel, technology and training aids from the advanced capitalist countries indicated the importance of continuing such cooperation if capitalism in Iran, which was vital for the West, was to continue. Hence, it is accurate to state that Iran was dependent on the U.S.[163]

One of the important steps the shah took to strengthen his ties with the Western Great Powers and the neighboring country was when he joined the Baghdad Pact, which comprised Great Britain, Turkey, Pakistan and Iraq, and was sponsored by the United States.[164]

The above-mentioned five features constituted the foundation of the Iranian state under the rule of Shah Mohammad Reza Pahlavi, who sought to achieve the following four objectives:

a) To pursue and bolster the secular Kemalist political and economic regime established by his father in Iran
b) To adopt contemporary education programs to rid his people of religious restrictions which perpetuated archaic thinking and backwardness among the people
c) To gradually liberate his country from foreign imperial influence by developing the national sources and technological capabilities to stop Iran's dependence on Western aid and expertise
d) To catapult Iran as an advanced military and economic power, thus achieving parity with the Western Great Powers

162 Fisher, op. cit., p. 528.
163 Halliday, op. cit., p. 67.
164 Gallman, Waldemar J. Iraq Under General Nuri (Baltimore: The John Hopkins Press, 1964), pp. 66-70.

These were quite lofty objectives Shah Mohammad Reza Pahlavi dreamed of attaining. However, he ignored a very important fact: in spite of his strenuous efforts to spread secularism, the majority of the Iranians remained deeply religious. His reform programs touched a thin layer of urban intelligentsia, but spiritual needs kept permeating the minds of all social classes of the populace. Pilgrimages to holy Shi'ite sites in Mashhad, Qum, and Najaf and Karbala in Iraq were performed regularly by millions of Persians regardless of the travel difficulties.

Negligence of religion and hostility towards the mullahs had dire consequences on Shah Mohammad Reza and his regime, in the long run, as will be illustrated in a later chapter.

Chapter 5

Gamal Abdel Nasser and Arab Socialism: The Downfall of Nasser

Historical Background

Egypt was the first Arab country to witness some aspects of social progress and modernization due to its invasion by Napoleon Bonaparte in 1798. Late in the eighteenth century, the authority of the medieval Ottoman Empire was quickly fading in the province of Egypt as the governing Mamluks grew more powerful and defiant to Istanbul. The weakness of the Ottomans and the social stagnation/backwardness promulgated by the Mamluks lured Napoleon Bonaparte to strategically invade Egypt, and his forces landed in Alexandria on July 1, 1798.[165] He destroyed the ragtag army of the Mamluks in the historical Battle of the Pyramids on July 22, and annexed Egypt to his domain. Yet the French occupation was brought to an end when Great Britain, fearing to lose control of the strategic routes leading to India, destroyed the French fleet in the Battle of Abiker on August l, 1798. The French army stayed in Egypt for three years and finally was allowed by the British and Ottoman authority to depart in 1801.

Short as it was, however, the French presence left a profound influence on the Egyptian society. Media and intellectual activities were

165 Qusay al-Husein, "Awda' Misr Wa Dhuhur Muhammad Ali," al-Khaleej, No. 10498, Feb. 4, 2008.

substantially enhanced and expanded by an Arabic press machine brought by Napoleon. Western literature was translated and spread among the educated elite, thereby altering the long-lasting traditional intellectualism based, by and large, on religion. Advanced military machines fascinated the Egyptian generals who were still using archaic weaponry.

After assisting the armies of the sultan against the French invaders, the British signed the Peace of Amiens treaty in 1802, which required them to leave the country, thus paving the way for the arrival of a new leadership in Egypt. Muhammad Ali, a highly ranked Ottoman officer, took advantage of the vacuity and turbulence that erupted following the departure of the British forces, and led his troops to overtake the reign of power and start his meteoric career. He was officially appointed governor of Egypt by the sultan.[166]

Many historians assert that nineteenth-century Egypt was largely the creation of Muhammad Ali, who must be recognized as one of the world's great rulers of his age.[167] Muhammad Ali's ascension to power coincided with the dawn of the Industrial Revolution in Western Europe and he became increasingly intrigued by the advantages of modern technology for his extremely primitive country.

Quoting the well-known historian Abdul Rahman Al Jabarti, Atif al Ghumri claims that before Muhammad Ali, Egypt had descended to the lowest level of economic and social decline. The peasants were illiterate and were using ancient elementary methods of agriculture; education programs were inadequate; epidemics invaded Egypt yearly; and annual deaths from bubonic plague and cholera killed 10 percent or more of the population.[168] From the onset of his arrival to power, Muhammad Ali realized that, in spite of the dire backwardness of Egypt, progress was by no means impossible. He embarked on a rigorously planned program of reforms concentrating on sanitation and education. A modern quarantine was built, and foreign councils in Alexandria were appointed to a Board of Sanitation, which was granted substantial funds and full authority. The effectiveness of these steps was

166 Kinross, pp. 447-448.
167 Fisher, p. 274.
168 Atif al-Ghumri, al-Khaleej, No. 10461, January 19, 2008.

evidenced as the eruptions of epidemics were drastically reduced.[169]

Ali's plans for education started by inaugurating a modern military school which included infantry, cavalry, engineers, navy and artillery. Most of the instructors were French. Distinguished male students were sent to European countries to pursue their higher education. As for industry, Ali imported textile plants and sugar factories, but the lack of capable technicians and crude resources hampered the efforts of industrialization. In sum, Muhammad Ali was attempting to extricate Egypt from the Middle Ages and propel it toward modernization.[170]

After Muhammad Ali's death, Egypt's ties with Europe were brought closer as a result of the construction of the Suez Canal by the French engineer Ferdinand de Lesseps in 1869, when Egypt was ruled by Khedeve Sa'id, a descendant of Muhammed Ali. The canal, a waterway 107 miles long that connects the Mediterranean Sea with the Red Sea, provides a shortcut between the western countries and the Far East. It became one of the most important routes of the world's commerce and substantially increased interaction between the Egyptian and European cultures, thereby causing a significant social and economic progress. The Renaissance in Egypt peaked in the twentieth century through the work of scholars like Ahmad Lufti al-Sayid, Qasim Amin, Salama Mousa, Taha Hussien, Abbas Mahmoud al-Aqqad, Ibrahim Abdul Qadir al-Mazinin and others. These thinkers, most of whom studied in Europe, began to preach new, previously unheard-of European ideas such as Darwinism, socialism, democracy, and nationalism, while the vast majority of the populace remained deeply religious.[171]

The modernizing current was rivaled by a militant religious movement called *al-Ikhwan alMuslimun* (Muslim Brotherhood). It was established in the 1920s by Sheikh Hasan al-Banna, a well-known and respected religious figure, as a vehement reaction to secularism and Westernization, and to stop deviation from Islamic beliefs. When Sheikh al-Banna was asked about his future program, he would answer:

169 Fisher, pp. 278-279.
170 Fisher, ibid. pp.178-180
171 Abdul Adheem Ramdham, Al-Ikhuan al-Muslimun: Wa al-tandheem al-sirri (The Muslim Brotherhood: The Clandestine Organization) (Cairo: Rose al-Yusif Press, 1982) p. 2.

> We are quite satisfied to be Muslims, and our program is the same program of Prophet Muhammad, may blessings of God be upon him. Our belief derived from the holy Quran and the prophet's traditions.[172]

The Brotherhood targeted the youth and infiltrated the military forces. A substantial number of young officers joined its ranks. But the intellectuals who believed in secularism and were preaching modernization perceived the Brotherhood movement as a reactionary ideology aiming to drag Egypt and the Arab world back to the medieval early Islamic era.

Hence, with the birth and spread of Kemalism after the downfall of the Ottoman theocracy, and the growth of the Western-educated middle class amidst the Islamic masses, the Middle East was set for a dialectical conflict between religious and secular ideologies.

Amidst all these competing ideologies and political effervescence, a boy was born in Egypt on May 1, 1918; his name was Gamal Abdel Nasser.[173] He was destined later in his youth, as a military officer, to become the hero of Arab national socialism, and his influence on the Middle East exceeded by far any other leadership or political movement.

This chapter discusses in detail the main characteristics of the secular, socialist and nationalist ideology—henceforth termed Nasserism—that was established by Colonel Gamal Abdel Nasser and overtook the political beliefs of the vast majority of the populace.

As a high school youth, Nasser was invariably rebellious, leading strikes, demonstrations and riots against the British occupation of Egypt since the nineteenth century, and the French-British control of the vital Suez Canal and its lucrative income. He joined the revolutionary radical movement of Young Egypt, which sought independence and social reform. The turning point of Nasser's life came in March 1937, when he was admitted to the military academy.[174]

Resentment among the Egyptian middle class against backwardness and colonialism constituted the major cause of upheaval in Egypt

172 Ibid, p. 30.
173 Robert Stephens, Nasser: A Political Biography (New York Simon and Schuster, 1971), p. 21.
174 Ibid, p. 39.

for decades. The revolt of Ahmed Arabi in 1881 against the corrupt Khedeve and his foreign advisors was crushed by the British army. Later in 1919, Sa'ad Zaghlul's revolt against colonialism, emphasizing Egypt's Arabic cultural background and insisting on demand for reform, led to the promulgation of the 1923 constitution defining the king's court. All these and other events showed that the core of Egypt's social, political and economic systems needed essential redress.

In April 1936, the young King Farouk ascended the Egyptian throne. A new election was held and the liberal Wafd Party obtained the majority of the seats in both houses of the Parliament. Chairman of the Wafd Party, Mustafa al-Nahhas (Pasha), a loyal royalist, became prime minister with a Wafd cabinet.[175] With such a powerful backing, King Farouk embarked on gradual social reform. The first step he undertook was to reform the educational system. Realizing the need for diversified specializations to meet the needs of modern life, the king began to facilitate admission of youth of lower classes to colleges of teachers, law, engineering, post-graduate studies and most of all the military academies, which were formerly restricted to the sons of prominent families. After World War II, the middle class steadily increased in number and influence as journalists, lawyers and professors, among others, utilized the new opportunities of growth and prosperity.[176]

However, the reform was not happening quickly enough nor widespread enough, as it hardly touched the large rural areas. Changes affected the large cities, while the peasantry, who constituted the people's majority, remained ignorant, disease stricken, and destitute. They were bullied by the police and dragooned to vote by their landlords or by the government through the officially appointed *omdahs* (headmen) or chiefs of the villages, and occasionally lured by leaders of political parties vying in the villages. The growing class of the urban industrial centers were not in much better condition. Dilapidated slums were proliferating faster than the reform plans in the cities, as the impoverished population migrated from the countryside seeking scarce opportunities of employment.

175 Fisher, p. 455.
176 Stephen, p. 46.

In foreign affairs, the 1936 treaty requiring England to terminate the protectorate protocol imposed in 1914 was not fulfilled, despite the efforts of the Egyptian leadership. Instead, Britain increased its military establishment in Egypt and announced that its naval headquarters in the Mediterranean was to be transferred from Malta to Alexandria, a decision which exacerbated the humiliation of the Egyptians.

After World War II, the Palestine issue became the focus of politics in the Middle East. The British government kept avoiding attempts of Arab leaders, especially Nuri (Pasha) al-Said of Iraq, to elicit a firm pledge to keep Palestine under the rule of the Palestinian Arabs.[177] Winston Churchill, an ardent Zionist who believed that a Jewish state in Palestine coincided with the British imperial interest in the Middle East, did not approve Nuri al-Said's demands.[178]

In 1948, Israel was created on the land of Palestine, and the Arab armies attacked the newly born foreign state in an attempt to retrieve the land for their Palestinian brethren. They were defeated. That war constituted a turning point in the mind of Gamal Abdel Nasser, the young, ardent nationalist and keen anti-colonialist Egyptian officer.[179]

Nasser attributed the humiliating defeat of the Arab countries to what he perceived as the reactionary and corrupt Arab rulers who were obsequious to the British and Western imperialism. He believed that the entire Arab world needed to be revolutionized and united in one powerful nation in order to achieve liberty and progress. After returning home from the war of Palestine, Nasser began to choose his close commanding officers for his clandestine movement. The movement was bolstered when Nasser was able to recruit General Muhammad Naguib, a highly respected patriotic older officer.

At that time, Egypt was ruled by young King Farouk, who had much wealth and political power. Strikingly handsome, youthful and rich, Farouk's profligacies and other self-indulgences, which were exaggerated by his foes, increased the negative opinions of the people

177 Zaki, Mamoon Amin, Izdihar al-Iraq-tahat al-hukm al-malaki (Prosperity of Iraq Under the Royal Regime), op. cit. pp. 178, 79.

178 Zaki, Mamoon Amin, Su'ud wa taraju' al-mashru' al-sihuni (The Rise and Retreat of the Zionist Project) (London: Dar al-Hikmah, 2007), p. 161.

179 Stephens, p. 85.

against the king's personal behavior. Riots, demonstrations and assassinations of politicians occurred, which led the government to hold relatively free elections in 1950. Campaigns revolved around the above-mentioned problems, and the Wafd Party under the leadership of Mustafa al-Nahhas (Pasha), a Western-style liberal political figure, won the election by a landslide.[180]

By October 1950, Prime Minister Nahhas, after several warnings, unilaterally abrogated the Anglo-Egyptian Treaty of 1936 and the Anglo-Egyptian Agreement of 1936, which established dominion over Sudan. This historical development prompted the British to impose counterproposals that were rejected by Egypt. Riots and demonstrations erupted in Cairo and several spots along the Suez Canal. Violent incidents became more frequent, and on January 25, 1952, a skirmish at Ismailia involving 1,500 British troops led to casualties. Egypt was ready for a profound historical change.

On July 23, 1952, the organization of Free Officers, led by Colonel Gamal Abdel Nasser, executed a coup d'état that dethroned the king, and after a few months abolished the royal regime and installed General Muhammad Naguib as president of the Republic of Egypt.

THE SECULAR SYSTEM OF GAMAL ABDEL NASSER

Sydney Nettleton Fisher, an American historian, describes the revolution in Egypt as three revolutions in one: a "French revolution" to get rid of a king and form a republic; an "American revolution" to drive out the British colonialism; and a "Kemal Ataturk revolution" to transform and regenerate the social and economic facets of an old civilization.[181]

Due to the effect of their programs on other parts of the Middle East, further comparison between Ataturk and Nasser is relevant.

An avid reader, Nasser, like Ataturk, was deeply influenced by the progressive philosophy of the Enlightenment, showing keen respect for the writings of Jean Jacques Rousseau, Voltaire, Claude Helvetius and others whose philosophies led to the French revolution.[182]

180 Fisher, p. 455.
181 Fisher, p. 693.
182 Stephens, p. 32.

Both leaders were military officers who utilized the army to execute revolutions and, upon seizing power, initiated profound social, political and economic changes that reflected on neighboring countries.

Both leaders believed in secularism, opposed intrusion of religion into politics, strictly restrained religious movements, emancipated women from religious constraints and advanced their educational and career opportunities.

However, Nasser's socialization of Egyptian economy and his economic development programs were more radical and far-reaching than the statism of Ataturk.

Nasserism spread among the masses of the Middle East much wider than Kemalism. Ataturk spoke Turkish and his audience was limited to the people of Turkey, while Nasser's well-organized propaganda in Arabic was heard by all Arabic-speaking countries. He was able to galvanize support from Morocco to Baghdad.

From the day Nasser ruled Egypt in 1954 until his death in 1970, the thesis of Nasserism overwhelmed other ideologies and mastered the minds of the majority of the Middle Eastern masses.

The coup, or the revolution of 1952, as some prefer to address it, was planned by a group of young military officers whose ranks were close to each other. Addressing themselves as the Free Officers, the group galvanized around one executive committee headed by Colonel Gamal Abdel Nasser, a young man of thirty-four at the time.

Once they controlled power, the officers selected from among themselves an organization they called the Revolutionary Command Council, which became the executive authority of the government.

Nasser admits that members of the Free Officers organization were not qualified to run a government. They were young men enthused by patriotic goals such as to remove "the corrupt and reactionary" royal regime and initiate general social changes.[183] In the beginning, their decisions were made as reactions to situations as they arose, to serve the instant needs of the people and the country.

Hence, Colonel Nasser, with his charismatic and dominant personality, was able to shape a rather clear program and lead his comrades

183 Fisher, p. 692.

to follow it. Right after the success of the coup, Nasser began to set and bolster the cornerstones of the new regime according to his perceptions, which were detailed in his book, *The Philosophy of the Revolution*, of how to attain the vital goals of the people and the country.[184]

Accentuating the belief that the revolution should lead to immediate essential reform of the society, the junta adopted the popular theme that the economy and political systems needed to be thoroughly cleansed before Egypt could become a modern country. Therefore the following steps were undertaken: all grandeur civilian titles denoting status, class and land ownership were eliminated; secret police and the police section of the royal palace were abolished; all political prisoners were freed; corrupt officials were arrested; and censorship of the press was eliminated.

In 1952, the cabinet decreed a new Agrarian Law No. 178 restricting ownership of land to two hundred square *fidan* per person, in comparison to the pre-revolution system when 0.4 percent of the population owned 20 percent of the arable land, while the rest were distributed to smaller land owners. Later the law was changed to restrict land ownership to twenty square *fidans* per family.[185]

The next step of fundamental social reform undertook by the junta under the guidance of Naguib and Nasser was to establish a more secular government. Gradually, religious endowments were discontinued by the end of 1952. Later, Muslim and non-Muslim religious courts in Egypt were abolished. The decrees did not repudiate sacred law, but henceforth precepts of sacred law were to be interpreted by civil judges.[186]

These steps were compared with the "Secular Kemalism" and set the new junta into direct disagreement with the ardent organization of the Muslim Brotherhood. The two sides stayed at odds until Nasser's death in 1970.

Due to the military nature of the new leadership, they imposed a draconian ruling system that did not allow any aspect of opposition or disagreement, and required full submission of political forces. Hence

184 Gamal Abdel Nasser, Philosophy of the Revolution (Cairo: Dar al-Ma'arif, 1955).

185 See al-Khaleej, October 17, 2002. For the text of the law, see Robert Stephense, pp. 115-116.

186 Fisher, p. 697.

a decree was passed to ban all political parties. On January 17, 1953, all political parties were dissolved and their properties were confiscated "for the popular interest." The parties were described as "practicing abominable partisanship, strictly pursuing their interests and exploiting the people."[187]

Hence the several-decades-old competitive, multi-party system came to an abrupt end upon the downfall of the royal regime. The commander in chief of the military forces promised that the transitional period would come to an end soon. However, it lasted throughout Nasser's rule.

Subsequent to the abolition of all political parties, there ensued a deep political vacuity which needed to be filled. Hence, the framework of the "Liberation Rally" or "L.R." was established by Anwar Sadat, a member of the Free Officers, to gain support for the government of the revolution. It was the first political order established during the early stages of the revolution, reflected Nasser's thoughts, and was formed around his leadership.[188]

The L.R. was not a political party. It was a program to organize the people and reestablish society on a new basis. Nasser described this system as a school by which the people learned how to elect their representatives. Nasser was attempting to reorient popular activities away from political parties and unite them under his new system.

The objectives of the L.R. were specified as "unity, order and work," and the slogan, "We are all Liberty Rally," indicated that the L.R. was for the entire people.

The mass media announced the reasons for the L.R. as ''to rally all the popular forces, except the feudalist and former leaders of the disbanded parties, to accomplish a major goal: to kick out imperialism and confront all anti-revolution forces."[189]

The second experience that was perceived and implemented by Nasser was the formation of a political order to bolster his position,

187 Buthaynah Abdul Rahman al-Tikriti, Gamal Abdel Nasser: nash'at wa tatawur al-fikr al-nasseri (Gamal Abdel Nasser: The Birth and Development of Nasserism) (Beirut: Center of Arab Unity Studies 2000) pp.174-176 .

188 Stephens, p. 121.

189 Abd Allah al-Imam, Al Nassiriya: Dirasah watha'iqiya li fikr Abdel Nasser (Nasserism: A Documentary Study of Abdel Nasser's Thoughts) (Cairo: Dar al-Sha'b, 1976), pp. 182-193.

and that was the establishment of the National Union (N.U.).[190]

In January 1956, Nasser gave several speeches in which he announced the end of the transitional period, attacked the previously active political parties as corrupt, announced several principles dealing with women's rights and equality, and decreed the need for the establishment of a National Union to encompass all patriotic forces that intended to build the new society.

Nasser thought that the N.U. would be the effective means to expedite the process of revolutionizing social changes towards progress.[191] He perceived that the N.U. would encompass the following social and economic forces:[192]

a. The technicians and intellectuals whose efforts and expertise are indispensable for the industrial and development plans. The development plans would create new opportunities for new jobs and eliminate unemployment, which would lead to the elevation of economic and social standards.
b. The laborers, whose duties and specialties are to be distributed within the public sector, which includes: consumptive industries, spinning, textile, and the services sector. The laborers were the real beneficiaries of the new industries and the improved old industries. The leadership of the revolution undertook new measures to solve the laborers' problems by passing new "Egyptianization" laws to bolster the plans that aimed to create a robust economy. They also passed labor laws that supported the rights of workers in industrial projects.
c. The peasantry: Peasants whose standard of living was extremely low during the former feudalist era constituted the majority of the population. The land reform laws were a clear expression of the revolution's support for the peasant and the liberation of the peasantry from the feudalist hegemony. For the first time in the country's history, the law specified minimum wage for the peasants, and the peasant became the owner of land to cultivate.

190 Ahmad (Nasser's Speeches), pp. 239-245.
191 Ibid, pp. 277-282.
192 Tikriti, Buthaynah Abdul Rahman, op. cit. pp. 180-182.

d. Egypt's capitalist class: Dealing with this social segment was not an easy task as interests of the bourgeoisie were interconnected with the leader of the old regime. However, Nasser thought that the N.U. would embrace the bourgeoisie along with the lower classes to form a patriotic front to confront imperialism.

The philosophy of the N.U. as perceived by Nasser was based on two principles: to attain national unity in a manner suitable to the peculiar nature of the Egyptian society, and to avoid the shortcomings of the single-party and multi-party systems. He explained that "from the experiences through which we had passed, the single-party system is monopoly of power while the multi-party system leads to division and disunity of the people which we worked very hard to build."[193]

Nasser thought that the N.U. would establish a forum for the different economic and social interests to discuss and eliminate disagreements and achieve national unity. Obviously Nasser's frame of thought during this period was characterized by the following:

a. Disbelief in class conflict
b. Perception of society as an organic entity integrated to achieve common interests for all
c. Belief that development of society depends on the efforts of all citizens, except the feudalists and traitors

Hence, the main objectives of the N.U. may be summarized as the following:

a. To establish a sound democratic life based on the six principles of the 1952 revolution
b. To secure the right of individuals to take part in building the country and to practice freedom of speech, mass media, expression of opinion and discussion and to be focused by the

193 Ahmad, see Nasser's speech on February 14, 1960, Vol. III, Section 2, Item 618, pp. 74-75.

opinion of the majority

c. To secure the rights of every member of the villages' committees to discuss the problems of their villages in order for the entire country to attain a general goal—a cooperative society
d. To achieve the unity of the Arab people who are liberated from any sort of imperial control
e. To outline the general policy of the country. The executive authority is to implement the planned matters to organize the laws of the local administrations on all levels. The main duties of the local councils are to implement the supreme policy of the state.
f. To reinforce the relations between the leadership and the people through the local councils, and to soundly build the political, social and economic conditions of the country[194]

Eventually Nasser realized that his attempts to reconcile class conflict and achieve harmony among the social classes were myopic and impractical. By 1958, the capitalists, who were able to infiltrate the N.U., began to show flagrant hostility towards the government's industrial plan to establish the "Industrial Order," which limited the profits of the stocks and concentrated more power in the hands of the working classes. As conflict between the capitalist and working classes intensified, Nasser realized that class conflict is unavoidable. Therefore, in July 1961, he announced his plans of nationalization of economic institutions, [195] which brought his system closer to the Marxist-Leninist regime of the Soviet Union.

In the late 1950s and early 1960s, the Soviet Union shook the entire world by achieving spectacular and historically unprecedented technological feats. On August 12, 1957, the Soviets successfully launched the first cross-continental missile to outer space.

On April 12, 1961, Yuri Gagarin, the Soviet pilot and cosmonaut, became the first human to journey into outer space when his Vaslok spacecraft completed an orbit of Earth.[196]

---

194 Ibid, Item 699, pp. 305-312.
195 Ibid, Item 804, pp. 767-775.
196 See Nasser's Congratulation Cable to Nikita Khrushchev, Ahmad, Vol. 3, Item 791, pp. 732-733.

These remarkable achievements were celebrated around most parts of the world. It seemed that the socialist Soviet Union unequivocally had attained the highest level of scientific and technological knowledge, outraced the imperialist capitalist Western world, and that socialism was inevitably going to prevail all over the civilized parts of the world. The dominant belief was that the capitalist system of the imperialist west had announced its bankruptcy, while the socialist Soviet Union was on the rise.

These assumptions aroused keen controversies. A very noteworthy point here is that the philosophical, political, educational and economic system of the Soviet Union was based on the atheist, antithetical-to-religion ideology of Marxism-Leninism, which denounces religion—all religions—as the opiate used by the ruling classes to subjugate the masses. So where was God? the masses asked. How could He allow such dazzling successes by such an ungodly country?

These arguments bolstered the secular beliefs such as existentialism, nationalism, Nasserism, socialism, Kemalism and especially communism, while the religious movements endured a deep recession.[197]

In Egypt, immediately after Gagarin's dramatic achievement, Nasser in July 1961 passed an aggregation of socialist laws that revolutionized most aspects of the country. These laws are summarized below.

THE NATIONALIZATION DECISIONS

In a speech he gave in Alexandria on July 26, 1961, Nasser announced what became known as "The July Laws of Nationalization." Some portions of that historical speech are as follows:

> Brother Citizens,[198]
>
> Our meeting today bears a new meaning. We used to meet here to celebrate the commemoration of the day in which we were

197 I still remember, as a student, the keen inclination of youth meeting in Baghdad, Tehran, Istanbul, Cairo, Damascus, Beirut, among others, to join those "progressive" movements while looking down on religious people as ignorant and reactionary.

198 Ahmad, Nasser's Speeches, Vol 3, Item 804, pp. 767-775.

able to liberate ourselves from everything against which we rebelled. But, we meet today in a different circumstance. Today we meet to fulfill social equality. In the past, 5 percent of the population ruled 95 percent of the entire people. But now the destitute peasant can feel a humanitarian treatment as he owns five acres of land, while the laborer, who used to work in a factory like an animal, now feels that he is a partner in that factory and that he works because he is represented in the board of directors, plus he receives 25 percent of the factory's profit.

Nasser announced the following statistical details, which revolutionized all aspects of the Egyptian society and became exemplary to other Arab and developing countries' revolutionary movements.[199]

1. Ownership of all banks, private insurance companies, and 149 industrial commercial companies were overtaken by the state. Ownership of stocks was restricted to no more than ten thousand Egyptian pounds.
2. Monopoly of the cotton industry and all sorts of imports were confiscated by the state.
3. Concessions given to Libon Company and Ahram Troly Company were abrogated and the state took over their contracts.
4. Wholesale and large department stores were overtaken by the state.
5. The progressive taxation system was adopted on large income and reached 90 percent on any individual's income exceeding ten thousand Egyptian pounds.

To explain his plans to the public, Nasser claimed that in outlining his socialist decisions, he had studied numerous models. He had closely scrutinized Titoe-ism, doctrines and practices in the Soviet Union, China, Cuba, Sweden and others in order to determine the system that he deemed suitable to Egypt's needs. He emphasized the need

199 Tikriti, pp. 189-193.

to establish an institution which he called the Arab Socialist Union (ASU), and he highlighted its functions in the Charter of National Work.

The promised National Charter was presented to the National Congress of Popular Force by Nasser in a lengthy speech he delivered on May 21, 1962.[200]

In the first paragraph, the Charter reaffirmed the Arab character of Egypt which is clearly proclaimed in the 1956 constitution.[201] Nasser claimed that the Egyptian revolutionary experiment had had far-reaching consequences on the life of the "entire Arab nation" as well as on the liberation movements in other developing countries such as Africa, Asia and Latin America. But he claimed the charter was designed for Egypt's domestic affairs.

This emphasis on domestic affairs rather than his essential foreign policy plan aiming at uniting the Arab world under his leadership, and the above-mentioned radical ideological changes are attributed to the big fiasco he suffered when Syria seceded in 1961 from the United Arab Republic.[202]

One of the major achievements which exalted Nasser's esteem among the Arab world was his decision to accept the request of the Syrian leadership to unite with Egypt to confront the Israeli menace. The two Arab countries were united on February 22, 1958, and the new country was officially called "The United Arab Republic."[203] It was ardently celebrated by the majority of the Arab populace, and perceived as the first step towards uniting the entire Arab world into one powerful, prestigious country under Nasser's leadership.

However, in 1961, due to the infiltration of the capitalist businessmen into the system of the newly born republic, antagonism erupted against the poor working class and the socialist laws, which, as mentioned before, forced Nasser to abandon his plan to melt all social classes in a single Egyptian melting pot system and a more radical economic

200 Tikriti, p. 197.

201 Ibid, p. 237.

202 Muhammad Abdul Mawla, *Al-Inhiar al-adheem: asbab qiyam wa suqut wihdat misr wa Syria* (The Great Crash: The Reason for the Establishment and Crash of the Unity between Egypt and Syria) (Beirut: The Center for Arab Unity Studies, 2000), pp. 180-182.

203 Ibid, p. 160.

system. Nasser realized that his attempts to harmonize all social classes under one patriotic umbrella under his leadership was impractical and that class conflict is unavoidable.

Furthermore, the disappointing secession of Syria from the United Arab Republic, and an uprising led by a group of disgruntled Syrian army officers, frustrated Nasser and pushed him to restore his efforts, at least temporarily, to concentrate on Egypt's domestic needs.

Between 1962 and 1964, the government took several complementary steps to the 1961 laws, which put most of the economic system under the state's control. At the same time several laws were passed on behalf of the working class (the proletariat). Labor time was restricted to forty-two hours per week, and for the first time in Egypt's history, a retirement law for the working class was passed, and a minimum wage of twenty-five qirsh per working day and a paid annual leave were implemented. Obviously Nasser was determined to impose a socialist system in Egypt to create a model to be followed by other Arab countries. He called his socio-economic system "Scientific Socialism." But he made sure to differentiate his system from the Marxist-Leninist socialism, followed by the Soviet Union, by refusing the concept and practice of the dictatorship of the proletariat. He believed in mixing socialism with democracy. He briefly discussed that system as follows:[204]

1. Liberating the citizen from all aspects of exploitation
2. Providing equal opportunities for the citizens for just share of the national wealth
3. Ridding the citizens from any source of worries regarding security of their future
4. Democracy is to mean the authority of the entire population, not the domination of one social class or another

As for the methods of structuring the socialist system, Nasser specified the following:

1. Creating a public sector capable of leading progress in all fields and bearing the main responsibility in the development plans

204 Tikriti, p. 192.

2. Keeping the cooperative ownership
3. Keeping a private sector that participates in the development within a comprehensive framework without exploiting others
4. Imposing popular censorship on the three sectors according to the general interest, especially the interest of the patriotic sector, which derives their benefit from the socialist system

Nasser announced his special method of implementing democratic socialism and his openness to the worldwide experience of socialism, which he detailed in "The Charter of National Work." He asserted that socialism is the only way that leads to social and economic progress.[205]

On May 21, 1962, the National Conference was held in which President Nasser submitted the project of the Charter of National Work and the creation of the Arab-Socialist Union. All suggestions were approved by the conference without any changes.

The discussions that led to the approval of the radical charter highlighted the mistakes and deviations that occurred in the past and specified the methods of avoiding them in the future. The Charter became a guide for the future plans of the government.

Discussion of the details of the Charter required eighteen sessions held by the preparatory committee between November 25 and December 31, 1961. The meetings were characterized by free and transparent discussions during which Nasser explained his ideas of class conflict, democratic socialism and the need to establish the Arab-Socialist Union.

The Charter is constituted of ten chapters:[206]

Chapter One: A general view dealing with the results of the pioneer revolutionary experience in all aspects of life, which was started and continued by the Egyptian people in extremely difficult circumstances.

Chapter Two: The necessity of revolution by which the Arab nation will be able to get rid of the chains and residues of colonialism, and to compensate the lengthy period of political, social and economic backwardness.

205 Ahmad, (Nasser's Speeches), Vol. 3 Item 802, pp. 758-759.
206 Tikriti, pp. 197-199.

Chapter Three: Elaborates on the roots of the struggle of the Egyptian people and the connection to Egypt with the Arab world, over the historical periods, which resembles the connection between the part and the whole.

Chapter Four: To learn from the consequences of the 1919 revolution and the despair it generated which paralyzed all desires or movements towards change.

Chapter Five: Deals with peaceful democracy. This chapter deals with the old Egyptian regime which was allied with the feudal and capitalists under colonial protection.

Chapter Six: The inevitability of socialism as a means to attain social freedom. The socialist solution was a fact imposed by historical destiny, the wide popular expectations and the world's conditions of the second half of the twentieth century.

Chapter Seven: Production and society. The battle of production is the real challenge by which man confirms the states he deserves under the sun.

Chapter Eight: The application of socialism and its impediments. Work is the only method by which society can accomplish its goals. Also, democracy must be applied in all cites of production. Leadership must be aware of widespread problems and be able to solve them.

Chapter Nine: Arab unity and highlighting Egypt's responsibility in generating and protecting progress in the Arab world.

Chapter Ten: Concerning the foreign policy of the Egyptian people which typifies and generates patriotism. It is based on: war against imperialism and hegemony, work for peace, and participating in international cooperation for prosperity.

The Charter became the comprehensive program for implementing Nasserism, i.e., to guide Egypt towards democratic socialism as perceived by President Gamal Abdel Nasser. The essential point that Nasser highlighted in the Charter was specifying the social classes and forces to be included in the single national coalition. They are the laborers and peasants, the intellectuals, the soldiers and patriotic capitalists. By cooperation, these social segments can achieve patriotic democracy. Excluded from the patriotic coalition are the feudalists, the bourgeoisie and the compradors, who are all allies of imperialism and were subjected to the decisions of socialism.[207]

The charter indicates a turning point in Nasser's thinking. It shows his change from attempting to follow peaceful tactics of cooperation and coordination to deal with class conflict to solving it by resorting to violence. After the fiasco of the unity agreement with Syria and his perception that the National Union was infiltrated by antagonistic elements, Nasser stated, "In the Charter we never excluded violence. We asserted that the reactionary will never ally with us; if they attack us or our society, we will use against it our utmost violence."[208]

THE ARAB SOCIALIST UNION (ASU)

On June 30, 1962, President Nasser announced that the National Charter was to be the program of a new order called the Arab Socialist Union. The ASU was to constitute the foundation of the system of the government. It aimed to create a solid popular aggregation in which all social differences were melted. It also endeavored to raise the spirit of hard work and loyalty among the citizens with a high level of social awareness and aspirations to solve all social problems.

In light of these details, President Nasser specified the mission of the ASU as the following:

a. The ASU is the comprehensive framework for the cooperating popular forces which includes the (peasants, soldiers, intellectuals and patriotic capitalists). President Nasser characterized the ASU as "this order helps fulfill the will and desires of the people." Hence, the ASU is the working popular force and personification of its interests and goals.
b. Nasser states that the ASU has a peculiar characteristic. "The ASU is not a political party, but a coalition of forces. It differs from the system of a party as the doors of the ASU are operated for all individuals of the working popular forces. It refuses the concept of hegemony of one class over another. It is based

207 Ahmad, (Nasser's Speeches), Vol. 3 Item 802, pp. 747-749.
208 Tikriti, p. 230.

on peaceful cooperation among all popular forces to attain the objectives of the Charter."[209]

Nasser continues, "The national unity generated by the alignment of these popular forces is capable of establishing the ASU, making it the authority that represents the people, stimulates the potential of the revolution and protects the values of sound democracy."[210] Hence, the ASU is a popular institution encompassing the popular working classes that are allied within the framework of the national unity, and it utilizes the charter as a guide of work.

c. The ASU is a complete popular entity, democratically evaluated by the revolutionary masses who use it to accomplish their goals. The ASU is the tool of the masses in guiding the patriotic work. President Abdel Nasser asserted in Chapter 5 of the Charter that "there is a pressing need to create a new political system within the framework of the ASU to recruit and organize all the elements that are suitable for leadership. The new political system should develop the revolutionary stimuli of the masses, feel their needs and find the right solutions for those needs."
d. Based on his personal perception, Nasser specified the main duties of the ASU were to raise and consolidate the revolutionary work, protect the principles and objectiveness of the revolution, liquidate the remains of the influence of feudalism and capitalism, struggle against the intrusion of foreign influence, struggle against the reactionary, which has been destroyed, struggle against opportunism, resist negativism and deviation, and forbid extemporization in patriotic work.

The expected objective of the ASU was to consolidate the relations among the people and the three authorities of the state—legislative,

209 Gamal Abdel Nasser, Hawl mafhum al-amal al-Siasi (Regarding the Concept Political Operations) (Cairo: Dar al-Waqif al-Arabi, 1973), p. 19.
210 Ibid.

executive and judicial.

These functions are briefly explained in the introduction of the law of ASU, which explains that the Arab Socialist Union is the pioneer socialist leader of the people. It represents their will, and directs and supervises the patriotic work according to the principles of the charter. The charter provides the framework within which all demands of the people are met.[211]

Nasser devoted his ultimate attention to accentuate the exceptionally wide authorities he granted to the ASU and to assure its permanent prevalence over the functions of the state. In the chapter of "sound democracy" the Charter asserts, "The authorities of the elected popular councils must emphatically and constantly exceed the authority of the executive systems of the state. Such is the natural situation to secure the popular sovereignty."

Being elicited by the people, the ASU has the right to propose suggestions to the executive council and ministries to direct their operations. The recommendations are binding to the council and ministries.

Any disregard towards the recommendations by members of the ministries and the executive council will be subject to inquiries according to the constitutional requirements.

Based on the above information, the methods of links between all levels of the ASU with the laws of the ministries and the local rules need strict control and keen supervision to secure their implementation without impediments.

a. The relation between the ASU and the judicial branch[212]

Democracy will never flourish or be sound unless it is implemented according to the sovereignty of law and away from deviation. And sovereignty of law will never be practically achieved unless it is implemented by independent judges who have no power over their decision but the law. No authority has the right to interfere in issues related to justice. The charter emphasizes that the independence and prevalence

211 Stephens, pp. 352-355.
212 Ibid, p. 207.

of the law are important props of liberty. In fact, accentuating and consolidating the sovereignty of the law is the final safeguard of liberty. However, due to the powers bestowed on it by the law and the presidential support, the Arab Socialist Union, as a representative of the popular desires, passes decisions that must be obliged by the judicial authority. This measure was undertaken to create a functional relation between the Arab Socialist Union and the judicial authority to reestablish the legislation according to the requirements of the new revolutionary, democratic socialist society.

b. The relation between the ASU and the unions cooperatives[213]

Principle No. 4 of the ASU states an important fact that the ASU does not replace unions, cooperatives and youth organizations. The charter of the ASU emphasizes the independence of these organizations. It states the popular organizations, especially cooperatives and unions, can play an effective role towards implementing democracy. The Charter accentuates that the development of cooperative and unions provides an inexhaustible source for the enlightened leadership (which directly touches the nerves of the masses and feels their pulse). The Charter also evaluates the role of the cooperative farms as "in addition to their productive role, they are capable of exploring peasants' problems and finding solutions to them." As for the laborers, they are no longer merchandizes exploited for production. They have become a labor power owning production itself, full partners in administration, sharers in profit, paid the best salaries and provided with the best working conditions. "The affiliates of the unions and cooperatives are the real owners of their interests."[214]

213 Ibid, p. 208.

214 Usmat Saif al-Dawlah, al-ahzab wa mushkilet al-democratiyah fi Misr (Political Parties and the Problem of Democracy in Egypt) (Beirut: Dar al-maseerah, 1977), pp. 125-126.

NASSER'S CONSTITUTION OF 1964[215]

Egypt witnessed the first secular constitution in 1923, during the premiership of Sidqi Pasha.[216] Then it was followed by five more constitutions, until under Gamal Abdel Nasser's rule, the 1964 constitution was promulgated.

The significance of this constitution is that it highlighted Nasser's perceptions of national and patriotic orientation. It also elaborates on his philosophical thoughts regarding adhering to and protection of democracy and socialism.

The first article of the constitution indicates that the United Arab Republic was a democratic socialist state founded on the coalition of all social forces.[217] This detail explains the meaning of "sound democracy."

The second clause of the first article denoted that "the people of Egypt are part of the Arab nation," which meant the adherence of Egypt to the concept of pan-Arabism.

Article 9 is the most specific and daring, as it accentuates Nasser's belief and perception of socialism. Socialism is the basic program for building and developing the national, and realizing sound democracy. Thus, Article 9 clearly indicates that "socialism is the economic system of the state."[218]

In his foreign policy, Nasser shook the Western world when he took a defying initiative and assumed a leading position in the non-alignment movement, thereby breaking a long-standing trend of pro-Western diplomacy followed by the Arab countries. The concept of the non-alignment movement was launched in the Afro-Asian Conference held in Bandung-Indonesia in 1955, in which Nasser played a key role.[219] The purpose of the movement was to "ensure that the independence, sovereignty, territorial integrity, and security of non-aligned countries in their struggle against imperialism, colonialism, racism and all forms of social aggression."

---

215 Ibid, p. 117.

216 Hamdi Riza, barlaman Misr 2005 (Egypt's Parliament, 2005) "al-Ittihad," Nov. 3, 2005.

217 Saif al-Dawlah, p. 117.

218 Tikriti, p. 238.

219 Miles Copeland, The Game of Nations: The Morality of Power Politico (New York: Simon and Schuster, 1959), p. 188.

He was the first Arab-Muslim leader to confront the formidable colonial powers of the Western world and dared to take such bold decisions as obtaining arms from the "infidel" Soviet Union, exchanging diplomatic recognition with Communist China, delivering bellicose speeches against Britain, France and Israel, among others.

These dramatic stances of patriotic anti-colonialism pleased the vast majority of the masses inside and outside of Egypt. Nasserism, with its principles of pan-Arabism, socialism, anti-colonialism and anti-Zionism, became the ideology that deluged the minds of the Middle Eastern people as the following details show.

The leaders of Syria, fearing aggression by Israel, turned away from a possible unity with Iraq to coerce Nasser to unite Egypt with Syria to form the United Arab Republic in 1958, with Nasser as its president.[220]

In Iraq, people of all ages, men and women, were mesmerized by Nasserism. The "Sound of the Arab" (Sout al-Arab) broadcasting station promoted Nasser as the savior of the Arab world and agitated the masses of Iraq to erupt in street riots and demonstrations praising Nasser, decrying the leadership of Iraq as stooges of the West, and demanding unity with Egypt.

In July 1958, a military coup d'état led by General Abdul Karim Qassim toppled the pro-West monarchy, marking the birth of the Republic of Iraq. The celebrating crowds were ecstatically carrying large pictures of Nasser while demanding an immediate unity with Egypt (the United Arab Republic). The second leader of the new Republic of Iraq, Colonel Abdul Salam Arif, the deputy prime minister and vice commander of the military forces, was an ardent pro-unity supporter under Nasser's leadership. Arif was supported by the powerful Arab Nationalist Movement espoused by renowned military and civil figures who were deeply influenced by Nasser.[221]

Elsewhere, Lebanon, Kuwait, Saudi Arabia, Oman, Qatar, Bahrain and most of the Arab countries outside the Arabian Peninsula witnessed a keen surge of pro-Nasserism movements.[222]

220 Stephen, p. 275.

221 For more details, see Zaki Mamoon Amin, Izdihar al-Iraq tahat al-hukm al-malaki, op. cit. p. 398.

222 See Noor al-Din Ben a-Hbib Hajlawi, Ta'theer al-Fikr al-Nasseri ala al-Khaleej al-Arabi, (The

Hence the secular revolutionary thesis of Nasserism permeated most parts of the Middle East and the Islamic world for almost two decades, while religious movements slumped into a deep recession.

It is relevant here to compare the influence of Kemalism with Nasserism, although Nasser, by far, had much deeper influence on the Middle East than Ataturk. Both men were military officers who used the army as a means to liberate their people from foreign colonialism. Both leaders established secular regimes in the countries among the sea of Islamic nations.[223]

However, Kemal Ataturk's reform programs were based on adopting programs along the framework of the liberal systems of the Western world, although he never succeeded in implementing democracy, while Nasser distanced himself from the Western world and its systems, and established a radical revolutionary regime close to the Marxist-Leninist system of the Soviet Union.

Regardless of the difference between the two leaders, it is a historical fact that the "secular (Y) thesis" launched by Kemal Ataturk in the 1920s was continued by Gamal Abdel Nasser's leadership until the late 1960s.

However, Nasserism suddenly collapsed after the Egyptian and Arab armies were pulverized by Israel in the 1967 war. On January 5, 1967, the Israeli air force attacked Egypt, Syria and Jordan, while its land forces advanced in a blitzkrieg that devastated the armies of the Arab countries. The war ended after only six days with a dramatic victory for Israel. After a cease-fire was declared, Israel enlarged its territory almost four-fold by occupying the Sinai Peninsula from Egypt, the West Bank from Jordan including East Jerusalem, and the Golan Heights from Syria.[224]

Nasser's fiasco marked the end of the secular era of nationalism (the secular X), and all the so-called ideas inspired by Nasser's leadership that deluged the Arab minds for almost two decades—such as

Influence of Nasser's Thoughts on the Arabian Gulf) 1951–1971 (Beirut: Markaz Dirast al-Wihdah al-Arabiyah, 2003).

223 Fisher, p. 693.

224 Zaki, Mamoon Amin Su'ud wa Taraji al-Mashru al-suhuni (The Rise and Retreat of the Zionist Project) op. cit., see chapter 8, pp. 271-316

pan-Arabism, retrieving Palestine from the Zionists, and liberation from colonialism—collapsed in six days.

Hence, a tremendous ideological and cultural vacuum befell the Middle East, and an ominous question overshadowed the entire region like a dark cloud—"What can we do now?"

The popular opinion was that Westernization, Kemalism, Nasserism, socialism, nationalism, and all other "imported" ideas had failed to fulfill the people's aspirations or encounter the enemy, and that the solution was to resort to the only unifying native faith—the religion of Islam,[225] the (Y) of secularism.

The strength of Islamic belief stems from its deeply rooted infiltration of the minds of the Middle Eastern people for almost fifteen centuries. The Islamic system provides for a comprehensive framework of law, brotherly relations, rules for peace and war, and family relations. These dogmas remained intact since the time of Prophet Mohammad regardless of some deviations. Therefore, even the ardent liberal intellectuals began to find refuge, after the 1967 catastrophe, in Islamic spirituality. Former Westernized writers such as Muhammad Hasanain Haikal and Abbas M. al-Aqqad, who were believers of H. Bergson, Bernard Shaw, H.G. Wells, the philosophers of Fabian socialism, began to explore the relevance of Islamic doctrines to the existing condition. Even Taha Hussein, the most influential twentieth century Egyptian writer, intellectual and figurehead for the Arab renaissance, whose sobriquet was "the dean of Arab literature," abandoned most of his antireligious ideas and turned to write about the advantages of Prophet Mohammed's leadership and the thriving aspects of the early Islamic era.[226]

Hence, religious outcries of three devout Muslim activists—Hasan al-Banna, Abu al-Ala al-Mawdudi and Sayyed Qutb—surfaced and prevailed on most parts of the Middle East. Al-Banna was the thinker who established the Muslim Brotherhood in Egypt in 1928, and al-Mawdudi created the Jamati-Islami in Pakistan, with followers in other parts of the Middle East. In the 1950s and 1960s, Qutb built upon and

225 Muhammad Hasanain Haikal, madafi' Ayatollah: Qissat Iran wal-thawrah (The Canons of Ayatollah: The Story of Iran and the Revolution) (Beirut: Dar al-Shurooq, 1983), p. 170.

226 Ibid, p. 170.

radicalized the ideas of al-Banna and al-Mawdudi and created an ideological legacy of jihad (holy war) that became the primary model for new revolutionary religious organizations across the Muslim world.[227]

This far-reaching religious surge had a profound political effect as evidenced by the dramatic increase in membership of the Muslim Brotherhood. New Islamic organizations appeared and gained strong influence among students of universities. In 1979, they were able to assemble about three hundred thousand young men praying for the *Eid al-Adha*, the sacrifice feast, in Cairo.

Calls for the "rule of God" resonated from Pakistan throughout the Arab world. They all announced one slogan:

> There is no ruler in Islam but God, and the Shari'ah is the law from God to rule the Earth. The civil ruler has no duty but to obey God's law and he has no right to change or add to that law.[228]

Hence, the era of Nasserism with its secular nationalism was quickly fading away, while a thunderous rise in Islamic belief began to overtake the Middle East.

Meanwhile, Nasser stayed in power and waged a war of attrition to regain some legitimacy and respect for himself and his regime. The war lasted until his death in 1970, yet he was not able to retrieve even one inch of the lands the Arabs lost to Israel.

Upon Nasser's death, Vice President Anwar al-Sadat was chosen as the next president of Egypt. His regime was characterized by his attempt to synthesize religion with a semi-liberal system. He attempted to cajole the growing forces of Islamic movements while allowing a multiparty political system, conducting parliamentary elections, eradicating socialism, and seeking rapprochement with the United States and the Western countries.[229] He also accentuated his religious devo-

227 Muhammad Hasanain Haikal, Kharif al-ghadhab: qissat bidayat wa nihayat anwar al-Sadat (The Autumn of Anger: The Story of the Beginning and End of Sadat Era) (Beirut: 2nd ed. 1983), pp. 288-290.

228 Haikal, Madafi' Ayatollah, op. cit. p. 171.

229 David Hirst and Irene Beeson, SADAT (New York: Vail-Ballou Press Inc., 1981), p. 173.

tion by performing publicized prayers in mosques and by establishing a *majlis shura*, a traditional Islamic consultation council, to function beside the elected parliament.

The highlight of Sadat's rule came in October 1973 when he conducted a well-coordinated war with the Syrian army and attacked Israel in what is historically known as the Yom Kippur War, because it occurred during the holy Jewish feast of Yom Kippur. The Egyptian army crossed the Suez Canal to attack the Israeli forces occupying the Sinai Peninsula in the south, while the equally large Syrian army attacked from the north front, and both Arab armies were thunderously shouting the traditional Islamic religious slogan, "Allah Akbar," or "God is the greatest." For two weeks the war progressed in favor of the Arabs until the United States extended an historically unprecedented military act which enabled the Israelis to check the Arabs' onslaught, and the war ended in a draw.[230] Yet, this war enabled the Arabs to regain some of the dignity they had lost after the disgraceful defeat of 1967.

President Sadat, however, squandered what the masses perceived as his brilliant achievement after he visited Israel in 1977 and signed a treaty with it in 1978.[231] He was vilified as a traitor by most Arab countries, and in 1981, he was assassinated by fanatic members of the Muslim Brotherhood.

The Islamic movements kept growing and marching on the Middle East until it reached its zenith when a roaring popular revolution, led by (imam) cleric Grand Ayatollah Ruhollah al-Khomeini, erupted all over Iran and toppled the Western-oriented modernizing system of Shah Mohammed Reza Pahlavi. Immediately after the departure of the shah, Iran, with its historical and strategic weight, was declared a full-fledged theocracy based on *al-Shari'ah al-Islamiyah*, the Islamic religious code.[232]

Upon assuming the position of Supreme Religious Jurist of Iran, Khomeini declared jihad and set on his campaign to export his Islamic revolution to the neighboring countries, threatening their leaders to

---

230 Zaki, Mamoon Amin, Su'ud wa tara ju' al-mashru' al-Suhiuni, op. cit., p. 351.
231 Camp David Treaty; see Hirst and Beeson, SADAT, pp. 296-306.
232 See Organization of Islamic Information, Khat al-al-imam al_Khomeini: Ardh lil mabadi al-a'amah (The Line of Iman al-Khomeini: His General Principles), pp. 71-72.

repent and return to the strict path of Islam or bear the consequences.

The religious frenzy spread like fire all over the Islamic world, through the secular Republic of Turkey and as far as the Soviet Union, where a large Muslim community resided.[233]

Back in Egypt, upon Sadat's assassination, Vice President Hosni Mubarak assumed the presidency. He pursued the same synthetic parliamentary and majlis shura system as his predecessor.

Mubarak was president for decades, supported by the Western powers as a secular force that could control the Islamic movements, until the surge of both revolutionary and religious passion overtook Egypt and Dr. Mohammad Morsi, a leading figure of the Muslim Brotherhood, was elected president, thereby catapulting the Islamic movement to the helm of the government, and putting the Republic of Egypt, for the first time, under the rule of an Islamic religious regime.[234]

Almost at the same time in Turkey, the Islamic Party of Justice and Development won the election of the majority of the parliament. The leader of the party, Recep Tayyip Erdogan, an ardent Muslim whose wife wears the traditional Islamic scarf, became the prime minister of the secular Kemalist Republic. It was the first time since the downfall of the Ottoman Empire and the birth of the secular Turkish Republic in the 1920s that an Islamic movement dominated the political system of Turkey and a religious figure assumed the premiership of the country.[235]

In the beginning of the second decade of the twenty-first century, it seemed like the spread of the Islamic ideology was unstoppable, and a powerful alliance between Egypt's Muslim Brotherhood regime and Turkey's Islamic government was established, while the Iranian theocracy loomed on the horizon.

233 Muhammad Hasanain Haikal madafi' ayatollah, op. cit., p. 176.

234 Bradley Hope, Rise of al-Azhar in New Egypt, The National (Abu Dhabi), December 27, 2012.

235 Zaki, Mamoon Amin, "Turkia min rajul awrupa al marid ila dawlah mihwariyah" (Turkey from the Sick Man of Europe to a Pivotal State), Al Khaleej, No. 11457, October 1, 2010.

Chapter 6

THE BIRTH OF THE IRANIAN THEOCRACY IN THE MIDDLE EAST

The rise or awakening of religious *salafism*, or fundamentalism, refers to the upsurge of Islamic ultra-conservative reform movement within Sunni Islam that deluged most parts of the Muslim world subsequent to the success of the religious revolution in 1979, which gave birth to the Iranian theocracy.

From Iran to Turkey to Egypt, Iraq, Syria, Tunisia, or Morocco, all over the Middle East there was a prevailing wave of religious fundamentalism. Even in the Republic of Turkey, the cradle of secularism, the religious movement steadily grew strong enough to control the several-decades-old secular Kemalist political system and reinstitute the religious parties' presence in the government.

In Iran, Shah Mohammad Reza's oppressive regime, his secular programs and Westernization plans outraged the majority of the pious masses and drove them to galvanize behind a clergyman, Imam Ayatollah Khomeini. Khomeini's charisma, rigorous anti-imperialism rhetoric, and calls to return to the glorious past Islamic rule and godly Shari'ah resonated among the vast majority of the Iranian people and its neighboring countries.

Khomeini (1902–1989) was born into a family of Shi'ite religious scholars in the small Iranian village of Khomein. He was trained at the Islamic seminary in the city of Qum and then became an instructor there. He opposed the policies of both of the Pahlavi shahs, accusing them of trying to break the power of the clergy and secularize the Iranian society. In 1963, Khomeini was arrested for publicly accusing Shah Mohammad Reza of following policies that were incompatible with the principles of Islam. He was arrested again when he would not relent in his criticism of the regime, and he was exiled to Turkey in 1964. Eventually he was given permission to reside in the Shi'ite holy city of Najaf in Iraq, where he stayed until he was deported by the Iraqi Ba'ath authorities to a suburb of Paris, France in 1978.[236]

The details of Khomeini's life strikingly resemble the lives of Shi'ite imams (descendants of Prophet Mohammad's households). He had been attacked, imprisoned and almost killed by an unjust secular ruler, and, like some of the imams, he was sent into exile. Like Ali and Hussein, he courageously confronted injustice and adamantly demanded true Islamic values. Like all imams, Khomeini was known to practice mysticism. Like Ali, whose son was killed in Kerbala, Khomeini's son, Mustafa, was killed by the shah's SAVAK.[237]

In 1977, the famous Egyptian journalist-writer Mohammad Hasanain Haikal, after paying a visit to Khomeini where he lived in exile near Paris, described the methods by which he directed his followers from his exile:[238] "Outside the villa where he lived, two pavilions were erected; in one of them the leader gave his speeches to his followers, while the other one was used to serve food for all his visitors."

What attracted Haikal's attention was the gathering of diversified crowds from all over the world. Students from the Sorbonne University, graduates from Harvard, Yale, Berkeley and other American universities, as well as members of good Iranian families could often be observed in attendance. Members of the Iranian Student Union in Paris were permanently present. Some of those students assumed the duty of armed guards to protect Khomeini's life.

After the dusk prayers, Khomeini would speak to his supporters. Haikal gave the following elaborate description of Khomeini's speech:

> He started with a very low, calm voice which I have never heard

236 Cleveland, op. cit., p. 427.

237 Coughlin, Con. Khomeini's Ghost (MacMillan, 2009), pp. 141, 142.

238 Haikal, Mohammad Hasanayn Madafi, Ayatollah, pp. 188, 189.

> such a serene sound. His voice was touching the ears of his audience in tender waves which elevated his listeners to a state of ecstasy. At the beginning Khomeini's grandson, Hussein, was translating (for Haikal) from Persian to Arabic, then I opted to concentrate on the influence of his words on his followers. It was a very strange situation. Khomeini was sitting there with his black Shi'ite turban, which exuded sadness, as if he was an Islamic leader who was resurrected from the seventh century. All the audience who represented the Iranian elite were listening in an absolute silence attempting to absorb every word he uttered.[239]

Haikal asserts that Khomeini was very well informed about the conditions in Iran. After all, he was a prolific scholar who authored forty books[240] and was fully aware that the conditions in Iran were ripe for an Islamic revolution. He was also aware that no political activity or leadership was capable to lead the revolution. Opposition movements and the remaining members of the old political parties were all encircled by the shah's forces, and they were utterly helpless. The religious leaders were in the same dire situation. But Khomeini believed that religion was the only force to bring about the revolution, and he was the capable man to lead it.[241]

Khomeini was aware that his statements and instructions were very well received by the masses, who obviously responded positively to him. Popular support was not a problem for Khomeini—his main concern was how to surmount the formidable oppressive powers under the command of the shah. There were fifty thousand SAVAK agents to protect the shah, but Khomeini aimed at recruiting the entire fifty-five million Iranian population to overwhelm the SAVAK. Furthermore, the shah's army was comprised of seven hundred thousand officers and soldiers,[242] so he felt the army had to be neutralized rather than con-

239 Ibid, p. 189.

240 Munadhamat al-Ii'lam al-Islami (Organization of Islamic Information), Khat al-Imam al_ Khomeini imam Khomeni's line), p. 16.

241 Ibid, pp. 15-18.

242 Coughlin, op. cit., pp. 90, 126.

fronted. Several of Khomeini's followers kept pressuring him to resort to armed resistance, but he informed them that this was impossible and the "only way to deal with the army was by stripping its weapons." He stressed that the chains that tied the military corps to the shah—the oath of loyalty and obedience—must be destroyed, one way or another. Khomeini's supporters did not understand how he would be able to disarm the military forces while he was far away from Iran in exile. It was easier said than done.

The shah had created a large elite force of highly ranked officers who received very lucrative incomes and enjoyed lavish privileges, and they were very loyal to him. Hence, by the beginning of 1977, Khomeini began to direct his revolutionary messages to these armed forces. The messages were simple: do not serve the shah, for the shah is Satan; he personifies the tyrant; military people are the blessed soldiers of God and should not shoot their Muslim brethren, because every bullet that hits a Muslim also hits the holy Quran. They were told to go back to their villages, their families, their mosques and to God.[243]

By mid-1977, official reports began to indicate some military personnel were fleeing the service. Although he received those reports, the shah was reluctant to believe them. By the autumn of 1977, Khomeini intensified his propaganda against military service. Previously, he had requested that the soldiers desert the military. He continued with that message but also began to instruct them to take their weapons with them. He told them, "You are the soldiers of God, leave your military units by small groups or one by one, but take your weapons with you; they are the weapons of God."[244]

In 1978, the efforts of Ayatollah Khomeini began to shift the opposition against the shah from a peaceful reform movement of the educated middle class to a widespread Islamic revolution. The shah became alarmed by the obvious shift and decided to wage a vehement defamation campaign against Khomeini. In November 1977, Farhad Masudi became editor-in-chief of the widely circulated *Etela'at* daily newspaper. He was ordered to publish a hostile attack against Khomeini,

243 Haikal, op. cit., p. 191.
244 Ibid.

in an article accusing him of corruption, sexual perversion and other personal vilifications. Masudi strongly objected to the article, fearing violent reaction by the people. He called the minister of information and expressed his concern that there would be a violent reaction from the citizens, telling him, "If we publish this article, our headquarters will be attacked." The minister called the royal castle and relayed his worries regarding the provocative article, but the shah insisted on publishing it. The minister of information attempted to pacify Masudi, telling him, "Do not worry, the Ministry of Interior will provide you with the required protection."[245] The anti-Khomeini article was published in the *Etela'at* newspaper, and was the catalyst that agitated the students and bazaar merchants in Qum to launch a huge demonstration protesting the article and denouncing the shah's regime. An army unit attacked and brutally foiled the demonstration, killing a number of demonstrators.[246]

The culmination of the uprising occurred in December, during Muharram, the Muslim month of mourning rituals for the martyrdom of Imam Hussein, Prophet Mohammad's grandson. In that year Muharram was used by the clergymen to direct the protest strictly within a religious framework. Waves and waves of protesters defied the regime's curfew and took to the streets wearing white gowns of martyrdom, signifying their willingness to imitate the sacrifices by Imam Ali and his son, Imam Hussein, who had achieved martyrdom while resisting the despots of their time. Hundreds of protesters were killed, but the demonstration kept escalating as Muharram continued.[247]

Due to the brutality against the demonstrators and in response to Khomeini's calls, the military foundation on which the shah's regime was built began to crumble. In January 1978, a battalion of five hundred soldiers camping in the holy city of Mashhad deserted their positions, and unrest continued to spread all over the country. The uprisings became so huge that the SAVAK and the police were not able to overcome them; the intervention of the army was required.[248]

245 Ibid, pp. 191, 192.
246 Cleveland, op. cit., p. 428.
247 Ibid, p. 430.
248 Ibid, p. 420.

Wisely, Khomeini instructed his followers not to engage in battle with the army under any circumstance, even though most of the military was still loyal to the shah. He instructed, "Those military ranks are your brothers, they have the same feeling like you and the rest of the people. All we need is one strike to disconnect the ring that connects them with the shah." In a letter he sent to the protestors, he instructed, "Do not attack the chest of the army, attack its heart, try to gain the hearts of the soldiers. If they fire on you to kill you, let them kill five, ten, twenty, a thousand. They are our brothers and we should welcome them and prove that the blood is more powerful than the swords."[249]

A noteworthy point here is that Khomeini, a frail old man, was a powerful charismatic leader unsurpassed by any other leader of modern time. His orders were blindly obeyed by the young, old, educated, illiterate, civilians, military, religious and secular to the extent that they exposed their chests to the bullets of the shah's army to achieve martyrdom. No other leader—not Ataturk, Nasser, nor Saddam Hussein—had such compelling influence on his followers. That is why many historians compare Khomeini with the imams or prophets of old time.

In one of his widely circulated notices, Khomeini spoke about the martyrs who were an important element of the Shiite tradition. He said, "They claim that the hero is the essence of history, but that is wrong, the martyr is the essence of history and the spirit that pushes history forward."[250] He instructed:

> Meet the soldiers with your barren chests, because the shah will give orders to the army and the army will obey the shah. We know that the army is confused because they are not sure what to do but they have to obey the orders. How can they disobey the orders while they are obligated by the military system? But, one day they are bound to liberate themselves from the system of Satan and return to the system of God.

249 Haikal, op. cit., p. 193.
250 Ibid.

> Meet those bullets with your chests. Your blood and the love you express towards them will convince them. The blood of every martyr is a bell that will awaken one thousand of the living people.

Khomeini kept repeating a word widely used in mystic literature, *wijdan*, which means subconscious or conscious hidden in human heart. Thus, Khomeini stressed, "You have to move towards the wijdan of the army."[251]

Astutely using this emotional and religious rhetoric, Khomeini was able to take advantage of the military system's weakness. All its sources of power—its huge size, the special attention bestowed on it by the shah, and its modern American equipment—would be useless if confronted by an entire determined nation. Thus, Khomeini was able to separate the higher-ranked officers from the soldiers and the lower ranks, and strip the army of its awesome weapons, or at least neutralize it, as a prelude to the final battle that toppled the shah.

Conscript troops refrained from the continuous killing of unarmed students and civilians, deserted their units, and joined the demonstrators. Overwhelmed by the brouhaha, the secularists and intellectuals joined forces with the clergymen because they knew that only Khomeini was able to command the grassroots support of the people. Dr. Shahpour Bakhtiar, a Sorbonne University graduate and a Moderate Freedom Movement fighter, agreed to become prime minister on the condition that the shah leave the country. Bakhtiar was courageously trying to protect Iran from falling under the rule of religious fanatics,[252] but it was too late for a liberal figure like Bakhtiar to stop the uprising. He was denounced by Khomeini, who issued a proclamation stating that politicians appointed by the shah were illegal, and to serve the shah's government was to betray Islam.

On January 16, 1979, Mohammad Reza Shah fled Iran, and a year later died of cancer while exiled in Egypt. On February 1, Ayatollah Khomeini victoriously arrived in Tehran. He was welcomed by

251 Ibid.
252 Coughlin, op. cit., p. 259.

millions. An unarmed popular revolution inspired and guided by an elderly member of the religious establishment had toppled the King of Kings (as Mohammad Reza called himself) and brought an end to the Pahlavi dynasty.[253]

CONSOLIDATING THE REVOLUTION AND THE ESTABLISHMENT OF THE ISLAMIC REPUBLIC

When Khomeini arrived in Tehran to a tumultuous euphoric welcome by millions of Iranians, the government, the army, the security, the economy and all other foundations of the state had collapsed. A typical situation synthesizing political movements from the secular/liberal to religious/conservative was fomenting within the entire country. The liberal system was vying for power against a powerful conservative movement aiming to turn Iran into a full-fledged theocracy.[254] While Khomeini was consolidating his position, many of the diversified movements that cooperated with him to topple the shah turned against him, into opposition. The country was in a state of labor that could give birth to two antitheses of the shah's despotic regime—either a true democratic-constitutional government, or a full antithesis, a theocratic regime.

For some politicians, the departure of the despotic shah was the main objective of the revolution and it was time to return to political stability and order. This was largely the attitude of Western-educated men like Karim Synjabi, Mahdi Bazargan, Ibrahim Yazdi, Sadeq Qotobzada and Abdel Hasan Bani Sadre.[255] But for Imam Khomeini and his followers, the downfall of the secularist shah was just the beginning of a revolution and the uprooting of all aspects of the old regime.

Khomeini took the initiative to bolster his position by forcing the liberal-minded Prime Minister Shahpour Bakhtian to resign in 1979, and he assigned Mahdi Bazargan as his own prime minister. Bazargan sought to pursue a national reconciliatory policy and concentrated on

253 Fisher, op. cit., p. 532.
254 Cleveland, op. cit., p. 430.
255 Ibid, p. 425.

restoring administrative order and economic stability.[256]

To restore law and order, Khomeini formed a local committee to reestablish the basic tasks of security and administration. Those committees were largely controlled by clergymen who were able to boost the influence of the militant religious forces. Furthermore, Khomeini ordered the formation of Revolutionary Guards (RG), an armed force that was separate from the official military corps. Constituted of destitute young men, the RG were very loyal to Khomeini. They were used to quell the opposition of the revolution, and they played an instrumental role in consolidating Khomeini's position.[257]

Other organizations that operated as part of the government were the revolutionary tribunals set up in February 1979. These courts were staffed by religious judges who prosecuted officials of the shah's regime and other individuals accused of counter-revolutionary activities. Several ex-parliament members, hundreds of SAVAK agents and highly ranked military officers were executed by these courts.[258]

In mid-1979, a group of ayatollahs formed the Islamic Republic Party (IRP) to establish an institution with a stable structure for the Islamic ideology. The IRP endeavored to gain more popular support for the Islamic Republic and to undermine the secular liberal groups. Being controlled by the religious scholars, whose contacts with the people were more personal and consistent through religious services in the mosques, the IRP was able to convince more people to support Khomeini and his new regime. The IRP was able to impose its principles on the people by using the Revolutionary Guards to raid opposition rallies and arrest suspected individuals.

Legitimacy was bestowed on the regime when a national referendum was conducted in 1979 and the replacement of the monarchy with an Islamic Republic was approved.[259]

In June 1979, Prime Minister Bazargan's government drafted a constitution that adopted the principles of an Islamic state but did not bestow any special administrative or judicial authorities to the

256 Ibid, p. 431.
257 Coughlin, op. cit., pp. 157-162.
258 Cleveland, op. cit., p. 432.
259 Coughlin, op. cit., pp. 161, 162.

religious establishments.

Alarmed by the text of the new constitution, which did not grant enough authority to the religious men, Khomeini hastened to address the first meeting of the Grand National Assembly and emphatically stated the constitution should be "one hundred percent based on Islam." During the deliberations, the GNA experts totally restructured the original draft and adopted a new constitution that required all of Iran's laws and regulations to be based on Islamic principles.[260]

In November 1979, Bazargan resigned along with his cabinet. His hopes for establishing a liberal constitutional democracy and cooperation with the Western world were frustrated.

Mohammad Ali Rajai, an ardent and loyal supporter of Khomeini, became prime minister. Supported by a powerful group of politicians which included Mohammed Behashti, Hussein Ali Montazeri, Mohammed Ali Raji and Ali Akbar Hashimi Rafsanjani, Imam Khomeini was able to outwit his opponents and end the synthesis period. The Western-educated leaders had proven to be politically less skilled than the mullahs. By the end of 1981, Khomeini and his clergymen virtually controlled all aspects of life in the country.[261] Thus the secular thesis of the Pahlavi dynasty that had lasted for almost six decades came to an end, and its theocratic antithesis was born in Iran.

The new constitution adopted the principle of vilayat-i-faqih, the governance of the Islamic jurist (explained in more detail later in this chapter), and Imam Khomeini was entrusted with the responsibility of serving as supreme Islamic jurist.

Diligently operating from outside of Iran, Khomeini had conducted a revolution that overthrew the shah and ended the reign of the Pahlavi Dynasty in 1979. He changed the name of the country to the Islamic Republic of Iran and set off the ultra-religious era in the Middle East.[262]

After assuming the highest position of spiritual leadership in Iraq, Khomeini was able to perform a spectacular achievement that

260 Cleveland, op. cit., p. 431.

261 Haytham Muzahim, "Al-Fikr al-siyasi al-she'i li Iran" (The Shiite Political Thought in Iran), Iran Bayn Thawratain (Iran Between Two Revolutions) (UAE: al-Misbar, 2013), pp. 62, 63.

262 Pipes, op. cit.

contravened many theories of modernization. He utilized religion, which is considered by many scholars of comparative policies to be a main factor of social stagnation, to consolidate and develop his newly born regime.[263]

Saturated with Shi'ite religious beliefs, Khomeini utilized Shi'ism, a religious sect of Islam explained in greater detail later, to bestow legitimacy on his regime and cajole the ardent vast Shi'ite majority of the Iranian populace. His decision concurred with the popular perception of legitimacy in the Western world, which is mutual respect and trust between people and their government.

A deep investigation into history reveals that, in certain cases, religion could be a source of legitimacy, social solidarity and modernization of traditional societies. A very unique example was the creation of the United States of America, currently one of the greatest democracies and most modern countries in the world. The American Calvinists at the time of the 1776 revolution did not quite agree with the secularist ethos of the founding fathers. Yet they gave the national struggle a Christian character so that they could fight alongside the secularists to create the democratic, capitalist republic of America.

Similar to that in the Islamic world, some fundamentalists were able to use religion to cajole the fanatics and legitimize adoption of certain aspects of modernization for their country. They were convinced that it is possible to be modern on other cultural terms than those followed by the Western world. For example, the royal family of Saudi Arabia, which is the hub of Islam, introduced their extremely traditional society to the requirements of life of the twentieth century. To gain the support of the fanatics who vehemently opposed any aspect of social change, King Faisal Al Saud (1964–1975) and his wife astutely referred to the Quranic verse which says, "Read in the name of thy God, the Most Bounteous, who taught by the pen, taught the human that which they knew not" (Quran:2-5), to introduce secular educational subjects such as modern medical methods and technology into schools.[264]

263 Cleveland, p. 430.

264 Zaki, Mamoon Amin, Saudi Arabia: The Modernizing Islamic Theocracy (International Development and Alternative Future: The Coming Challenge, ed. Mekki Mtewa/Bombay: Allied Pub. Ltd. 1990), Ch. 12.

The Iranian revolution of 1978–79, which sought reform and legitimacy, used the same methods. Imam Ayatollah Khomeini used religious dogma to agitate the people of Iran to take to the street to protest against the oppressive methods of SAVAK and the unconstitutional, reactionary policies of Mohammad Reza Shah. Khomeini compared the shah with Yazid, son of Mu'awiyah, the abhorred Umayyad caliph who ordered the killing of Imam Hussein, son of Ali, at Kerbala (i.e., the personification of the unjust ruler, according to Islam). Muslims opposed injustice, and the mass of people, who were disillusioned with all nationalist ideologies, responded to Khomeini's policies, which concurred with their deepest religious beliefs.[265]

As the leader who successfully guided the revolution that toppled the Pahlavi dynasty, Imam Ayatollah Khomeini never assumed a public office. He became the supreme religious leader of the Islamic Republic of Iran, and the first decision he made was the adoption of a polity that was strictly based on Islam. Yet, his ideology is derived from the dogma of the Shi'ite sect.

A Background on Shi'ism

For numerous centuries, Shi'ism has been the subject of profound debates on whether it is a religious sect or a political movement. After Prophet Mohammad's death, the Islamic community was overtaken by turmoil to determine who was more eligible to succeed Mohammad to rule the Islamic state. A very powerful political group was claiming that the most suitable man to become the caliph was Mohammad's cousin and son-in-law, Ali Bin Abi Talib.[266] This political group included a number of companions of the prophet such as Ammar Bin Yassir, Al-Miqdad Ibn Al-Aswad, Abu Dhar Al-Ghafari and Sulayman Al-Farisi. They acquired the title of Shi'ite Ali, which means the followers or the party of Ali. They were adamant in their belief that Ali should assume the caliphate and they based their argument on a speech Prophet Mohammad had given during his last pilgrimage to Mecca before his

265 Esposito, op. cit., p. 18.

266 Nabil al-Altoom, al-tatatwur al-siyasi il jamburiyah al-islamiyah al-Iraniyah, 1980–1993 (The Political Development of the Islamic Republic of Iran 1980–1993), op. cit, pp. 160-162.

death, in which he had instructed the Muslims, saying: "As if I've been summoned (by God) and I have acquiesced, I am leaving with you two burdens: the book of God and my household. You will never be shattered as long as you adhere to both of them."[267]

The Sunni Muslims disputed the Shi'ites' claim and set forth a different version of the prophet's last speech, claiming that he asserted: "I've been summoned and acquiesced. I am leaving you two burdens, the book of God and my Sunnah (tradition). You will never be shattered as long as you adhere to both of them."

Professor Ali Jaleel Al-Wardi, a well-known Shi'ite scholar, supports the Sunni version of the prophet's speech.[268] In fact, the Sunnis' claim, which accentuates the prophet's instruction to adhere to God's book and the prophet's tradition, makes much more sense because the two main sources of the Islamic tenet are the holy Quran and Mohammad's "Sunnah-Hadeeth" tradition, i.e., the tradition is the second most important source of information of the Islamic religion. So how is it possible that the prophet neglects his tradition and emphasizes the role of the descendants of his household? The controversy persists until today and probably will never be solved.

Based on their perception of the prophet's speech, the Shi'ite Muslims believed that Ali Bin Abi Talib was prevented from assuming the caliphate by a conspiracy, which led to Abu Bakr Al-Siddeeq becoming the first caliph of the Rashidun era after the prophet's death. The Shi'ite followers kept insisting that Ali was the most legitimate successor to the prophet because he was the first child to adopt Islam, he was the son-in-law of Mohammad, and he was a great fighter for Islam.[269]

Ali's death threw the Muslims into disarray as his followers kept insisting that the leadership should be kept within Ahl al-Bayt—i.e., the household of Prophet Mohammad and Ali Bin Abi Talib. On the

267 See the Shi'ite-Sunni debate about Prophet Mohammad's recommendation regarding his successors in al-Wardi,
wu'adh al-sulatin, (Advisors of the Sultans), (Beirut: al-Furat Publishing Co.), pp. 249-252.

268 Al-Wardi, ibid, p. 250.

269 Al-Taweel, Mohammad Amin Ghalib, Tarikh al-Alawayeen (History of the Alawite), 4th ed. (Beirut: Dar al-Andalus: Printing, Publication and Distribution, 1981), pp. 125-127.

other hand, the powerful Sunni Umayyad family was consolidating its position in Syria and accentuating Mu'awiyah Bin Abu Sufyan's claim to be the caliphate of the Muslim world.[270]

In the city of Kufa, Iraq, Ali's eldest son Al Hasan was declared caliph and the second imam, and he mobilized a large army to fight Mu'awiyah to reclaim the leadership of the entire Muslim community. A wise and mature man, Hasan decided to defuse the tense situation and avoid profuse bloodshed among the Muslims. He agreed to concede the political position of caliph to Mu'awiyah while maintaining for himself the religious title of imam,[271] and bequeathed that religious title to the descendant of Ahl al-Bayt.

After both Mu'awiyah and Hasan died, Al-Hussein, the second son of Ali, was urged to fight the Umayyads and claim the caliphate, as well as proclaim himself the third imam, following his brother Hasan.

Al-Hussein became known to Muslims as a martyr.[272] Followers of Ahl al-Bayt did not acknowledge the caliphate of Yazeed, the son of Mu'awiyah who inherited his father's position. Hussein mobilized a large army in Kerbala, Iraq, to march on Yazeed son of Mu'awiyah to retrieve the caliphate to the "rightful people"—Hussein, the descendant of Ali.[273]

However, Hussein was betrayed, as his army and followers deserted him. He and his direct family were "martyred," as they were savagely slaughtered by Mu'awiyah's army. The brutal killing of Hussein and his family in Kerbala marked the beginning of deep animosity between the two factions of Shi'ite and Sunni Muslims.[274] Hussein's death is still passionately mourned by the Shi'ites every year during Muharram, the first month of the Islamic Hijri lunar year, during which Hussein was killed.[275]

The fourth imam was Ali Zayn Al-Abideen, the son of Hussein, who frequently prostrated to God in piety; thus he was named Al-Sajjad, the

---

270 Fisher, op. cit., pp. 57, 58.

271 Al-Taweel, op. cit., pp. 176, 177.

272 Ibid, p. 181.

273 Ghalib, Mustafa, Tarikh al-Da'wah al-Isma'I liyah (History of the Ismailiyah Movement) (Beirut: Dar al-Andalus, 1965), p. 115.

274 Ibid, p. 117.

275 Imam Khomeini's Line, op. cit., p. 58.

prostrator. Like his uncle, Hasan, he did not have political ambitions. He did not claim the caliphate and was satisfied to keep the religious title of imam.[276]

The fifth imam was Mohammad Al-Baqir. He was a widely informed man and hence was dubbed Al-Baqir, which means the all-around erudite man.

The sixth imam was Jafar Al-Sadiq, son of Mohammad Al-Baqir.[277] He was entitled Al-Sadiq, the truthful, because he always told the truth and never lied. He was considered by many as one of the most outstanding Muslim thinkers whose profound jurisprudential contribution changed Shi'ism from just a movement into a well-structured Islamic creed.[278]

Imam Al-Sadiq had six sons, and each one of them was suitable to be imam. Imam Al-Sadiq nominated his eldest son Ismael to become imam after his death, but Ismael died before his father, thereby causing deep confusion among the Shi'ite people. How could this happen when the position of imam is destined by God to be inherited in the same line from father to the eldest son until doomsday, as the Shi'ite creed states?

Some Shi'ite moved to solve the problem by announcing Jafar Al-Sadiq's son Abdallah, nicknamed Al-Aftah (which means the flat nose), would become imam, even though his father never nominated him as was required by the creed. But Abdallah died a few weeks after his father, which exacerbated the predicament of the imamate.[279]

After Abdallah died with no heir, the Shi'ite decided to designate Jafar's other son, Musa Al-Kadheim, as the seventh imam. However, Al-Kadheim was poisoned and died in Baghdad, causing more confusion and disarray among the Shi'ites.

In order to preserve and bolster their strong belief in the godly destined inheritance by the oldest son of the imam, which was shaken by the fatal interruption of the succession, the Shi'ite invented a new concept, the absent imam. The Mawsawiyah, followers of Musa

276 Ghalib, op. cit., p. 121.
277 Armstrong, op. cit., p. 57.
278 Ibid, pp. 66, 67.
279 Al-Katib, op. cit., pp. 104, 105.

Al-Kadheim, asserted that Imam Musa never died, but disappeared in time and was bound to reappear sooner or later.[280] This Messianic concept added a new principle which affected the creed of Shi'ism until modern times.

After Jafar Al-Sadiq's death, the dispute about the imamate's eligibility divided the Shi'ite into two main branches: the Imamiyyah (later known as the Twelvers) and the Ismaelis (later known as the Seveners). The Imamiyyah believe in all twelve imams; they constitute the majority of the Shi'ite community worldwide and the religious majority of Iran presently. The Ismaelis are the minority and are scattered across several countries.[281]

The eighth imam was Ali Al-Ridha, who lived during the reign of the Abbasid caliph, Al-Mamun, son of Harun Al-Rashid, who was a supporter of Ahl al-Bayt. Al-Mamun announced that Imam Ali Al-Ridha was his heir apparent to become caliph after his death. Al-Mamun also arranged the marriage of his daughter to Al-Ridha's son. This rapprochement with an imam from Ahl al-Bayt alarmed the Abbasids, who feared losing their power to their rivals. They threatened mutiny against Al-Mamun, in order to replace him with his uncle. Al-Mamun realized the futility of his attempt and decided to pacify his followers by poisoning Al-Ridha to death to bring down the final curtain on this matter.[282]

The ninth imam was Mohammad Al-Taqi. The tenth imam was Ali Al-Hadi and the eleventh imam was Al-Hasan al-Askari. Al-Taqi and Al-Hadi held the positions of imam and died quietly. But al-Askari played a significant role in perpetuating the needs of the Twelvers until the present time. He claimed that he had a son, Mohammad Al-Mahdi, who became the twelfth imam, from which the Imamiyyah derived the name the Twelvers. Yet there was some vagueness about the twelfth imam, as some disputed his existence and even his birth, because Imam Al-Askari never had any children. The main purpose of spreading this metaphysical belief was to save the creed of the Imamiyyah Shi'ite from being discredited. Without this myth, the continuation of the Twelvers

280 Al-Taweel, op. cit., pp. 200, 201.
281 Ibid., p. 20.
282 Ibid, pp. 224, 225.

would be in jeopardy because of the lack of a person who qualifies for the imamate. Thus the Twelvers were able to continue their creed by bestowing the Messianic quality on Al-Mahdi to keep the believers waiting indefinitely for him.

The Imamiyyah believe that Al-Mahdi Sahib Al Zaman (owner of time) had gone into his minor occultation that lasted for seventy years, during which he contacted only four of his deputies. Then he went into the major period of occultation, during which he will not contact anyone. Eventually he will emerge simultaneously with Jesus Christ, and they will both spread justice and prosperity all over the world.[283]

The Imamiyyah Shi'ites base their ideology on four beliefs: the infallibility of the twelve imams, the conviction that al-Mahdi will return, *intidhar* and *al-taqiyyah* (privacy and secrecy), and Muharram, the continual recollection of the tragic massacre of the third Imam Al-Hussein, son of Ali.[284]

Infallibility

During the first Hijri century some Shi'ite thinkers, such as Hisham Ibn Al-Kindi, Hisham Ibn Salim Al-Jawaliqi and Ali Ibn Ismael Ibn Swayh, among others, began to exaggerate their belief in revering Ahl al-Bayt, and they accentuated the concept of their infallibility according to the holy Quran, in order to justify the call for absolute obedience to the imams. The Sunnis rejected this interpretation of the verse, saying that infallibility belongs only to God. The Shi'ite argued, "How can we blindly obey a person (the imam) if he was fallible or he misconceives or commits mistakes? The imams are not ordinary people, they are chosen and guided by God. Hence they should be blindly obeyed."[285]

Professor Al-Wardi, the renowned sociologist, believes that the ultra-exaggeration of reverence towards Ahl al-Bayt was a sort of rebellious measure against the tyrannical Sunni Umayyad rulers whom the Shi'ite perceive as "deviants from Islam," to counter their oppressive

283 Ibid, pp. 232, 233.
284 Al-Wardi, wu'adh al-silatin, op. cit., p. 333.
285 Al-Taweel, op. cit., pp. 234-236.

regime, and their animosity towards Ahl al-Bayt.[286]

The theory of the infallibility of the twelve imams is challenged by several Muslim scholars based on the belief of Ahl al-Bayt. Prophet Mohammad, Ali Bin Abi Talib and all his descendant imams never claimed infallibility—in fact, they all adamantly rejected it. Prophet Mohammad claimed, "And I am not but a regular human being like you, but I receive religious inspiration from God." All twelve imams absolutely disclaimed infallibility and kept proclaiming that they were ordinary people—sometimes they were wrong, and sometimes they were right, and they sought people's advice, and opposed them if they committed any wrong deed. In a detailed speech he gave in the mosque of Kufa, Iraq, Ali Bin Abi Talib, the first of the twelve imams, stated that he did not claim any extraordinary feats and that he was merely another servant of God, similar to all other good believers.[287]

The objection to the concept of the imamate infallibility is that it abolishes the practice of Al-Shura (the consultation), which was upheld and pursued by Prophet Mohammad and the four Rashidun caliphs who succeeded Mohammad. Al-Shura is the process of deliberation of various opinions for the purpose of arriving at appropriate decisions in matters related to social life. It is required procedure that is ordered by the Quran, as God instructed Muhammad to consult with his disciples before making any decision (Chapter 3: Al Omran 139). In another chapter of the Quran it instructs: "And they deal with their matters based on consultation" (Chapter 13, Al-Shura, 37).

These are very detailed and clear verses that depict the practice of Al-Shura. In all these Quranic verses, the just ruler is expected not to be tyrannical and not to pass an opinion or a decision without seeking the advice of his followers. Therefore, Prophet Mohammad kept instructing the Muslims to consult among themselves to deal with their regular matters of life. "Prophet Mohammad was a leader of a mission, not a tyrant."[288]

286 Al-Wardi, op. cit., pp. 329, 340.
287 Al-Katib, op. cit., pp. 29, 30.
288 Al-Wardi, wu'adh al-sulatin, op. cit., p. 254.

AL-MAHDI

The second firm belief of the Imamiyyah Shi'ites is the concept of the Al-Mahdi, Sahib Al-Zaman (the awaited deliverer, the owner of time, or the Messiah) (see the book of Isiah, chapter eleven and Matthew 24, which both discuss the Messiah). The Messiah is the one on whom God bestowed wisdom, understanding, the spirit of knowledge, or the man who is guided by God to save the world and fill it with peace and justice. The Imamiyyah Shi'ites accorded the same attributes to Imam Al-Mahdi.

The concept was instigated by the Twelvers for two purposes. First, they aimed to keep their faith active after the eleventh imam, Al-Hasan Al-Askari, died without having a son or an heir apparent, which jeopardized the system of imamate as protected by God (as they asserted). Therefore, they claimed that Al-Hasan Al-Askari had a son called Mohammad Al-Mahdi, who was born on 15/Sha'ban 255H, 869 A.D., and he assumed the imamate when he was only five years old because God made him omni-knowledgeable.[289] He was the twelfth and last of the infallible imams. They claim that in the year 266H, he and his mother entered a basement of a house in the city of Samara, Iraq, and he disappeared, while his mother watched him, into two periods of occultation, the minor period and the major period. His minor occultation period lasted for seventy years, during which he contacted only four of his deputies to send instructions to his followers. At the end of that minor period of occultation, upon the death of his fourth and last deputy, Abdul Hasan Ali Al-Sammari, Al-Mahdi sent a letter to his followers, conveyed by Al-Sammari, in which he declared the beginning of his major occultation period, which would last until the end of time, and he declared he would not contact any one of his followers. He also declared he would reappear to come back to salvage the world and fill it with justice and peace.[290]

The second aim of the Twelvers was encouragement of a belief that the awaited-for Al-Mahdi would return to the caliphate. The

289 Al-Taweel, op. cit., p. 232.

290 Al-Hasan Bin Musa al-Nawbakhti, Firaq al-Shiah (The Shi'ite Schools of Thought) (Beirut: Dar al-Adhwa', 1984), pp. 94-97.

descendants of the household of Ali Bin Abi Talib had made several unsuccessful attempts to recover the caliphate from the Umayyads, so the Twelvers wanted to encourage their followers to believe in and wait for their Sahib Al-Zaman to come back and restore justice for them.

INTIDHAR AND TAQIYYA

The third belief of the Shi'ite is *intidhar* and *taqiyya* (waiting and secrecy). Waiting for the Al-Mahdi was practiced in privacy to avoid the unbearable brutality of the tyrannical rulers. It was based on the secrecy practiced by Prophet Mohammad and his followers, at the beginning of the Islamic call, to protect themselves from the brutality inflicted on them by the tribe of Quraysh. Later in Islamic history, taqiyya was utilized by the Shi'ite as a tactic to tolerate all sorts of abuse by their enemies while they waited for Al-Mahdi to eliminate all aspects of unfairness and establish the rightful world for all humans.

The messianic belief in the awaited Al-Mahdi gave the Shi'ite hope and optimism about their future. That strong faith helped them to withstand unbearable conditions of persecution by the brutal rulers. Without that well-entrenched belief that Al-Mahdi would return, the Shi'ite sect would probably have disappeared in time. Also, the practice of taqiyya helped the Shi'ite to conceal their belief throughout the period of occultation, until the awaited Al-Mahdi comes back. Taqiyya protected the Shi'ite from possible annihilation by the tyrannical caliphs and sultans under whom they lived.[291]

However, waiting and secrecy affected the general attitudes and behavior of the Twelvers and led them to fully withdraw from any sort of political activities or even resist injustice inflicted on them by brutal rulers. This period was characterized by the negative attitude of the Twelvers whereby they suspended almost all functions of the state such as collecting the Zakat (an obligatory payment made annually under Islamic law), which is one of the five main pillars of Islam and which all Muslim believers are required to pay.[292]

291 Al-Wardi, op. cit., p. 333.
292 Al-Katib, op. cit., pp. 188, 189.

MOURNING OF MUHARRAM

The fourth practice that is passed from generation to generation by the Shi'ite is the annual mourning commemorating the massacre of Imam Al-Hussein Bin Ali and his family.

In the past, the Shi'ite used to secretly meet in isolated rooms to commemorate the tragedy of the "martyrdom" of Imam Al-Hussein. In those gatherings, they would rally their supporters who dissented against their oppressive rulers. Eventually the mourning rituals became part of the Shi'ite identity, resembling the pilgrimage and gathering of all Muslims in Mecca.[293] The mourning rituals developed over time to include the Shi'ite punishing themselves by hitting their foreheads with machetes to shed their blood, pounding their backs with chains while crying and shouting "O Hussein," and reciting sad chants about him.

In Iran, Imam Khomeini integrated the rituals of Hussein mourning as one procedure of his regime. He stated:

> No one understands the significance of these mourning sessions all over the world. We are described as a weeping people because they are not aware of the Godly rewards that are bestowed on these accessions. They certainly are not aware of the untold goals and the rewards of these prayers. The political aims of the mourning sessions are to face God and to mobalize all energies towards Islamic goals. The main objective of the mourning sessions is not just to lament and weep on the Master of the Martyrs, but more important are the political goals which were outlined by our imams during the first period of Islam.[294]

CONFUSION AND UNCERTAINTY

The rigid determination to continue the concept of waiting led to a serious crisis among the thinkers of the Twelvers regarding the

293 Khomeini's Line, op. cit., p. 61.
294 Ibid.

functions of the government. One difficult question was how to deal with such basic functions of the Islamic government as collecting the Zakat, and other taxes. All these religiously vital functions, according to the Twelvers, were strictly the duties of the Imam al-Mahdi (and no one else), when he returned and established his virtuous government.

So when the Shi'ite were attacked and won the battle with its booty—and were subsequently required to pay one-fifth of the spoils to the legitimate ruler in accordance with the Shari'ah, and the only legitimate ruler was the absent imam—the Shi'ite were in full confusion. They did not have any guide or written instructions regarding how to deal with collecting war booty or levying the one-fifth tax while the imam was occulting, both of which are required by the laws of Prophet Mohammad. Some suggested to just discard the booty and ignore the tax, while others suggested to hoard the booty underground until the absent imam came back from his occultation and managed these matters.[295]

The second source of Shi'ite confusion was the elimination of the procedures of the shura (consultation), which was discussed previously. The holy Quran exalts, "Those who responded to their Lord and performed prayers and dealt with their affairs by consulting among them, and spent from what we gave them" (Quran 3,158).

By entrusting the political system to an infallible imam who is chosen by God, the Shi'ite utterly uprooted the procedure of shura that was ordered and practiced by Prophet Mohammad and his four pious successors. The Shi'ite thinkers were not able to explain this belief, which contradicted the Quran and Prophet Mohammad's instructions.

The third source of confusion was the elimination of the procedure of *Bay'ah* (fealty), or the practice of legitimately electing the ruler of the Muslim populace.[296] The fealty was instructed by Prophet Mohammad before his death, when some of his closest disciples approached him and inquired, "O messenger of God, we do not know how long you will stay with us to guide us. Please name one to succeed you to become our refuge after you are gone." He replied, "I can see his place; and if

295 Ibid, p. 187.

296 See Armstrong, op. cit., p. 25. Also, al-Taweel, op. cit., provides details about "Al-Baya'ah the fealty," or, election practiced by the four Rashideen "rightly guided" caliphs, pp. 143-157.

I nominate anyone you will desert him, just like the Israelis deserted Aron, son of Omran."

So Mohammad left the matter of succession to his followers—that is, the most pious four successors, the Rashidun caliphs (the wise successors): Abu Bakr Al-Siddeeq, Umar Ibn Al-Khattab, Uthman Bin Affan and Ali Bin Abi Talib. All were sworn into their offices after obtaining fealty from all Muslims.[297] Some Islamic pundits believe that the prophet wanted to suggest his cousin and son-in-law, Ali Bin Abi Talib, as his successor, but Mohammad died before having a chance to express his desire.

Thus the four Rashidun caliphs used the system of fealty to legitimize their claim to the caliphate. The Rashidun caliphs invariably invited suggestions and exhorted criticism from all Muslims—men and women.

The Twelver Shi'ite, by attributing infallibility on the imams and requiring blind obedience to them, eliminated the concept of al-bay'ah and ascribed a totalitarian authority to their rulers. It is historical fact, though, that the election-fealty or bay'ah system was stopped by the Sunni Umayyads, who changed the Islamic political system into a hereditary dynasty. Then the authoritarian dynastic governments were pursued by the Abbasids and the Ottomans[298] until Mustafa Kemal Ataturk announced the birth of the secular Republic of Turkey in 1924. Yet authoritarianism and totalitarianism are criticized by Islamic thinkers.

KHOMEINISM

The bewilderment of the Shi'ite lasted for centuries until Imam Ayatollah Khomeini reached prominence as a leader and formulated a rigorously outlined new philosophical understanding of Shi'ite Islam—referred to as Khomeinism. The main significance of Khomeinism is that it is based on a deep understanding of pragmatic and spiritual

297 Ibid.

298 In his book *The Middle East: A History*, Professor Sydney Nettleton Fisher, op. cit., provides comprehensive details about the characteristics of the four Islamic empires: the Rashideen, the Umayyads, the Abbasids and the Ottomans.

needs. The process of co-influencing religion with politics, as was done by Khomeini, was unique.

Ayatollah Khomeini was a *faqih* (an expert in Islamic law), a Shi'ite clergyman (ayatollah), a prolific author, a religious ideologue, and a political leader who in 1979 led the thunderous revolution that toppled the powerful shah Mohammad Reza Pahlavi of Iran. He converted Iran into the first theocracy in modern time, and unleashed a religious wave that overtook almost the entire region of the Middle East.[299]

Khomeinism represents a typical Hegelian dialectical antithesis that was born in the womb and opposed the secular-nationalist ideologies that overtook the Middle East after the collapse of the Ottoman theocracy in the 1920s. The early twentieth-century intellectuals and some military officers promoted what they perceived as secular philosophies (which were largely derived from the secular Enlightenment Era), by which they would liberate and modernize their countries. However, when those philosophies failed to be accepted, to accomplish the goals expected by the populace, their religious antithetical movements quickly spread and culminated in the widely supported theocratic Khomeinism.[300]

In his lectures, Khomeini boldly challenged the traditional Shi'ite thinkers and clergymen. By combining religious beliefs with political plans required by life, Imam Khomeini established his pragmatic leadership and stated his perception of the daily needs of the people. He altered the metaphysical, indefinitely postponed, daydream-like Messianic idea of the Al-Mahdi into a solid umbrella that encompassed the pragmatic social, political and economic matters of the people.

Although he acknowledged the deeply rooted Shi'ite belief in Imam Al-Mahdi, Khomeini asserted that waiting for the absent imam did not preclude satisfying the needs of life. The state must not depend entirely on the return of the absent imam. Hence it was the duty of the religious leaders to establish the state in which absolute justice could be pursued, similar to that which would be created by the awaited imam.[301]

299 Esposito, op. cit., p. 38.
300 Haikal, op. cit., p. 167.
301 Ibid.

By accentuating the necessity for the religious man to assume political leadership, Khomeini reversed a basic principle of the Shi'ite philosophy and came closer to the Sunni Islamic concept of the caliphate.

Khomeini determined that during the period of occultation of the infallible Al-Mahdi, the Muslim ruler must possess the following eight characteristics:

1) Full knowledge of jurisprudence, which is the highest priority
2) Sound mind
3) Piety and devotion to Islam
4) Justice
5) Deliberation and administration
6) Manhood
7) Purity of birth
8) Generosity (not stingy, thrifty or greedy)[302]

Khomeini acknowledged that authority may be managed by ordinary people regardless of their sanctity, which is the same concept on which the position of the caliphate was established and practiced for centuries after the death of Prophet Mohammad. The caliphate position was assumed by followers of Mohammad who obtained popular consensus or assignment. The four caliphs of the Rashidun era, who ruled for three decades, became successors of Mohammad (caliphs) as a result of the fealty pledged to them by the majority of the people, while the Umayyads, the Abbasid and Ottoman caliphs pursued a dynastic hereditary system of caliphate. None of these rulers claimed sacredness or divinity.[303]

Their legitimacy was based on tribal or family loyalty. Contrary to that, the Shi'ite political philosophy believed that leadership was a divine career. That is why the awaited imam is the only leader who is authorized to complete the duties that were started by the prophets. Any other system of authority is considered as trespassing on the divine role outlined by God for the deliverer imam.[304]

302 Muzahim, op. cit., p. 12.
303 Fisher, op. cit., Part I and Part II.
304 Muzahim, op. cit., pp. 61-63.

By recognizing the basic Shi'ite belief of the imamate and synthesizing it with the system established by Prophet Mohammad and his successors that allows popular participation, Khomeini gave birth to a new version of Wilayat Al-Faqih. Khomeini modified the old concept of the absolute authority of the faqih to more accurately meet the requirements of the present time.[305]

Khomeini was denounced by numerous well-known Islamic thinkers and Salafi leaders who considered Khomeinism a flagrant deviation from the foundational principles and institutions of Islam. Included in that group were renowned leaders such as Abu Al-Aala Al Mawahdi, Mohammad Baqir Al-Sadr, Al-Sayid Mohammad Hussein Fadl Allah, Hussein Tabatabai, Sayyid Qutb, and Taqui Al-Din Al-Rahim, as well as many other influential thinkers who disagreed with Khomeini's attempt to modify the Islamic dogma according to the modern political systems.[306]

Khomeini countered his critics by asserting that the caliphate system followed by Prophet Mohammad's four Rashidun caliphs was based on the approval and the selection of the *ummah*, the Muslim populace, which was not substantially different from modern political systems. The caliphate system was not based on a divine power as predicated by the Shi'ite.

Khomeini represented a uniquely sophisticated path which became a paragon for most Islamic movements that aspired to enter the political arena. Khomeini's success provided a practical foundation for a modern religious state.[307]

Thus, Khomeinism practically implemented the theory of Wilayat Al-Faqih as an earthly state, and as a temporary period of waiting for the return of Al-Mahdi.

THE REPUBLIC

A critical point forged by Khomeini is the belief in the system of a democratic republic. Khomeinism stimulated several controversial opinions, as it combined the religious theory of Wilayat Al-Faqih with

305 Mahboobah, op. cit., p. 166.
306 Khomeini's Line, op. cit., pp. 10, 11.
307 Mahboobah, op. cit., pp. 166, 167.

the modern concept of limited government. One of the very contentious points which provoked keen debates was the addition of "Iran" to the name of the republic (the Islamic Republic of Iran).

Dictionaries of the world define a republic as a state in which the head of the government is not a monarch or other hereditary ruler. The supreme power in a republic rests in the hands of citizens entitled to vote and is exercised by representatives chosen by the people. This definition coincided with Ayatollah Mohammad's definition of the Iranian Islamic Republic as a type of government temporarily elected by the people and whose laws are based on Islamic Shari'ah.[308]

The republican system is the most modern political practice followed by the Western world, which separated religion from the state. It came after the long centuries of the medieval era, when humanity was ruled by absolute hereditary dynasties and tyrannical clergy. The diminishment of the clergy's power began with the birth and growth of the scientific-minded middle class during the Renaissance. Then came the secular freedom philosophers of the Enlightenment Era who denounced the tyrannical authorities of the kings and the church, and called for limiting the powers of the rulers by means of electing legislative authorities who served the interest of the masses. Most of their philosophers like Voltaire, Jean Jacques Rousseau, Helvetius, and Diderot, among others, preached secularism, abolishing monarchies and replacing them with democratic republics.

The earliest republic in modern history was born in the New World when, in 1776, George Washington, who was deeply influenced by the Enlightenment philosophy, personified and implemented it in his newly born country. He refused to be crowned as a king and preferred to be democratically elected as the first president of the Republic of the United States of America. Soon after George Washington declared his country's independence from the empire of Great Britain, he was approached by Moses Seixas, the tycoon financier and the head of the Jewish community in the New World, who congratulated the new president in the name of the children of the prophet Abraham. Washington thanked him and retorted that America is neither Christian nor Jewish

308 Ibid.

nor Muslim.[309]

Then the French Revolution erupted in 1789, which was also brought to fruition from the Enlightenment philosophy, that toppled the Bourbon dynasty and turned France into a secular republic. Subsequently the republican system spread to most countries of the European continent.

In the Middle East, the popular election of rulers had been unknown since the early stages of the Islamic state and the end of the Rashidun era (632 CE to 661 CE), during which the Muslim people expressed their support to the caliphs by declaring fealty to them. After more than one thousand years of rule by totalitarian theocratic dynasties, the Middle East region, for the first time, experienced the modern style of popular elections when in 1924, atheist General Mustafa Kemal Ataturk was elected as the first president of the republic of Turkey.

Hence, by announcing Iran as a democratic republic, Khomeini was accused by the fundamentalist clergy of imitating the system of the infidels and deviating from the path of Islam. Yet, Khomeini, with keen political acumen, appeased the masses, and moved to establish the Shi'ite type of government of Wilayat Al-Faqih as a temporary period of waiting for the occulting al-Mahdi to rise and come back to establish his promised perfect state.[310]

Imam Khomeini placed particular emphasis on women's rights. He believed that women shared an equal role with men in the struggle for achieving the Iranian revolution. Women deserve particular attention with regard to social progress in Iran; they constitute over 50 percent of the university students and probably have the most progressive political participation of any other Muslim country. Women were regular members of the Iranian parliament. It is rather paradoxical that the Iranian Revolution of 1979, which is based on the strict religious Shar'ia, encouraged the growing influence of women in Iran.[311] During the shah's secular regime before the revolution, most women were not allowed by their husbands or fathers to leave their homes. The male members of the

309 Zaki, Mamoon Amin, "Su'ood wa taraju," op. cit., p. 61.

310 See, Sashidina, Abdul Azeez, tabee'at hukm al-faqih fi Iran (The Nature of the Rule of the Faqih in Iran) (al-Misbar), op. cit., pp. 105-136

311 Khomeini's Line, op. cit. pp. 64, 65.

families felt it was immoral for their female relatives to be seen in public without being accompanied by a male relative. Contrary to that, Imam Khomeini only requested women to wear the Islamic *hijab* or just to dress modestly. By promoting the use of the hijab, Khomeini succeeded in removing many restrictions on women's behavior. By complying and dressing modestly or wearing the *hijab*, women were able to attend school, participate in public life and, most importantly, work and earn their own income. Khomeini based this tenet on the following Quranic verse, which advocates women's work and earning:

> And do not wish for that which God has given some of you more than others. For men is a share of what they earn and for women a share of what they earn and ask God for his bounty. Indeed, God is the omni-knowledgeable.[312]

One of the most significant signs of progress of women in Iran was the award of the 2003 Nobel Peace Prize to lawyer Shirin Ebadi for her efforts in serving human rights. Ms. Ebadi was the first Iranian woman—or rather, the first Muslim woman—to win the Nobel Prize.

Khomeini averred that the valiant march of women in this struggling country was an achievement to be proud of in modern Islamic history. To bestow religious character on women's participation in the revolutionary struggle, Khomeini recalled that the struggle of women in Islamic Iran was similar to the struggle of Khadija, the mother of believers (he was referring to Prophet Mohammad's first wife, who adamantly stood beside him), Lady Fatima, Grand Zainab, Imam Hussein's sister, who supported his revolution, and other women's struggles during the "glorious era of the Islam" and its aftermath.[313]

After the success of his revolution, Khomeini's main concern was to consolidate the foundations of his theocratic regime and protect it from its numerous opponents. By the time Khomeini returned to Iran, the social structure had almost broken down. The state, the army and the police forces had disintegrated; the economy had collapsed and political

312 The Holy Koran: Chapter One: Women, verse 32.
313 Khomeini's Line, op. cit., pp. 64, 65.

organizations from the far left to far right had begun to vie for power. It led to tumultuous chaos, the outcome of which could not be known.[314] These circumstances prevailed for a while, and were exacerbated by the dialectical conflict between secular and religious forces, and some other emerging autonomous revolutionary movements. The common intent among these movements during the early years of unrest was to determine the future of the Iranian society, i.e., whether to submit to the control of the religious establishment and become an Islamic theocracy, or to rise as a constitutional state under moderate reformers.[315] The resolution of this conflict cost thousands of lives and resulted in the total domination of the religious establishment over Iranian life.

Imam Khomeini pursued the path he had begun at the onset of the revolution. He banned magazines, closed down publishing houses, banned Western music, controlled television programs by replacing Western shows with recitation from the Holy Quran, and forbade alcohol. His crusade was aiming "to erase all the filth of the Western world that was poisoning the Islamic Republic of Iran."[316]

Khomeini named a close follower, Mahdi Bazargan, a freelance freedom fighter who had studied in France, to the position of prime minister. Bazargan's main task was to restore administrative and economic stability. Bazargan and his cabinet of moderate elements sought to control the revolutionary organizations and attempted to form a liberal governing institution. However, the range of Bazargan's government authority was limited by the power of a religious organization known as the Council of Islamic Deputies. Composed mainly of ulema and under the guidance of Khomeini, the council wielded supreme administrative and legislative power in Iran. It passed laws and decrees and possessed the power to veto policies adopted by Bazargan to implement his programs.

Frustrated with the paralysis of the clerical opposition, Bazargan resigned in November 1979, paving the clergy's way to full control of the government.[317]

314 [105] Cleveland, op. cit., pp. 430, 431.
315 [106] Ibid.
316 [107] Ibid.
317 Coughlin, op. cit., p. 174.

Khomeini ordered the establishment of semi-military forces and judicial organizations to eliminate certain institutions of the previous regime. The semi-military forces were joined by a large number of poor urban youth who were strictly devoted to Khomeini. Other organizations that operated to consolidate the new regime were the Revolutionary Tribunals, whose main objectives were to prosecute and eliminate SAVAK, the personnel and high-ranking military officers of the shah's government.

In order to provide an organizational structure and an ideology for the Islamic revolution, a group of ayatollahs formed the Islamic Republic Party (IRP). The IRP tried to gather popular support for the new Islamic regime and undermine secular movements. Due to the close relation between the ulema and the populace through the mosques, the IRP rapidly grew to become a major force in Iran. The IRP hegemony was imposed with the help of the Revolutionary Guards to thwart opposition rallies and their leaders. All liberal or leftist movements which tried to gain support of the educated middle class were considered to be the enemy.[318]

In 1979, a national referendum was conducted which approved converting Iran from a kingdom to an Islamic Republic. In June 1979, after the downfall of the liberal-minded Mahdi Bazargan and his aborted attempt to promulgate a moderate constitution that is less dependent on the clergy, Imam Khomeini in December took the initiative to draft a constitution that is based "hundred percent on Islam" 84 (footnote) and Wilayat Al-Faqih.

Khomeini's successful theocratic revolution in Iran in 1979, which toppled the tyrannical secular system of the mighty Shah Mohammad Reza Pahlavi, caused a seismic effect within and outside the realm of the Muslim world, and was considered a miracle. Later in 1989, the spectacular triumph achieved by Osama Bin Laden's al-Qaeda against the Great Powers, "atheist" Soviet Union was cheered by the Islamic and Western worlds. Then in 2002, the downfall of the secular Kemalist regime in Turkey occurred upon the election of the Islamic Justice and Development Party under its pious leader, Recep Tayyip Erdogan; all

318 Moslem, op. cit., p. 5.

these dramatic accomplishments attained by the Islamic movements were interpreted by the believers as undisputable proof of divine support. Hence a large number of youths who were frustrated with their countries' backwardness, corrupt leadership and the failure of all previously prevalent ideologies were inspired to create and spread jihadist organizations to fight the Western colonial powers and infidels everywhere. These organizations are discussed in detail in the next chapter.

Chapter 7

THE INTERNATIONAL FUNDAMENTALIST TERRORIST ORGANIZATIONS

ON MARCH 22 and 23, 2016, CNN, BBC Arabic and English, and other worldwide broadcasting channels erupted with the news that terrorist attacks claimed by the Islamic State in Iraq and Syria (ISIS—or in Arabic, DAESH) had hit B russels, the capital of the Kingdom of Belgium, leaving thirty people dead and more than two hundred wounded.[319]

The terrorist explosions in Brussels caused deep panic all over Europe. *Al Khaleej,* a UAE newspaper, revealed that the explosions were connected with those that had almost simultaneously hit several locations in Paris, France, on November 13, 2015, leaving 130 people dead and several hundred wounded. *Al Khaleej* printed the names and pictures of the persons who planned and carried out the attacks in both European capitals; they were members of ISIS, and part of a larger group of dormant cells located in several parts of Europe.[320]

At the end of President Obama's tour of Europe in 2016, James R. Clapper, U.S. Director of National Intelligence, revealed that ISIS has secret cells in Britain, Germany and Italy, and requested that the Europeans increase their participation in combating terrorism.

In Sweden, local intelligence agencies received details that ISIS was possibly planning an attack on the capital, Stockholm. The information

319 CNN, BBC, Arabic and English, March 23, 24, 2016.

320 *Al-Khaleej* (Arabic), No. 3459, Friday, March 25, 2016.

was reported by the *Express* newspaper and was broadcast by Sweden. The *Express* also reported that Swedish police received intelligence information from Iraq concerning seven or eight terrorists from ISIS who had entered Sweden to attack civil targets.[321]

Salah Abdul Salam was one of the terrorist leaders captured by the Brussels police in a raid after the Paris attacks. The British newspaper the *Daily Mail* opined that because Salam had backed out of detonating his explosives in the Paris attacks, ISIS had become suspicious of him and thus hastened to expedite the attacks in Brussels for fear that Salam might break down and inform Belgium police about the pending attacks.[322]

The police were also after two men from Russia, Alex Dovabish and Murat Yusif, who both converted to Islam, joined ISIS, fought in Syria and had committed other terrorist attacks.[323] This information revealed the international nature of the membership of ISIS. From Afghanistan to Yemen, Egypt, Iraq, Libya, Tunisia, to countries in Europe, are all constantly susceptible to attacks by Islamic militant fundamentalists.[324]

A noteworthy point here is that the Paris and Brussels attacks were carried out by ISIS-DAESH, even after several months of intensive bombardment by the Western allies in Mosul, Iraq, Syria, Yemen, Libya and other locations of the movement's headquarters; the allies' efforts did not do much damage. Also, the ISIS-DAESH movement has a network of bureaucratic leadership that keeps recruiting young individuals, and trains them and prepares them to execute terrorist attacks against specified targets.[325]

After extensive research, the government of the United Arab Emirates issued a report exploring effective methods to counteract terrorism. The report focused on the practical implementation of Federal Law No. (7) of 2014, promulgated by the president of the UAE, His Royal Highness Sheikh Khalifa bin Zayed Al Nahyan, regarding terrorist crimes.[326] The law was announced by all UAE mass media to expose

321 Ibid.
322 *Al-Khaleej*, No. 3457, Wednesday, March 23, 2016.
323 Ibid.
324 Report by al-Mizmat, Center for Studies of Research, Sada al-Watan, No. 9, p. 24 (Arabic).
325 Ibid, pp. 24, 25
326 Ibid.

the names and locations of those terrorist groups, to warn and enable other nations to confront them.

The Mizmat Center for Research and Studies published a comprehensive review entitled "*Huna Taskun Kull Shuroor al-Dunia*" ("Here lie all evils of the world"), revealing names and locations of no less than eighty-five fundamentalist organizations in different parts of the world whose purpose is to await orders from their leaders to wage terrorist attacks against designated targets. The list of the terrorist organizations, as confirmed by the UAE cabinet, includes the following names in both Arabic and English :[327]

English	Arabic
1. The Emiratis Muslim Brotherhood	جماعة الاخوان المسلمين الإماراتية
2. The Call for Reform (The Reform Organization)	دعوة الإصلاح (جمعية الإصلاح)
3. Fatah Movement of Islam in Lebanon	حركة فتح الإسلام اللبنانية
4. The Islamic League in Italy	الرابطة الإسلامية في إيطاليا
5. The Jihad (Holy War) Cells in the EUA	خلايا الجهاد الإماراتي
6. The League of Supporters in Lebanon	عصبة الأنصار في لبنان
7. The Islamic League in Finland	الرابطة الإسلامية في فنلندا
8. Al- Karamah Organization	منظمة الكرامة
9. Al- Qaeda Organization in the Maghreb Islamic country	تنظيم القاعدة في بلاد المغرب الإسلامي

327 Ibid, pp. 24-26.

10. The Islamic League in Sweden	الرابطة الإسلامية في السويد
11. The Nation's Parties in Gulf	أحزاب الامة في الخليج
12. The Battalion of Supporters of Shari'ah in Libya	كتيبة أنصار الشريعة في ليبيا
13. The Islamic Order in Norway	الرابطة الإسلامية في النرويج
14. Al- Qaeda Order	تنظيم القاعدة
15. The group of Shari'ah Supporters in Tunisia	جماعة أنصار الشريعة في تونس
16. The Organization of Islamic Aid in London	منظمة الإغاثة الإسلامية في لندن
17. DAESH (al- Dawla Al- Islamya fi Al- Iraq Wa al- Sham)	داعش
18. The Movement of Holy Fighters in Somalia	حركة شباب المجاهدين الصومالية
19. The Kordova Organization in Britain	مؤسسة قرطبة في بريطانيا
20. Al- Qaeda Order in the Arabian Peninsula	تنظيم القاعدة في شبه الجزيرة العربية
21. The Boko Haram Group in Nigeria	جماعة بوكو حرام في نيجيريا
22. The corps of Islamic Aid, part of the international organization of the Muslim Brotherhood	هيئة الإغاثة الإسلامية التابعة لتنظيم الاخوان المسلمين الدولي
23. Supporters of the Shari'ah (Yemen)	أنصار الشريعة (اليمن)

24. The Murabitoon battalion in Mali	كتيبة المرابطون في مالي
25. Taliban Movement in Pakistan	حركة طالبان باكستان
26. The Order and Group of the Muslim Brotherhood	تنظيم وجماعة الاخوان المسلمين
27. The movement of Supporters of Religion in Mali	حركة أنصار الدين في مالي
28.The Battalion of Abu Dhar al- Ghafari (Ghaphari) in Syria	كتيبة أبو ذر الغفاري في سوريا
29. The Islamic Group in Egypt	الجماعة الإسلامية ف مصر
30. The Haqqani Network in Pakistan	شبكة حقاني الباكستانية
31. The Brigade of Unity in Syria	لواء التوحيد في سوريا
32. The Egyptian Group of Supporters of Bayt al- Maqdis	جماعة أنصار بيت المقدس المصرية
33. The Pakistani Group Li Shukur Teebah	جماعة لشكر طيبة الباكستانية
34. The Battalion of Unity and Faith in Syria	كتيبة التوحيد والإيمان في سوريا
35. The Group of Egyptian Soldiers	جماعة أجناد مصر
36. The East Turkistan Movement in Pakistan	حركة تركستان الشرقية في باكستان
37. The Green Battalion in Syria	كتيبة الخضراء في سوريا

38. The Mujahideen Shura (consulting) Assembly	مجلس شورى المجاهدين
39. The Wing of Bayt al- Maqdis	أكناف بيت المقدس
40. Mohammed's Army in Pakistan	جيش محمد في باكستان
41. The Abu Bakir al-Sididq Battalion in Syria	سرية أبوبكر الصديق في سوريا
42. The Houthis Movement in Yemen	حركة الحوثيين في اليمن
43. The Army of Mohammed in Pakistan and India	جيش محمد في باكستان والهند
44. The Battalion of Talhah Bin Ubayd Allah in Syria	سرية طلحة بن عبيد الله في سوريا
45. The Saudi Hizb Allah (Party of God) in Hijaz	حزب الله السعودي في الحجاز
46. The Indian Mujahdeen (holy fighters) in India/ Kashmir	المجاهدين الهنود في الهند/ كشمير
47. The Battalion of Al- Sarim in Al- Ratter (the sharp sward) in Syria	سرية الصارم البتار في سوريا
48. Hizb Allah in the States of the Gulf Cooperative Council	حزب الله في دول مجلس التعاون الخليجي
49. The Islamic Principalities of Caucasia (the Chechen Holy Fighters)	إمارة القوقاز الإسلامية (الجهاديين الشيشانيين)
50. The Battalion of Abdullah Bin Mubark In Syria	كتيبة عبد الله بن مبارك في سوريا

51. Al- Qaida Organization in Iran	تنظيم القاعدة في إيران
52. The Islamic Movement in Uzbekistan	الحركة الإسلامية الأوزبكية
53. Battalion of the Caravan of Martyrs in Syria	كتيبة قوافل الشهداء في سوريا
54. The Organization of Badir in Iraq	منظمة بدر في العراق
55. The Philippine Group of Abu Saif	جماعة أبو سياف الفلبينية
56. The Battalion of Abu Omar in Syria	كتيبة أبو عمر في سوريا
57. The Gangs of Right Owners in Iraq	عصائب أهل الحق في العراق
58. The Council of American Islamic Relations	مجلس العلاقات الأمريكية الإسلامية (كير)
59. The Battalion of the Free Shammar in Syria	كتيبة أحرار شمر في سوريا
60. The Battalion of Hezbollah in Iraq	كتائب حزب الله في العراق
61. Organization of Kanfas in Belgrade, Serbia	منظمة كنفاس في بلجراد، صربيا
62. The Battalion of Sareat Al Jabal in Syria	كتيبة سارية الجبل في سوريا
63. Abu al- Fadhil Al- Abbas Brigade in Syria	لواء أبو فضل العباس في سوريا
64. The American Islamic Organization (MAS)	الجمعية الإسلامية الأمريكية (ماس)
65. Al- Shahba Battalion in Syria	كتيبة الشهباء في سوريا

66. The Battalions of the Brigade of the Doomsday (Iraq)	كتائب لواء اليوم الموعود(العراق)
67. Union of the Muslim Knowledgeable Men	اتحاد علماء المسلمين
68. The Battalion of Al- Qa'qa in Syria	كتيبة القعقاع في سوريا
69. The Brigade of Ammar Bin Yasir (Syria)	لواء عمار بن ياسر (سوريا)
70. Union of Islamic Organization in Europe	اتحاد المنظمات الإسلامية في أوروبا
71. The Battalion of Revolutionary Sufian in Syria	كتيبة سفيان الثوري في سوريا
72. The Iraqi Group of Supporters of Islam	جماعة أنصار الإسلام العراقية
73. Union of Islamic Organization in France	اتحاد المنظمات الإسلامية في فرنسا
74. The Battalion of Worshippers of God in Syria	كتيبة عباد الرحمن في سوريا
75. Al- Nusra Front in Syria	جبهة النصرة في سوريا
76. The Islamic League in Britain	الرابطة الإسلامية في بريطانيا
77. The Battalion of Omar Bin al- Khattab in Syria	كتيبة عمر بن الخطاب في سوريا
78. Movement of al- Sham Free People in Syria	حركة أحرار الشام في سوريا
79. The Islamic Gathering in Germany	التجمع الإسلامي في ألمانيا

80. Al- Shayma' Battalion in Syria	كتيبة الشيماء في سوريا
81. The Army of Islam in Palestine	جيش الإسلام في فلسطين
82. The Islamic League in Denmark	الرابطة الإسلامية في الدنمارك
83. The Battalion of Right in Syria	كتيبة الحق في سوريا
84. The Battalion of Abdullah Azzam	كتائب عبد الله عزام
85. The Islamic League in Belgium	الرابطة الإسلامية في بلجيكا (رابطة مسلمي بلجيكا)

The above list, detailed as it is, is not up to date. After the government of the UAE published and disseminated it to the rest of the world, waves of refugees from Syria, Iraq, Libya, and Lebanon, among other troubled countries, migrated into the European nations. Many historians believe that, with the tens of thousands of refugees entering Turkey and Europe, the migrants have been infiltrated by an unknown number of members of terrorist organizations who have settled all over Europe. No one knows how many terrorist groups are mixing with the waves of fugitives and penetrating the European continent to form clandestine cells just waiting for orders from their leaders to attack.

Obviously terrorism has become a worldwide threat and no country is immune from attacks, regardless of its power. However, it helps to understand that these terrorist movements share two common characteristics. First, they adhere to the ideology established early in the twentieth century by Hassan al-Banna, Hassan al-Hudhaybi, Abu al-A'ala al-Maududi and other first-generation leaders of the Muslim Brotherhood movement. Second, they were inspired and emboldened by the success and viability of the Iranian Islamic theocracy founded in 1979 by Imam Ayatollah Khomeini,[328] although sectarian strife has not

328 Shakir al-Nabulsi, Bin Laden wa al-aql al-Arabi: kaif fakkar al-Arab ba'd 11 September 2001

put the Sunni and Shi'a groups in direct conflict.

Due to the large number of known and unknown terrorist organizations, which would require numerous volumes to scrutinize adequately, only a few who have acquired wide notoriety will be discussed in detail, as examples of the rest.

One of the earliest fanatic Islamic movements that typifies the above-mentioned groups is the al-Qaeda movement, under the leadership of Osama Bin Laden, Ayman al-Zarqawi, Abdullah Azzam and their compatriots. Most of them are Egyptians and Saudis who were the product of the international intricacies of the tumultuous 1970s and 1980s. Al-Qaeda and its leadership gained international notoriety in 2001 when its members brazenly attacked targets within the most powerful country in the world—the United States of America.

September 11, 2001, or 9/11 as it became historically known, was an infamous benchmark of terrorist attacks that led to war and bloodshed. Nine men hijacked four commercial airliners. One of them fell into a field. Another crashed into the Pentagon, and the other two slammed into the twin towers of the World Trade Center in New York City. The death toll for that day was 3,200, including the passengers aboard the four aircraft.[329] The U.S. authorities and most of the world accused the al-Qaeda organization and its leader, the Saudi Arabian young billionaire, Osama Bin Laden, the terrorist fugitive living in Taliban-controlled Afghanistan.

Taliban is a Muslim fundamentalist movement that at that time was ruling Afghanistan. Historically, both Taliban and al-Qaeda were born as a reaction to the Soviet Union invasion of its adjacent Muslim country, Afghanistan, in 1979, which led to the involvement of the U.S. and the Muslim countries in a lengthy war against the Russian invaders. In fact, al-Qaeda and the Taliban are almost identical organizations, as both developed out of the Afghan jihadist fighters.

(Bin Laden and the Arab Mind: How the Arab Thought After 9/11) (Kolen, Germany, 2007), pp. 259-262.

329 Doug Wead: The Iran Crisis (USA, Haven Books, 1980), pp. 137-139.

A History

In December 1979, the Soviet army crossed the border of its Muslim neighbor and stormed the palace of Afghanistan president Hafizullah Amin, killed him, and occupied the capital, Kabul.[330]

The Soviet invasion was the culmination of decades of competition with Great Britain to control Afghanistan due to its strategic and vital commercial location. It had been occupied by the British Empire since 1879. Afghanistan fought and gained its independence from British colonialism in 1919, but Great Britain kept some of its military forces and its influence on the country's policies. Prince Amanullah Khan (1919–1929) rebelled and forced Britain to end its presence in his country. In 1926, Afghanistan was proclaimed a kingdom with Amanullah enthroned as its king.[331]

Amanullah, who made several trips to Europe, was deeply impressed by Europe's social progress and intended to westernize his undeveloped country. His reform plans precipitated severe conflict among the tribal chiefs, who accused him of impiety and desertion from Islam. In 1929, Amanullah was forced to abdicate and flee the country, and Afghanistan fell into destructive upheaval until 1933, when Mohammed Zahir Shah inherited the throne. He also attempted to pursue modernization programs. He succeeded in obtaining the League of Nations membership for Afghanistan, but he was unsuccessful in initiating democracy or achieving substantial reform in his country. Finally, Zahir's long reign came to an end when, while he was visiting Italy in 1973, his cousin and prime minister, Prince Mohammad Daoud Khan, carried out a coup d'état, overthrew the government, abolished the monarchy, and proclaimed Afghanistan a republic with himself as its president.[332] He was able to crush the recalcitrant leadership of the Islamic movements. Then, in 1979, Communist forces led a military coup d'état, Mohammad Daoud Khan and his family were killed, and Hafizullah Amin was appointed as president. President Amin and the Soviet leadership wanted to impose Communism on

330 Nabulsi, op. cit., pp. 24, 25.

331 Ibid.

332 Ibid.

the extremely traditional Islamic society of Afghanistan, which incited a nationwide religious reaction. Too weak to confront the Islamic movements, Hafizullah Amin was removed by the Soviet Union and replaced by a strong man, Soviet puppet Babrak Karmal, a leader of the Khalq People's Democratic Party of Afghanistan.[333]

Supported by an enormous number of Soviet troops, air and armorial forces, Karmal and his party attempted to appeal to the Afghan populace by adopting some reform measures like modernizing educational curricula, allowing women's schooling, and economic reform, among others. But the "atheist" Soviets and their puppet regime met a stiff jihadist resistance by the pious local tribes, the Islamic world and the U.S., which was leading the Cold War against Communism.[334]

A historically significant question arises here. Why would the Soviet Union, the second-greatest power in the world, invade a destitute, barren country whose vast majority of the population are illiterate? Because the Soviets believed they would achieve the following advantages:

1. The invasion put the Soviet air force within a short distance of the Hormuz Straits and the extremely oil-rich countries.[335]
2. They wanted to use Afghanistan as a base to confront the influence of Islamic activities in the adjacent countries as well as within the Soviet Union. The Communist rulers were leery about their 28 million devout Muslim minority, which constituted 20 percent of the entire population who were impervious to the Communist ideology. They remained faithful to their religion, performing prayers and other Islamic duties, including even the younger generations who were born, raised and inculcated in Marxism. When the Iranian Ayatollah Mohammad Shariatmadari called for the Muslims throughout the world to support the Afghan mujahideen against the Soviet invaders, the enthusiastic response by the Muslims of Soviet Central Asia

333 John Laffin, The Dagger of Islam (USA: Bantam Books, 1981), p. 158.
334 Nabulsi, op. cit., p. 26.
335 Wead, op. cit., p. 140

awed the Communist authorities.[336]

3. The Soviets wanted to explore the possibility of the existence of natural gas and other sources of wealth within the Afghan land.
4. They desired the historically important commercial location of Afghanistan like the old Silk Road, which connects the Eastern world with the West.[337]

The Soviet military command miscalculated the strength of the resistance of the mujahideen, who were well-informed about the details of the extremely rough Afghan terrain, in contrast to the Soviet soldiers' unfamiliarity with the topographic nature of Afghanistan. Plus, they underestimated the unexpected powerful negative reaction of the Islamic world to the invasion of a Muslim country by the godless Communist USSR. The religious reaction included Muslims from Africa through the Middle East to Pakistan, the Orthodox Muslim country adjacent to both the Soviet Union and Afghanistan, and played a strong role in helping the mujahideen.

In addition to the Islamic world, the United States was deeply concerned with the occupation of Afghanistan, which consolidated the Soviets' foothold in the Middle East.[338]

When the Soviet Union invaded Afghanistan, Pakistan was ruled by President Mohammad Zia-ul-Haq, a devout Muslim. President Zia-ul-Haq felt threatened by the Soviet occupation of Afghanistan and hastened to undertake serious steps to protect his country from what he thought was an approaching Communist menace. He summoned his strong military aide, General Akhtar Abdur Rahman, chairman of the Joint Staff Committee and director general of Inter-Service Intelligence (ISI), to assess the situation facing Pakistan.[339]

Akhtar presented his report to President Zia-ul-Haq, emphatically recommending that Pakistan should support the Afghan jihadist resistance. He explained that aiding the Afghan resistance not

336 Nabulsi, op. cit., p. 26.

337 Mohammad Yousaf, Afghanistan The Bear Trap: The Defeat of a Superpower (Havertown, PA, Casemate), p. 25.

338 Yossef Bodansky, Bin Laden: The Man Who Declared War on America (New York: Forum, 1999), pp. 15-17.

339 Yousef, op. cit., p. 12.

only defended Islam but also Pakistan. He advised that the Afghans' resistance should become the front battlefield of Pakistan's defense lines against the Soviets, because if the Soviets succeeded in occupying Afghanistan, the next step would certainly be to invade Pakistan. Hence, Akhtar's plan was not limited to resisting the Soviet attacks, but to prepare for large-scale guerilla warfare to defeat the Soviet Union.[340] He believed that with the help of the Islamic world, the Afghanistan resistance movement could create a quagmire for the Soviet Union, similar to the quandary and ultimate defeat of America in Vietnam. He urged President Zia to support the Afghan guerillas with arms, ammunition, money, intelligence, training, and operational advice, and to provide sanctuary for the wounded and refugees.

President Zia agreed to Akhtar's military suggestions because they concurred with his grand plans for the future of the Islamic world. He aspired to integrate the Muslim countries into one powerful united entity. He was hoping to surmount the weakness of the Muslims by creating an Islamic power block stretching from Iran through Afghanistan to Pakistan, reaching all the way to the Uzbekistan, Turkman and Tajik provinces of the USSR itself.[341]

With the Soviets' occupation of Afghanistan and the reaction of the Muslim world and the United States, the situation in the region evolved into a serious international crisis. The tension exacerbated the ongoing Cold War between the two superpowers. The Middle East was strategically and economically too vital for the United States to lose to its archenemy, the USSR. However, President Zia's plans to unite the Islamic world, far-fetched as they were, equally worried the United States, as an integrated Islamic entity would jeopardize Israel and the American interests. Thus, Washington was confronted with a dilemma regarding its goals in the Middle East: deal with either a powerful and expanding Communist presence or a huge integrated and unpredictable Islamic bloc. The State Department anticipated that a potentially powerful fundamentalist Islamic state would be more harmful than a Communist takeover.[342]

340 Ibid.
341 Ibid, p. 12.
342 Ibid, pp. 8, 9.

On August 17, 1988, a Pakistani air force C-130 transport aircraft crashed. The dead on board were President Zia-ul-Haq, and the man who might have succeeded him had he survived, the loyal General Akhtar Abdul Rahman Khan. Gone were the two most powerful men in Pakistan, as well as the two staunchest supporters of the Afghan mujahideen. Although President Zia-ul-Haq had numerous enemies and had survived several assassination attempts, many believe that it was the American CIA that contrived the plane crash to get rid of President Zia-ul-Haq and his grand Islamic state plans.[343]

Meanwhile, the war in Afghanistan continued and became a typical conflict of a secular atheist ideology against a fundamental religious belief.[344]

The formidable modern Soviet army was fighting backward fighters whose steadfastness was derived from sheer courage and fervent religious belief. The Afghan mujahideen were fighting a holy war against godless infidels or "Kuffar," as they were called. As devout Muslims, they closely followed the instructions of their holy book, the Quran. Once a jihad was declared by the ulema, it became the duty of all men to carry weapons to protect their faith, to defend their honor, to safeguard their independence and to shelter their land and families. Boys in their early teens and old men in their seventies honored the call to join the jihad. That is what made the mujahideen a formidable force.[345] Volunteers from Arab and Muslim countries kept pouring into Pakistan and Afghanistan to join the mujahideen against the Soviet invaders. One of the first volunteers from Saudi Arabia was Osama Bin Laden, the creator of the fanatical al-Qaeda organization.

THE BIRTH OF AL-QAEDA

In 1980, about one year after the Soviet invasion, Osama Bin Laden arrived in Afghanistan. At twenty-seven, Bin Laden, a devout Sunni Muslim, was willing to sacrifice his youthful and lavish lifestyle for the cause of Islamic solidarity and to lead the resistance crusade

343 Yousef, op. cit., pp. 8, 9.
344 Nabulsi, op. cit., p. 29.
345 Yousaf, op. cit., p. 33.

against the atheist Soviet invaders of an Islamic country.

Shortly after arriving in Afghanistan, Bin Laden met Sheikh Dr. Abd Allah Yusuf Azzam, a fanatic who had a major role in founding the international Legion of Islam, the highly devout international Islamic jihadists.[346] Dr. Azzam, a member of the Muslim Brotherhood branch of Jordan, was born in 1941 in Palestine. While still a child, his family sent him to Cairo to get religious education, where he remained to pursue his studies to receive both M.A. and Ph.D. degrees in principles of Islamic jurisprudence from the prestigious Al-Azhar University in Cairo.[347] He taught Islamic jurisprudence in several Arab countries, but in the 1970s, after the Afghan declaration of jihad against the godless Communists, he left teaching and went to Afghanistan to become one of the first Arabs to join the Afghan jihad. But he was asked by the fighters' leaders to pursue his teaching career. Azzam formulated and taught the doctrine of the centrality of the jihad to achieve liberation of the Muslim world from the strangling Western colonialism. He instructed his students: "Jihad and the rifle is your only effective method."[348]

Older and the more educated of the two, Azzam deeply influenced Bin Laden and became like his spiritual father. Furthermore, he became the founder of the ideological belief of several fanatic Islamic movements. Azzam and Bin Laden exploited the Soviet-Afghan war to attain a turning point by globally spreading jihad to an extent never known before. The holy warriors kept drawing volunteers from different parts of the world and support from Muslim and non-Muslim countries and sources. The new jihad call spread worldwide and became the common rallying cry for holy war against Islam's enemies in Europe and Central Asia, among others.[349]

In 1989, Azzam and some members of his family were mysteriously assassinated by an unknown person. After Azzam's death, Osama Bin Laden assumed sole leadership of the fanatic Islamic politics, supported by an Egyptian medical doctor, Ayman al-Dhawahiri (also known

346 Bodansky, op. cit., p. 11.
347 Ibid, p. 19.
348 Ibid.
349 Nabulsi, op. cit., p. 135.

as "al-Zawahiri").

Al-Dhawahiri had been born into a wealthy, prestigious Egyptian family. He studied and was deeply influenced by Sayyed Qutb's thought, especially the concept of "God's rule of the government." Al-Dhawahiri became involved in politics after President Anwar Sadat signed the Peace Treaty with Israel. In the 1980s, al-Dhawahiri visited Afghanistan as a doctor and a sergeant to treat the wounded Afghan fighters. There he met Osama Bin Laden, and the relationship between the two leaders grew closer as they agreed to expand and intensify the jihad against the enemies of Islam. He became one of the leaders of the Order of al-Jihad al-Islami, a fanatic religious movement that operates under the umbrella of the Muslim Brotherhood. Al-Jihad al-Islami was accused of several international terrorist activities, including in 1995 an attempt to assassinate Egyptian President Hosni Mubarak and the slaughter of fifty-eight tourists in Luxor in 1997—a crime for which al-Dhawahiri was sentenced to death in absentia.[350]

Throughout the 1980s, increasing numbers of Arab mujahideen kept arriving to Pakistan to volunteer to join the holy war. Bin Laden established a guest house in Pakistan to accommodate the volunteers on their way to the battlefront in Afghanistan, and he decided to set up his own camp to galvanize the Arab mujahideen forces who became known as the Arab Afghans.[351] Eventually Bin Laden established a military organization in Afghanistan which he named al-Qaeda, which means "the base." Thus, al-Qaeda, one of the most notorious Islamic terrorist movements, was born, with an initial membership of three thousand men.

Along with the Arab world, Washington was very supportive of the Afghan jihadists. The United States was convinced that it was supporting a truly national liberation movement, despite the fanatic Islamic ideology. America kept supplying large amounts of funds to sustain the holy war and confront the Communist regime and the Soviet presence in Afghanistan. Both the United States and Saudi Arabia cooperated to save Afghanistan from the Communist occupation. For every dollar

350 John L. Esposito, Unholy War: Terror in the Name of Islam (Oxford University Press, 2002), p. 91.

351 Nabulsi, op. cit., p. 147.

supplied by the U.S., another dollar was added by the Saudi Arabian government. The combined funds, amounting to hundreds of millions of dollars a year, were deposited in a special account in Pakistan under the control of the Inter-Service Intelligence (ISI), and it was crucial to the efforts of war against the Soviets.[352] Substantial amounts of these funds were earmarked for training camps as thousands of volunteers from the Arab and Muslim world kept coming to join the Afghan mujahideen. In the mid-1980s, approximately sixteen thousand to twenty thousand Arab mujahideen had already trained with Afghan fighters. The Pakistani ISI kept training an average of one hundred Arab mujahideen every month.[353] All of these factors contributed to the establishment and support of al-Qaeda.

While Al-Qaeda was founded in 1988 by Osama Bin Laden, Ayman al-Dhawahiri, Abdulla Azzam and several other Arab warriors to defend the Islamic religious against the Soviet (Kuffar) non-believers' invasion of Afghanistan,[354] it was Osama Bin Laden, with his bold, charismatic personality, generous financial donations and ardent religious devotion who assumed the leadership of this terrifying organization.

Bin Laden gained his respectable status among his comrades because he believed his sole duty was to be on the jihad battlefield, where he gained a reputation as a valorous and resourceful commander. He personally participated in several hand-to-hand battles commanding Afghan and Arab-Afghan fighters against larger forces of the ruling Communist regime and the Communist army. He fought fearlessly, seeking to attain martyrdom.[355]

Osama Bin Laden, a Background

Osama Bin Laden was born in 1957 in Riyadh, Saudi Arabia. He was the thirteenth son of Mohammed Awad Bin Laden, who had fifty-five children from several wives. Mohammed Awad was an immigrant from Hadramout, who became a multibillionaire. Taking advantage of

352 Yousaf, op. cit., pp. 81, 82.
353 Bodansky, op. cit., p. 18.
354 Nabulsi, op. cit., p. 147.
355 Bodansky, op. cit., p. 19.

certain propitious circumstances, Mohammed Awad was able to befriend the Saudi royal regime. Both King Abdul Aziz and King Faisal Al-Saud granted Mohammad Awad large properties and lucrative contracts, which augmented his already enormous wealth. Amid these fortuitous circumstances, Bin Laden was born, raised and educated. He was the only child of his mother.[356]

After graduating from secondary school in 1979, Osama entered King Abdul Aziz University in Jeddah, Saudi Arabia, to study public administration, the same year that the Soviet Union invaded Afghanistan. At the time, King Abdul Aziz University was a hub of vibrant Islamic intellectual activities, where the best and most knowledgeable educators were providing lessons and guidance for the youths. The message to the young seekers of knowledge was quite simple and clear: Only an absolute and unconditional return to the fold of conservative Islamism could protect the Muslim world from the inherent dangers and exploitations of the West.[357]

King Abdul Aziz University contained a large number of Saudi, Egyptian, Palestinian and other Arabs who were members of the Muslim Brotherhood and other fundamental Islamic movements. Osama was immersed in these activities, influenced by the thoughts of the Muslim Brotherhood, and became a strong believer in Sayyid Qutb's concept of "the rule is by God only." Sayyid Qutb's thoughts were taught by his brother, Professor Mohammad Qutb, who was a mentor of Osama Bin Laden at King Abdul Aziz University.[358]

Osama's belief in Sayyid Qutb's ideas was what motivated him to form comradeship with Ayman al-Dhawahiri, the leader of the jihadist group. And they both became among the earliest Islamic Arabs to rush to Afghanistan to join the Afghan jihadist resisting the Soviet occupation.[359]

Pursuing his deep studies, Osama Bin Laden was influenced by several other fundamentalist thinkers besides Sayyid Qutb, one of whom was Ibn Taymiyyah (1263–1328), the medieval Islamic theologian

356 Nabulsi, op. cit., pp. 129, 130.
357 Ibid, p. 130.
358 Ibid.
359 Esposito, op. cit., p. 10.

who is considered the first inspirer of the Islamic Salafi movement.

Ibn Taymiyyah came from an old family of ulema who belonged to the Hanbali School of Thought, the Islamic faction that believes in the strict values of al-Shari'ah and al-Sunnah, al-Nabawiyyah, the Islamic law and the traditions of Prophet Mohammad.[360] He was a jurist, an historian, and a prolific author of numerous books, all emphasizing strict adherence to the literal principles of Islam and attacking any *buda'a* (innovation or new ideas).

After the defeat of the Abbasid Empire by the Mongols, Ibn Taymiyyah accentuated the role of jihad as a main principle of Islam. He asserted that the only reason why the Muslims were deteriorating was because they had forsaken jihad.

Ibn Taymiyyah is considered the mentor of Mohammad Abdul Wahhab, the initiator of the draconian Wahhabi sect, which is the foundation of the government systems of Saudi Arabia and some other countries of the Arabian Peninsula.[361] Osama Bin Laden was born, raised and educated amid the Wahhabi ethos. Abu al-A'ala al-Mawdudi, the fanatic Muslim Brotherhood ideologue, also influenced the thought and decisions of Osama Bin Laden.

When the Soviet Union occupied Afghanistan to bolster the Communist regime there, and Osama Bin Laden decided to establish al-Qaeda in 1988, he was able to recruit three thousand men distributed in training camps located in eastern parts of Afghanistan and adjacent to the Pakistani border. The endeavor was fully funded and blessed by the Saudi government. Before the end of the 1980s, the number of members was increased to eleven thousand well-trained Egyptians recruited by Ayman al-Dhawahiri, Saudis and volunteers from other Islamic countries.[362]

Bin Laden kept the structure of al-Qaeda rather simplified to keep it from being discovered and infiltrated by undesirable elements. Even the American FBI was not able to collect enough data about its shadowy system. Al-Qaeda does not consist of only terrorists and fighters. There are diversified functions based on division of labor. Its

360 Armstrong, op. cit. p. 104.
361 Ibid, p. 135.
362 *The Guardian*, London, September 22, 2001.

membership includes physicians, nurses, electronic and computer experts, and engineers specialized in building roads and bridges to facilitate transportation of its fighters and materials. The organization also contains laborers, drivers, chefs and guards to meet all the requirements of training and fighting.[363]

Al-Qaeda's management institutions are the following: majlis shura (the traditional Islamic consultation assembly), committees of military operations, financial committees and intelligence agents. The leaders communicate with the loosely scattered rank and file by means of modern technological devices, which makes attempts to detect them extremely difficult, even for the most powerful and sophisticated intelligence agencies in the world.[364]

Following are the main objectives Bin Laden sought from creating al-Qaeda.

1. Establish archives to record the names of the Arab mujahideen, their dates of arrival and entry into the Afghan mujahideen. He also aimed to register the names of the martyrs, with dates and details of their martyrdom, in order to establish accurate records for all operations. By keeping these records, Bin Laden gained experience to avoid future blunders. Also, he was able to shrewdly conceal the details of the blueprint of al-Qaeda and enhance the combative efficiency of his terrorist groups scattered from Sudan through the Arab world to Afghanistan and other places.
2. Assure the continuation of jihad against atheism, the West and Zionism all over the world, even after ending the Soviet occupation of Afghanistan.
3. Combat all socialist systems in the Arab world with special emphasis on the socialist government.
4. Overthrow all existing Arab regimes and replace them with an Islamic caliphate.
5. Consider al-Qaeda the first nucleus for the founding of the

363 Bodansky, op. cit., p. 46.
364 Nabulsi, op. cit., pp. 150, 151.

Islamic state with its own position of *amir* (prince) as the head of its government.

Al-Qaeda's three thousand volunteers were situated in several training camps located along the border with Pakistan. Bin Laden was aided by assistants like Ayman al Dhawahiri, Mohammad Atif (Abu Hafa al Miari), a number of wahhabi Saudis and the majlis shura. Subsequently the membership grew from sixteen thousand to twenty thousand mujahideen from Yemen, Egypt and other Arab Islamic countries, primarily from Saudi Arabia.[365] Due to Bin Laden's overwhelming leadership and the large number of Saudis, al-Qaeda became like a branch of the fanatic Wahhabi movement in Afghanistan.

Contrary to Moscow's expectations, the war dragged on for years and it was extremely costly in lives and finance. The combination of valor and their staunch belief in the holy objectives for which they were fighting made the mujahideen too formidable to defeat.[366] They were fully convinced that God the Almighty was on their side and would stand beside them, provide them with all that they need, and help them to defeat their enemies. Their battle cry was "Allah u Akbar," or "God is the greatest." They shouted this traditional Islamic idiom as they rushed to kill their enemies or die. The mujahedeen's willingness to sacrifice their lives stems from their Quranic belief that God promised the *shaheed* (martyr) full forgiveness of all sins, and any mujahid who dies in a battle for the sake of God is assured a place in paradise.[367]

The morale of the Afghan mujahideen was bolstered by the waves of volunteers arriving from their Arab-Muslim brotherhood and the flow of shipments of weapons from different parts of the world, paid for by Saudi Arabia and the United States. Also, American technical and intelligence aids enhanced the accuracy of the mujahideen to target the confused Russian soldiers who were lost in the maze of Afghanistan's rough lands. Furthermore, the American CIA paid for thousands of copies of the Holy Quran to be translated into Soviet Usbek language and for production of several books describing Soviet atrocities

365 Ibid, pp. 146, 147.
366 Yousaf, op. cit., p. 33.
367 Ibid.

against Muslims. The books were smuggled inside the Soviet Union by Afghans who crossed the Amu River to distribute them among the Muslim population there.[368]

The mujahideen began crossing the borders to collect intelligence, and the number of people who wanted to cooperate was impressive. Some wanted weapons, some wanted to join the Afghan resistance fighters, while others wanted to participate in operations inside the Soviet Union.

In 1985, the mujahideen, after being trained and equipped by the CIA, began to wage continuous military operations inside the Soviet Union using rockets to hit vital targets and to ambush soldiers. As the attacks intensified, Moscow began to show obvious concern. The newspaper *Izvestia*, which usually avoided discussing the Afghan war, ran an article denouncing the border attacks.

The American consulate in Peshawar, Pakistan, closely watching the Kremlin's reaction, detected information stating that the mujahideen have the military capabilities to carry out larger attacks.[369]

In addition to the setbacks and the unexpected stiff resistance they were meeting in the battlefield, the Soviet military began to hear unnerving news of serious domestic unrest inside their country caused by the beginning of Mikhail Gorbachev's *glasnost* and *perestroika* (openness and restructuring) reform plans.[370]

By the mid-1980s, the hope for a quick victory by the Russian army faded away and the soldiers were frustrated and demoralized.

The CIA began to receive authentic information that Moscow was deeply worried about how the war was going. News began to arrive to the United States that the Soviet Union was experiencing serious losses in Afghanistan. In a more significant instance, a Soviet Politburo member confided to the U.S. ambassador in Moscow, Arthur Hartman, that the war in Afghanistan was indeed more costly than anyone would

368 Peter Schweizer, Reagan's War (New York: Anchor Books, 2003), p. 235.

369 Ibid.

370 Zaki, Mamoon Amin," perestroika: al-tanaqudh bayn al nadhariyah wa altatbeeq fi al-fikr al-shiu'i,

(Perestroika: The Contradiction Between Theory and Practice in the Communist Thought) (Afaq Araliyah, No. 2, February 1990, pp. 14-25.

have imagined.[371]

Finally, in January 1989, the Soviet Union began to withdraw in the traditional manner of a vanquished army. By the middle of the month, the bulk of the Russian army was gone, and by February, the withdrawal was completed.[372]

The pious mujahideen and al-Qaeda fighters claimed credit for playing a major role in defeating an atheist superpower by depending on their religious creed and the help of God.

Osama Bin Laden returned home to Saudi Arabia a hero. He was a wiser man toughened by experience. His political and religious views were more radicalized. A large number of Arab-Afghans and indigenous Afghans whom he guided considered him their spiritual leader. He was well received and respected by the Saudi government as a role model for the Muslim youth because of his heroic role in the Afghan war.

After the remarkable triumph in Afghanistan against the infidel superpowers, Bin Laden became more confident that nothing and no one could stop the Muslim nation from achieving its goals, once it was committed to the righteous practice of Islam.[373]

For a short while, Bin Laden seemed to turn his attention on his business and family. Riyadh's pleasure with Osama's religious activities was manifested by the enormous profit he gained from large government and private projects. He resumed his lucrative job with the Bin Laden Company of construction business, but he kept adhering to Wahhabi fundamentalist Islamic principles of austerity by moving his own family to a modest apartment, and kept practicing and advocating piety.[374]

The Gulf

In August 1990, Iraq shook the Arab and Muslim world when it invaded its tiny Arab neighbor, Kuwait. The invasion took place after a

371 Schweizer, op. cit., p. 204.
372 Yousaf, op. cit., p. 213.
373 Bodansky, op. cit., p. 28.
374 Ibid.

sharp disagreement between the Iraqi ruling Ba'ath party and the rulers of Kuwait, the al-Sabah family.

Lengthy negotiations between the two governments reached an impasse when the Iraqi government accused Kuwait of stealing crude oil from Iraq's oil fields adjacent to the borders of the two countries. Kuwait's persistent demands that Iraq remit the $12 to $14 billion loans that Kuwait lent Iraq during the eight years of the Iran-Iraq war only exacerbated the tension.[375]

In reality, President Saddam Hussein used the dispute as an excuse to invade Kuwait and achieve an old goal sought by all previous Iraqi leaders since the rule of King Ghazi in the 1930s. They all wanted to annex Kuwait to elongate the small shorelines in the Gulf. This claim is based on the historical fact that Kuwait was an administrative unit of Mesopotamia's port of Basra when Iraq was a part of the Ottoman Empire.[376]

Iraq had a more friendly relationship with Saudi Arabia, as the two countries in 1989 had signed a non-aggression pact which stipulated the principle of non-interference in the internal affairs of the two sisterly countries and non-use of force and armies between the two states.[377]

Yet, following the Iraqi invasion of Kuwait, the United States warned Saudi of Iraq's aggressive intention on the Saudi kingdom, even though Saddam Hussein kept attempting to reassure the Saudi king by referring to the 1989 non-aggression pact. The Saudi kingdom felt utterly defenseless and vulnerable to an invasion by Iraq's formidable army.[378] The flow of Kuwaiti refugees into Saudi Arabia, led by the amir who was pursued by the Iraqi forces, exacerbated the panic in Riyadh.

Upon learning about the invasion, Osama Bin Laden began contacting the Saudi highest authorities, offering them detailed plans for self-defense of the kingdom without the need for any foreign aid. He stressed his capability to mobilize equipment and a strong core of

375 Dilip Hiro, Iraq: In the Eye of the Storm (New York: Thunder's Mouth Press/Nation Books, 2001), p. 33.

376 Zaki, izdihar al-Iraq that al-hukm al-malaki, op. cit. p. 148.

377 Hiro, op. cit., p. 130.

378 Bodansky, op. cit., p. 29.

combat-hardened Arab-Afghan fighters whom he was willing to recruit.

He passionately reiterated in Riyadh that if the Muslim nations could evict the great Soviet Union from Afghanistan by declaring jihad, it certainly could defeat the Iraqi invading army. He assumed that the Muslim Iraqi soldiers would mutiny and join the jihadist forces.[379]

Bin Laden also warned Riyadh against bringing Western "infidel" forces into the holy land of Saudi Arabia because such invitation would disagree with the principles of Islam and would provoke the Muslim world. Bin Laden was deeply concerned about the legitimacy of the Saudi royal family as the custodian of the holy city of Mecca and the sacred shrine of Al-Ka'abah and who should defend them.[380]

Here again the Iraqi occupation of Kuwait acquired the nature of conflict between religious and secular ideologies, and it touched the core of political Islam. The invasion of Kuwait and the removal of its royal al-Sabah family was perceived by the Islamic world as a prelude to a flagrant attempt by Saddam Hussein to impose his Ba'athist Party secular, nationalist pan-Arabism ideology over the theocratic regime of Saudi Arabia and other Gulf countries. For the Saudi ruling family, defeating Saddam in the long run would not only stop the menace of secular Iraq, but would also secure the future of Islam and Saudi Arabia's own theocratic legitimacy.[381]

For America and the Western world, the purpose of waging the Gulf War was to defend the pro-West Saudi theocracy and to curtail Saddam Hussein's anti-West despotic regime from controlling the enormous oil reservoirs, restore the ruling al-Sabah family, and keep the oil-rich Kuwait under the protection of the West.

Regardless of the circumstances surrounding the Gulf War and Iraq's possible intentions, Bin Laden remained adamantly against the interference of the Western world, and he kept demanding that the Saudi rulers depend on the Islamic forces to defend the kingdom. But his warnings and objections were ignored as King Fahd and his coteries were terrified by the sight of the awesome Iraqi forces invading Kuwait and felt utterly vulnerable. Riyadh opened its gates for the entrance

379 Ibid.
380 Ibid.
381 Ibid.

of the U.S.-led coalition, including several Arab armies that in 1991 defeated Iraq in what is historically known as the Gulf War.[382]

The United States forces' presence in Saudi Arabia agitated not only Osama Bin Laden, but all senior ulema who were also categorically against the American presence in the Muslim holy lands. Yet the Saudi high command asserted that they were unable to defend the kingdom against the Iraqi onslaught alone. After the U.S. defense secretary, Dick Cheney, promised that the American troops would leave as soon as they were no longer needed, the Saudi king, at a meeting of 350 ulema at Mecca, overcame the opposition and agreed to the temporary stay of the U.S. troops until the crisis was resolved.[383]

News of disagreements between the Saudi royal family and the ulema quickly spread among the Islamic circles of Saudi Arabia and the rest of the Islamic world. Discontent was exacerbated by the American male and female troops pursuing their own cultural "sacrilegious" behavior of drinking alcohol and sexual promiscuity in the Muslims' holy land.

When the Gulf War ended and the Iraqi forces were forced out of Kuwait, Saudi Arabia still allowed the foreign forces on Saudi soil. Hence started Osama Bin Laden's al-Qaeda animosity against its allies and staunch military and financial supporters—the United States and the Saudi government.[384] With the increased hostility and the mounting pressure by the Saudi authorities, Bin Laden, fearing for his and his extended family's well-being, took them all and went into exile in the new haven of Islamic fundamentalism, Hassan al-Turabi's Sudan.[385] There he started lucrative business projects to finance his movement. Later he moved to Afghanistan and Pakistan to start jihadist activities against his enemies.

On the night of June 25, 1996, two men drove a tanker truck into the Saudi compound that encompassed the American headquarters in the Al-Khobar military facility near Dhahran. The men left the truck, which later blew up in a tremendous explosion that caused extensive

382 Hiro, op. cit., p. 139.
383 Bodansky, op. cit., p. 30.
384 Esposito, op. cit., p. 12.
385 Nabulsi, op. cit., pp. 73, 74.

damage, including the collapse of many nearby buildings, killing dozens, including nineteen American servicemen, and wounding hundreds, many of whom suffered serious injuries.[386]

The Dhahran explosion indicated that the construction and explosion of the five thousand pounds of military-class high explosives was carried out by a highly trained group of experts. Hezbollah International claimed responsibility, with Bin Laden's help.

In the beginning of 1996, Osama Bin Laden and Ayman al-Zawahiri became involved in important diversified political and strategic activities. In Iran, the wise and experienced leadership were aware of and appreciated the lessons of the above-mentioned activities and operations. They established Hezbollah International, the foundation of the future aspects of jihadist activities, which began to carry out jihadist activities in several Arab countries.[387]

The campaign of Islamic terrorism continued gaining momentum, and its membership kept growing. Several attacks and assassinations that took place in different parts of the world were claimed by al-Qaeda, and this encouraged a large number of new jihadists to sacrifice their young lives, believing that they were serving the will of God, who would reward them by sending them to paradise. [388]

The highlight of al-Qaeda's operation was the notorious 9/11/2001 terrorist attacks against several American targets, leaving several thousand dead and injured. It became historically known as the 9/11 event. It was the most damaging attack against America since the 1941 Japanese air attack against Pearl Harbor, which propelled the United States into World War II and declaring war against the Axis countries. [389]

In May 2011, Osama Bin Laden was assassinated in one of his hideouts in Pakistan, by a special American squad. But al-Qaeda is still active, conducting terrorist attacks in several parts of the world under new leadership.

From al-Qaeda evolved a more violent and merciless terrorist

---

386 Bodansky, op. cit., p. 153.
387 Ibid.
388 See detailed report of *al-Khaleej*, No. 12906, September 19, 2014.
389 Nabulsi, op. cit., p. 274.

movement called the Islamic State in Iraq and Syria (ISIS; in Arabic, DAESH), which, since it was instituted in 2014, has spread horror in different parts of the world. Shortly after its inception, it took control of large territories in Iraq and Syria, declaring itself the State of the Islamic Caliphate. ISIS will be detailed in a later chapter after chronologically briefly discussing other jihadist movements that preceded it, such as the Taliban and Hezbollah International organizations, and the Islamic Justice and Development Party under the leadership of the pious Recep Tayyip Erdogan, the president of the Republic of Turkey.

THE TALIBAN MOVEMENT

In 1996, Afghanistan witnessed the rise of a militia that would later control around 65 percent of the country and rename it the Islamic Republic of Afghanistan. After eighteen years of Soviet occupation, followed by a destructive civil war, this new Islamic radical movement was able to spread its authority and, under its control, bring the chaotic situation to an end.[390]

Taliban is a fundamentalist Islamic political movement active in Afghanistan, waging jihad (holy war) against the enemies of Islam. The name is derived from "talib," the Arabic name for student. The predominantly Pashtun[391] Taliban is a movement led by students of *madrasa* (seminaries specialized in teaching Islamic theology), ulema and some middle class *salafi*, individuals who believe in traditional Islamic ideology.[392]

The main source from which Taliban drew its ideology was the Egyptian Muslim Brotherhood, especially Sayyid Qutub's and Abu al-A'ala al-Maududi's idea that the rule must be only by God. Also influential were al-Maududi's thoughts mentioned in his book, *Concepts of Religion and State*, in which he attacks the Western democratic systems as they are based on human legislations, while God is the only legitimate legislator.[393]

390 Cleveland, op. cit., p. 561.
391 Pashtun is a tribe that ruled Afghanistan for centuries.
392 Esposito, op. cit., p. 15.
393 Al-Nabulsi, op. cit., p. 57.

In 1989, the Soviet troops, which had invaded Afghanistan in 1979, withdrew after being defeated by the mujahideen—Islamic fighters aided by the U.S., Saudi Arabia, and a few other Islamic countries. The Soviets left behind a vulnerable communist government headed by Mohammad Najibullah. Afghanistan entered into a period of an unstable and weak national government that was unable to stop a civil war fought mainly along tribal, political and military lines between the mujahideen as a united front supported by the United States, against the communist government of Najibullah, supported by the Soviet Union.[394] Finally, the mujahideen defeated the government forces, invaded Kabul, hanged Najibullah, enforced stability and imposed their fundamental *salafi* Islamic ideology on the country.

In 1994, as part of enforcement of their laws, the Taliban government began its combat against *munkarat* or religiously abhorrent social aspects. Among the munkarat are the following:[395]

1. Spreading the beliefs of democracy, which the Taliban consider as corrupt and immoral
2. Sodomy
3. Forced marriage of girls
4. Looting commercial convoys
5. Combating armed gangs wreaking havoc all over the country
6. Tax impediments imposed on commercial convoys
7. Women going out of their homes without the traditional "hijab" coverings
8. Women's education and females' schools
9. Allowing women to work
10. Listening to music and songs
11. Possessing and playing with dogs
12. Watching television (as soon as Taliban took control of the government, they collected all televisions and hung them from trees all over Afghanistan)[396]

394 Ibid, p. 31.
395 Ibid, pp. 30, 31.
396 Cleveland, op. cit., pp. 562, 563.

These principles became tantamount to the Taliban manifesto or its ideology, which was announced on December 27, 1997. The announcement of this manifesto attracted a large number of mujahideen, who joined Taliban's ranks.

Upon taking control of the government, Taliban hastened to implement their principles. They removed weapons from the streets, stopped corruption and embezzlement and imposed strict Shari'ah Islamic law. Initially they succeeded in gaining popular support as a reform movement. However, eventually they were exposed to be ruling the country by tyrannical means by imposing a puritanical form of Islam with strong support from the Wahabi Saudi government and Pakistan. By 1998, Taliban was able to control 90 percent of Afghanistan and drove their adversaries into a small cave in northwestern Pakistan.[397]

Taliban claimed that its government has a collective political leadership that operates on a consultative and consensus basis rather than ruled by one individual. By adhering to the Shari'ah in Kandahar, the Taliban claimed that it was following the same policies of the thirty-year-long system of the *Rashideen* (rightly guided) caliphs who ruled the Islamic world after Prophet Mohammed's death in 632. However, Taliban's decision-making process evolved to become highly centralized, secretive and dictatorial.[398]

The Taliban's highest decision-making entity was the Supreme Shura, which was based in Kandahar. The Shura Council was dominated by Mullah Mohammad Omar, the commander of the mujahideen. The Taliban rallied around Mullah Omar and nominated him to be the *Amir al Mu'mineen,* prince or commander of the faithful. It is a title assumed by most Muslim caliphs after the death of Prophet Mohammad. By assuming this title, Mullah Omar became the undisputed leader of the Afghan mujahideen.

To bestow legitimacy on his position as a leader of a genuine Islamic system, Mullah Omar appeared on the roof of a building in the center of Kandahar, wrapped in the cloak of Prophet Mohammad, which had been dug out of its nearby shrine. Omar wrapped and unwrapped the

397 Esposito, op. cit., p. 16.

398 Ahmad Rashid, Taliban: Militant Islam, Oil and Fundamentalism in Central Asia (New Haven: Yale University Press, 2000), p. 95.

cloak around his body and dramatically held it high while the wind fluttered it. He was warmly applauded by the large throng of mullahs who gathered in the courtyard below, and they cheered him as Amir al-Mu'mineen. [399]

The procedures conducted by Mullah Omar gained him the trust and camaraderie of Osama Bin Laden. Under the protection of Mullah Omar in Afghanistan, Bin Laden felt safe enough to issue his declaration to intensify jihad against America and all enemies of Islam, vowing "the walls of oppression and humiliation cannot be demolished except in a rain of bullets."[400] By then the CIA had set up a special force to track the activities of Bin Laden and his connections with other Islamic militants, and to plan how to capture him.

After shrewdly eluding the CIA, Bin Laden found a safe place to hide in Kandahar. On February 23, 1998, he called for all groups supporting Taliban and al-Qaeda to hold a meeting sponsored by what he called the "International Islamic Front for Jihad Against Jews and Crusades." The meeting issued a manifesto stating that for more than seven years the United States had been occupying the land of Islam and the holiest places in the Arabian Peninsula, plundering its riches, dictating its rules, humiliating its people, terrorizing its neighbors and turning its bases in the peninsula into a spearhead through which to fight the neighboring Muslim people.[401]

The meeting also issued a fatwa: the killing of Americans and their allies—civilians and military—is an individual duty for every Muslim who can do it in any country in which it is possible to do. Osama Bin Laden was announcing himself as the liberator of the entire Muslim world.

After the defeat and withdrawal of the Soviet Union from Afghanistan, Osama Bin Laden was visited by an influential Sudanese Islamist politician, Hassan al-Turabi, who convinced him to move to Sudan. Between 1992 and 1996, Bin Laden invested substantial wealth in Sudan infrastructure, but he continued his jihad against the enemies of Islam. He was accused of conducting bombing and terrorist attacks

399 Ibid, p. 42.
400 Ibid, p. 133.
401 Sharif, op. cit., p. 134.

in several parts of the world, which angered the U.S. and other countries, who subsequently pressured the government of Sudan to banish him from the country. He was deported as a persona non grata,[402] but he was welcomed back to Taliban Afghanistan by Mullah Omar. During his time in Sudan, Bin Laden's investment of large amounts of wealth earned the Taliban movement substantial financial power.[403]

By the end of 1998, Bin Laden was fully entrenched in the Taliban Afghanistan. Mullah Omar provided a sanctuary and expressed his admiration for Bin Laden's enduring struggle and his jihadist activities.

To bolster his organic relations with the Pashtun powerful tribe of Afghanistan and Pakistan, Bin Laden married his oldest daughter to Mullah Omar, while he himself married a young Pashtun woman as his fourth wife. Because Bin Laden now had become related to Pashtun elite by blood, his defeat by outsiders, especially non-Muslims, had become unthinkable. The ferocious Pashtun tribe became obligated to defend him against his attackers as the tribal code required.[404]

The Taliban government granted Bin Laden Afghan citizenship, which enabled him to undertake military commandment and international duties, while Mullah Omar assumed control of the religious and spiritual activities of the movement. Bin Laden provided the Taliban with the following:[405]

1. Acted as communication links that connected Taliban with the rest of the world, especially with the similar-thinking fundamentalist Islamic movements
2. Exploited his strong connection with the Pakistani intelligence agency, which protected Bin Laden while he was previously living in Pakistan
3. Utilized his high military position to send experienced Arab-Afghan and Taliban fighters to fight on the side of the pro-Pakistan Muslim Kashmiri fighters against the atheist Indian Hindus. Pakistan provided Bin Laden with all the information

402 Al-Nabulsi, op. cit., pp. 144, 145.
403 Bodansky, op. cit., p. 40.
404 Ibid, p. 307.
405 Al-Nabulsi, op. cit., pp. 185-189.

he needed for his operations. Also, in return for his services, the Pakistani intelligentsia protected the Pakistan-Afghanistan borders against possible infiltration of Western agents who may have attempted to abduct or kill Bin Laden.

4. Utilized his profound military and administrative experience, which he gained from commanding al-Qaeda in the war against the Soviet Union, to guide the military and administrative requirements of the mujahideen of Taliban. He ordered his highly experienced Arab-Afghan warriors to train the fighters of the Taliban movement and he effectively formulated its political and internal administration policies.
5. Donated large amounts of funds to build hospitals, schools, elderly and child care centers, and other vital utilities necessary for Taliban's infrastructure.

Bin Laden's steadily growing charismatic leadership in Pakistan and Afghanistan, as well as his sacrifice, sincerity and dedication, attracted a large number of Arab and Muslim followers; among them, prominent believers such as Ayman al-Zawahiri, an Egyptian physician and a member of the Muslim Brotherhood, Rifai Taha Musa a prominent leader of al-Qaeda and a leader of the Egyptian banned Gama'a Islamiyah, and two sons of Shaykh Omar Abdul Rahman, the blind cleric who was accused of participating in the assassination of President Anwar Sadat. Most of these men were suspected of involvement in the bombing of the World Trade Center in 1993.[406]

Thus the leaderships of al-Qaeda and the Taliban merged to form a partnership to wage jihad against those whom they perceived as enemies of Islam. Bin Laden was extremely impressed by what he described as the ideal and correct implementation of genuine Islam. He maintained that the Taliban government system represents the resurrection of the "spirit of the original Islam." In comparison, he denounced all other Islamic governments, including Saudi Arabia, the host of the holiest Islamic shrine, and considered them as aberrant from the real Islam.[407]

406 Esposito, op. cit., pp. 18, 19.
407 Al-Nabulsi, op. cit., p. 185.

The Taliban political ideology was influenced by the Pakistani Jamiyyat-i-Ulama-i-Islam (JUI) religious party with rigid militant anti-American and anti-non-Muslim cultures and religions. The Taliban founded training camps to inculcate the JUI ideology to thousands of volunteers from different Muslim countries under the auspices of Osama Bin Laden. That was the main reason why, despite its control of most of Afghanistan, the United States and most countries of the world never acknowledged the legitimacy of the Taliban government.[408]

These trainees were prepared to carry out terrorist attacks against targets specified by al-Qaeda and Taliban. In early 1998, Bin Laden and Al-Zawahiri began to plan to attack vulnerable American targets in nearby Africa. On August 7, 1998, two bombs exploded almost simultaneously, close to the embassies in Nairobi, Kenya, and Dar al-Salam, Tanzania, 450 miles apart. The bombing left more than 250 people dead and more than 5,500 injured. The two operations were carried out by a network of well-coordinated forces of Islamic jihadists, and it was masterminded by Osama Bin Laden and Ayman al-Zawahiri. Bin Laden and al-Zawahiri commanded the elite forces of jihadists whom they prepared in the Taliban-Afghan training camps, as well as al-Qaeda combatants who fought against the Soviet Union.[409]

Recounting the 1996 bombing in Saudi Arabia and claiming responsibility for the two bombings in East Africa, a call from the Islamic Army for the Liberation of Holy Places (a "military wing" of Bin Laden and al-Zawahiri's International Front), promised to escalate its campaign of anti-U.S. terrorism until the following demands were met:[410]

1. The withdrawal of U.S. and Western forces from Muslim countries in general and from the Arabian Peninsula in particular, including civilians
2. The lifting of the naval blockades imposed around the Arabian Peninsula (since the invasion of Iraq in 2003), and the withdrawal of warships from Islamic waters
3. The release of ulema and young Muslim prisoners in the United

408 Esposito, op. cit., pp. 18, 19.
409 Bodansky, op. cit., pp. 231, 267.
410 Ibid, pp. 267, 268.

States, Israel, and most of all Sheikh Omar Abdul Rahman and Sheikh Salman al-Udah (both sought after by Arab and American authorities for terrorist activities)
4. A halt to the expropriation of Muslim wealth, especially the oil of the Arabian Peninsula and Muslim countries
5. An end to all forms of U.S. support to Israel
6. An end to the campaigns of eradication being waged by the United States with aid of governments in its pay against young Muslims under the pretext of fighting terrorism
7. An end to the campaign of extermination conducted by the United States against certain Muslim nations in the guise of economic sanctions

The Islamic Army for the Liberation of Holy Places emphatically announced its determination to pursue its attacks against American interests all over the world until all its demands are met.

As he claimed to be the leader of Islamic resistance, Bin Laden was absolutely sure that the Afghan forces that defeated two great empires, the IS and Soviet Union empires, were also capable of defeating the United States empire.[411]

Threats of attack kept coming out of Afghanistan until, in July 2001, the U.S. CIA intercepted secret intelligence information showing a strong likelihood that al-Qaeda would soon attack the U.S. It was a message of scattered dots that the CIA was able to decipher, which strongly suggested that a huge terrorist attack was being prepared against the United States. But they were never able to figure out the nature of the attack or the date chosen for its implementation.[412]

On September 11, 2001, the notorious attacks occurred, and the United States and its allies subsequently imposed strict security measures on travel centers as part of the effort to combat terrorism anywhere in the world.

Many writers and analysts began to speculate about who the perpetrators were, accusing several different organizations from different

411 Al-Nabulsi, op. cit., p. 195
412 Bob Woodward, State of Denial (London: Pocket Book, 2007), pp. 82, 83.

parts of the world, until Osama Bin Laden appeared on al-Jazeerah television and proclaimed a vague statement bragging that the valorous Muslim fighters were the ones who carried out the attacks. But the unequivocal answer came out when Sulayman Abu al-Ghayth, the official spokesman of al-Qaeda, clearly announced that the 9/11 operation was planned and executed by al-Qaeda.[413]

Being aware that Bin Laden was living in Afghanistan and protected by the Taliban government, who allowed al-Qaeda to pursue its terrorist activities, the United States in October 2001 began its invasion by extensive bombing of vital Taliban and al-Qaeda targets. Also, a covert CIA paramilitary mission code-named Jaw-Broken advanced into Afghanistan in a land onslaught. The invasion was designed by President Bush to capture Bin Laden, topple the Taliban regime and send a warning for any other country that might shelter terrorist organizations.[414]

The U.S. attack on Afghanistan was widely supported by the international community, as about thirty-seven nations contributed troops or offered other aspects of support. The military campaign succeeded in toppling the Taliban government, but Bin Laden, his followers, and most of the Taliban fighters remained at large. In 2004, the U.S. assigned Hamid Karzai, a former member of the mujahideen and an outstanding politician, to head a friendly government in Afghanistan.[415]

However, the Taliban never gave up. Before the end of 2003, its fighters began to regroup and to wage attacks against the Western allies in Afghanistan and against Karzai's government. Karzai's regime was weak, unstable, and the economy was in shambles, which caused young desperate boys to fall prey to the recruitment of the Taliban.

Yet a noteworthy point is that Karzai, with the help of the U.S., attempted to reestablish his extremely primitive country on the basis of democracy. His initiatives precipitated significant progress in religious freedom and education, especially among women, which led to the growth of the middle class. According to the UN, nearly 40 percent

413 Al-Nabulsi, op. cit., p. 274.
414 Woodward, op. cit., p. 78.
415 Cleveland, op. cit., p. 252.

of the country's eight million students are girls.[416] Education of girls is one of the few social aspects Karzai successfully instituted—a significant achievement after girls for so long were forced to stay home and forbidden by Taliban from going to school.

After the downfall of the Taliban government, Afghanistan changed; the people were happy with democracy in spite of the messy and unstable conditions of the country. Karzai's government urging men and women to practice their freedom and rights for elections was popular. In March 2014, a short time before Election Day, the voter registration station at a girls' school in Kabul was packed. A large crowd flocked through the heavily guarded gates of the school. Supervisors of the elections claim that as many as seven hundred people a day had been arriving, waiting for a long time to receive the registration cards which allowed them to cast their votes. The large number of women who crowded the registration centers was spectacular. More than three hundred women signed up to run in provincial-council elections. Habiba Sarabi, a woman who ran for second vice president on Zalmai Rassoul's ticket, states, "We have always been ignored. This is the opportunity to show that women can be in a position of power."[417]

Throughout March and on presidential and provincial Election Day on April 15, a wave of bloody terrorist attacks occurred in Kabul and other parts of Afghanistan to hamper the election process. Yet, despite the escalating violence, people remained impressively enthusiastic to take part in the election. Bold defiance and perseverance of women was dramatic. Says Waliullah Rahmani, director of the Kabul Center for Strategic Studies, "A few months ago, no one even thought there would be an election. Now you can see the momentum."[418]

Yet, equally adamant to consolidate their ideology and enforce the Islamic Shari'ah are the Taliban. They are expanding their presence all over the country, waging fierce attacks against the coalition forces to push them out of Afghanistan in order to take over power. They are receiving considerable amounts of funds and modern weapons, from al-Qaeda and Iran, to be used against U.S. and NATO forces. A senior

416 Krista Mahr/Kabul, "Waiting for the Taliban," *Time*, April 14, 2004, p. 24.
417 Ibid, p. 23.
418 Ibid.

Taliban commander attributes his successful operations against the coalition forces to weapons supplied by Iran. "We are ambushing the Americans and planting roadside bombs. We never let them relax."[419]

This is a mid-Asian Islamic country and it is also experiencing the same scenario of an unstable conflict between religious and secular ideologies and will likely do so for years to come.

419 Coughlin, op. cit., p. 334.

Chapter 8

HEZBOLLAH

HEZBOLLAH WAS ORIGINALLY the name of the Lebanese-based Iranian-sponsored Shi'ite religious fighters. The name means "Party of God." Currently the name Hezbollah indicates a larger institution sponsored, financed and controlled by Iran, which includes any guerrilla organization with branches located in the Gulf States, Palestine, Iraq, Yemen or other countries, all of which could be combined under the name "Hezbollah International."[420]

In an interview conducted by the *al-Ahram* Egyptian newspaper with the leader of Hezbollah, Sayyid[421] Hassan Nasrallah, he explained the reason for choosing the name, asserting that:

> "God gave this name to the people who obey Him and his messenger, and since we claim to be among this group, we believe we have the right to use this name."[422]

The political career of Nasrallah and the roots of the Hezbollah party are traced back to the *Harakat al-Mahroomeen* (Movement of the Deprived or Dispossessed), the predominantly Shi'ite popular reform movement established in 1974 by Imam Musa al-Sadr, an Iranian-born Lebanese cleric. The movement aimed to rectify the prejudicial

420 Bodansky, p. 407.

421 "Sayyid" is a respected title indicating a religious status, or it could be used as "mister."

422 Nicholas Noe (editor). Voice of Hezbollah: The Statements of Sayyid Hassan Nasrallah (London: Verso 2007), p. 213.

Lebanese political and economic systems that favored the Christian and Sunni Muslim communities while relegating the Shi'ite to an abject second-class citizenship.

Al-Sadr, the charismatic Shi'ite leader, was able to gain a substantial number of followers whom he urged not to fatalistically accept their poor conditions. He asserted: "Whenever the poor involve themselves in social revolution, it is a confirmation that injustice is not predestined."[423]

He coerced the Lebanese government to grant the Shi'ite better recognition, which boosted his status with the masses. Out of the Harakat al-Mahroomeen (The Movement of the Deprived) al Sadr, with his comrade, Hussein al-Husseini, established the Amal Party, which means Party of Hope.

Motivated by religious and political feeling, Hassan Nasrallah, at the tender age of fifteen, and his brother joined the Amal Party. Notwithstanding his young age, Hassan Nasrallah became the deputy of his village in the party's structure.[424]

Similar to the circumstances that led to the birth of al-Qaeda, which was Islamic Afghanistan's reaction to the invasion of the USSR, Hezbollah was born in 1982, subsequent to Israel's invasion of Lebanon.

Several times since the 1970s, Israel had attacked the Palestinian Liberation Organization (PLO), which had been located in southern Lebanon since Jordan's army, under the command of King Hussein, brutally drove them out. Finally in 1982, after violent skirmishes with the PLO across the borders, Israel invaded Lebanon with a formidable army, stormed the locations of the PLO fighters, and forced them to withdraw and regroup inside the capital, Beirut. The Israelis then prepared to raid Beirut and crush the PLO, but U.S. President Ronald Reagan stopped the invaders and allowed the PLO fighters to scatter to several Arab countries.[425]

Lebanon continued to be subjected to the brutality of the Israeli occupation as the soldiers defiantly roamed the streets and caroused in

423 Augustus Richard Norton, Hezbollah (Princeton University Press, 2007), p. 18.

424 Rif'at Sayyid Ahmad, Hassan Nasrallah, tha'ir min al-junoob (A Rebel from the South) (Damascus: Dar al-Kitab al-Arabi, 2006), p. 18.

425 Zaki, The Rise and Retreat of the Zionist Project (Arabic), Op. cit. pp. 420, 421.

the Lebanese plush entertainment centers. Israel established a permanent military headquarters in Beirut, which caused widespread feelings of frustration and humiliation all over Lebanon, as their government was utterly helpless in the face of the Israeli aggression.

However, a group of young patriotic citizens decided to take the initiative to confront the occupation and liberate their country. Thus the Hezbollah party was born, as a last resort after all other methods had failed to achieve any effective result against the Israeli military occupation.

Hezbollah's birth was timed with the rising of the Islamic revolutionary spirit instigated by the occurrence of the Islamic revolution in Iran and the birth of a new generation of Islamic revolutionary fighters. The nucleus of the party took root in the southern city of Ba'alabek.[426]

At the outset, the newly born party remained reticent and did not even announce its identity until after the occurrence of the first suicide mission carried out by "martyr" Ahmad Qassir, who on November 11, 1983, drove at the Israeli military headquarters in a car loaded with an enormous amount of explosives. The explosion was so violent it shook the adjacent villages. Thus began the wave of suicide attacks, which inflicted severe damage and against which the mighty Israeli military machine was utterly helpless. Hence Hezbollah arose amid the inferno of war.[427]

One of the party's most prominent leaders who rose through the military branch was then 22-year-old[428] Hassan Nasrallah. Nasrallah originally gained the attention of his two religious mentors, Sheikh Raghib Harb and Sayyid Abbas al-Musawi. Both leaders were impressed by his brilliance, breadth of knowledge, sincerity, courage and planning capabilities.

The leadership of Hezbollah perceived that the regular methods of resistance, like the limited raids by some Palestinian fighters, had all hitherto proven ineffective, and new tactics must be devised to achieve better results. The party's new methods were based on the following:[429]

---

426 Ahmad, op. cit., pp. 6, 7.

427 William Booth, "Israel on alert over growth of Hezbollah," *The Washington Post*, Sunday, July 24, 2016.

428 Both titles of sheikh and sayyid carry a high religious and social status.

429 Ahmad, op. cit., pp. 10-12.

1. Full belief in God and His support
2. Correct and accurate arrangement of priorities
3. Readiness of the leadership, not only the rank and file, for martyrdom and sacrifice of their lives

Motivated by these principles, Hezbollah launched its resistance activities. Hassan Nasrallah was at the forefront of the party's fighters against the occupation in the territory of Iqleem al-Tiffah, boldly roaming on all battlefronts. In February 1984, when the ideologue leader Raghib Harb was killed while he was engaged in a battle against the occupation army, the rank and file of the party became even more motivated to attain martyrdom in pursuing their struggle against the occupation.[430]

The chain of attacks by martyrs of the party relentlessly continued and the party began to gain recognition and the respect of the Arab-Muslim world. However, sharp disagreements erupted among the Shi'ite community regarding the 1982 Israeli invasion of Lebanon. When the PLO forces were banished from Jordan and fled across borders to Lebanon, the Lebanese Shi'ite of the south welcomed the Palestinians with open arms. The Lebanese even invited them to their houses as temporary brotherly guests. Yet, as time passed, it became obvious that the Palestinians were in Lebanon to stay. They became well-entrenched, organized their armed forces, developed into a state within a state and began to abuse their Lebanese hosts.[431] Yasser Arafat, the leader of the PLO, was giving orders and making decisions as if he was the legitimate ruler of Lebanon. Thus the Shi'ite attitudes began to change from welcome to deep resentment.

The leader of the Amal Party, Nabih Berri, a prominent lawyer, began to rally frustrated fellow Shi'ite under his command, and violent clashes erupted between the Amal Party's members and the PLO.

The 1982 Israeli invasion of Lebanon against the PLO constituted a turning point in the lives and inter-relations of the Lebanese Shi'ite community. The Amal Party welcomed the Israeli invasion because it

430 Ibid.
431 Hala Jaber, Hezbollah: Born with Vengeance (New York: Columbia University Press, 1997), p. 14.

removed the dominance of the PLO from southern Lebanon. Amal leaders Nabih Berri and Dawud rejoiced to be liberated from the heavy-handed Palestinian control of their country, and they sought a *modus vivendi* with Israel and the United States.[432] On the other hand, notwithstanding the Palestinian's abusive behavior, some Lebanese kept their pro-PLO attitude as their comrades in their struggle against their common enemy, Israel. That disagreement led to the division of the Lebanese Shi'ite into two factions, one under the leadership of Nabih Berri, and the other under Sayyid Abbas Mawsawi, a staunch Islamic fundamentalist and enemy of Israel.

Berri and his followers believed that the Israeli occupying forces would leave Lebanon upon completion of their mission of liquidating the PLO. Thus Berri began to cooperate with the Israeli forces to end the Palestinian presence and their guerilla activities across the Lebanese-Israeli borders in order to achieve social stability, after Israel withdrew from Lebanon.[433] However, that attitude began to change as the Shi'ite realized that the Israeli forces were not planning to withdraw and appeared intent to stay in Lebanon indefinitely, despite having achieved their goal of pushing the PLO out of the south.

In early 1983, the Israeli Defense Force (IDF) outlined the first draft of their plan to found the "Organization for a Unified South." The scheme, in effect, was putting southern Lebanon under the direct occupation of the Israelis, similar to the one used in the West Bank and other Arab lands occupied by Israel. Consequently, the Shi'ite realized that the Israeli army, which had been considered their liberator from the PLO, now was regarded as an occupier.[434] Nervousness began to prevail among a community renowned for its keen sense of independence.

The Lebanese Shi'ite learned good lessons from the Palestinian and Israeli occupations—or, for that matter, any other occupier of their small country: that is, how to wage an effective armed resistance. They also learned not to leave their dwellings, to avoid what happened to the Palestinians who were terrorized and forced to have their country

432 Norton, op. cit., p. 23.
433 Jaber, op. cit., p. 54.
434 Ibid.

occupied by Israel.

In the beginning, the number of volunteer civilians who started the resistance activities against the Israeli occupation was rather small. But the number of core fighters began to grow, and an official resistance organization was formed, called the Lebanese National Resistance (LNR), dominated by the Amal Party.

The LNR and all other movements were not effective enough to satisfy the Lebanese ambitions for independence. Hence a new, more religious radical movement was born, which was deeply influenced by the success of the Iranian theocratic regime. The new movement took the name "Hezbollah" and it departed from Nabih Berri's rather secular Amal Party. Hezbollah began to appear within the resistance scenario and formed its military branch, which it called *al-Muqawamah al-Islamiyah*, meaning the Islamic Resistance.[435]

The leaders of this nascent religious institution were fundamental clerics who had studied Shi'ite theology in Najaf, the predominantly Shi'ite holy city in Iraq. The new movement impressed a larger number of fighters and became widespread in Lebanon, including Beirut. Hassan Nasrallah, who defected from the Amal Party, in which he previously had a prominent position, became the head of the Hezbollah Party. He hastened to outline his new party's objectives in its first month of foundation. Iran's influence on Nasrallah and Hezbollah became obvious, as pictures of Ayatollah Khomeini began to appear in many Lebanese villages, announcing the birth of a movement which derived its revolutionary ideology from Iran and not from other sources.[436] Members of the Hezbollah Party consider Ayatollah Khomeini the greatest personality in the world, without rival.

STRUCTURE OF HEZBOLLAH PARTY

In early 1983, Hezbollah formed a central leadership body which consisted of three prominent members. They became Hezbollah's first majlis shura (constitutional assembly) and they were managing the

435 Ahmad, op. cit., pp. 6-7.

436 John L. Esposito, The Islamic Threat: Myth or Reality? (Oxford University Press, 1999, 3rd ed.), p. 147.

party's operations in Beka Valley, Beirut and south Lebanon. The main function of the majlis shura is to perceive, interpret and implement decisions regarding military, political and other social and economic issues according to the Islamic dogma.

A letter from the majlis shura, representing the first major account and the main source of information about the aims of the party, was addressed to the "oppressed people," and it starts with a question: "Who are we and what are our duties?" The answer is written in a document stating:[437]

> We are the sons of Hezbollah in Lebanon, we greet you and through you we talk to the entire world, persons and institutions, political parties, humanitarians and mass media without excluding anyone. Because we are concerned to convey our call to all to comprehend our suggestions and understand our purposes ... We are the sons of Hezbollah, consider ourselves as part of the nation of Islam in a world which is being subjected to the aggression of Western and Eastern pressures.

The main objectives of our party are the following:[438]

1. Specifying the main enemies of Islam which are Israel, France and America.
2. Force Israel out of Lebanon as a prelude to its final eradication and liberation of the holy Qudus city (Jerusalem).
3. Our Imam Khomeini accentuated repeatedly that America is the mother of all evils and we have the right to fight it. Evicting America, France, their allies and any imperialist hegemonic power from our country.
4. Prosecuting all individuals and groups that collaborated with and encouraged by America to commit crimes against Muslims and Christians.
5. We adhere to Islam, but we do not impose by force on other

437 Ahmad, op. cit., pp. 35-41.
438 Ibid.

> people: O free oppressed people. We are a nation that believes in the message of Islam, and our Sublime God says "there shall be no compulsion in religion (Quran: The Cow 2:256). Our people will have the freedom of self-determination and freely choose the type of rule they prefer. We urge all to understand the Islamic system which secures peace, justice and dignity for all, and it alone prevents the attempts of infiltration of imperialism into our society.

The leader who masterminded the formation of the main ideas of Hezbollah and guided it, in spite of his young age, was (Sayyid) Hassan Nasrallah.

WHO IS HASSAN NASRALLAH?

Hassan Abdul Karim Nasrallah was born on August 31, 1960, in the town of Bazoorah, east of Lebanon. His father was Abdul Karim Nasrallah, and Hassan was the oldest of eight children, with three brothers and five sisters. He was raised in the "al-Karanteena neighborhood," one of the poorest suburbs of East Beirut, where he received his elementary and middle education.

Hassan's father ran a grocery store and Hassan used to help his father in the store. There he noticed a picture of Imam Musa al-Sadr hanging on the wall. Musa al-Sadr was an Iranian-born clergyman of Lebanese parents, a Shi'ite philosopher and religious leader who descended from a deeply rooted family of well-known Shi'ite clerks. The young Hassan used to sit opposite the picture of the holy imam and dream of becoming like him.[439]

Hassan was not like other boys who spent their time playing soccer or swimming. He preferred to walk a long distance to the al-Ta'akhi mosque to pray and listen to the ceremonies of Sayyid Muhammad Hussein Fadlallah. Fadlallah was a prominent Shi'ite imam and *marja*, (authority in Islamic dogma), who guided the prayers in the mosque.[440] From an early age, Hassan was an avid reader, and whenever he went to the city center, he bought used books. He read whatever he could, but

439 Ibid.
440 Noe, op. cit., p. 117.

his special interest was to concentrate on treatises about Islam.

Although his family was not fanatically religious, young Hassan was openly pious and studious in implementing religious requirements, and was consumed by his interest in Imam Musa al-Sadr. At the age of fifteen, he graduated from high school and joined the Shi'ite Amal Party.

After a few months, Hassan decided to travel to the Iraqi Shi'ite holy city, al-Najaf, to study the Quranic religious details. In al-Najaf, he met Sayyid Abbas al-Musawi, a prominent Lebanese cleric and one of the earliest leaders of Hezbollah, who became like a brother mentor to Nasrallah. (Al-Musawi was killed by Israeli forces in 1992.) Al-Musawi supplied the penniless newcomer with clothes, books and a small monthly stipend,[441] and Hassan entered the educational system of the *Hawzeh* (the Shi'ite high seminary). The Hawzeh is divided into three stages. The first stage is preparatory or the general entrance to the religious and scientific education. The second, or middle, stage is called "al-Sutooh," which is preparatory to the third stage.

The third stage is the external research period. In this stage it is mandatory for the students to undertake a research project without reviewing published books. The researchers are required to obtain the opinions of jurisprudents and professors to prepare their thesis to graduate.

Abbas al-Musawi was the instructor for the young students. He was very strict and was able to qualify his students to graduate in two years instead of the customary five years.[442]

By 1978, Nasrallah, an outstanding student, had successfully passed the first stage. However, after that, his dreams were shattered as he was compelled to stop his studies. In that year, Saddam Hussein, the leader of the ruling secular Ba'ath party in Iraq, crushed the al-Da'wah Islamic Shi'ite religious-political movement and waged a campaign against religious centers. The al-Da'wah party had originally been an Islamic Iraqi party whose ideology was established by the followers of Ayatollah Khomeini in Najaf. When the Iraq-Iran War erupted in

441 Ahmad, op. cit., pp. 18, 19.
442 Ibid.

1980, Saddam Hussein considered the al-Da'wah party and all Shi'ite political movements as fifth column controlled by Khomeini and his theocratic regime.[443]

When the Iraqi police raided al-Hawzeh al-Shi'iyah in Najaf, Sayyed Abbas al-Musawi was in Lebanon and he was advised not to return to Iraq, as he was wanted by the authorities. The Lebanese students who were pursuing their religious studies in al-Hawzeh were detained for a short while, then deported to Lebanon. Luckily for Hassan Nasrallah, he was not in al-Hawzeh, and he left Najaf and returned to Lebanon.

In Ba'alaback, Lebanon, Nasrallah had a second chance to realize his aspiration to continue his education, as Sayyid Abbas al-Musawi recruited a number of qualified teachers to start a religious school there. Hassan was simultaneously admitted as a student as well as a teacher, because of his wealth of knowledge.

In 1982, the Amal Party elected Hassan as its political envoy to the Beqaa province. By this position, he became a member of the party's central political office. In the same year, he was promoted to the third stage of his studies.[444]

In spite of his heavy political duties and staunch commitment to the party, Nasrallah was determined to pursue his studies to become an expert jurisprudent and a *mujtahid*, a judiciary competent scholar qualified to analyze and infer the correct legal ruling.

Once again, fortune interfered. In June 1982, Israel invaded Lebanon, which constituted a turning point not only in Hassan Nasrallah's life, but in the interrelation among the Shi'ite community and the course of struggle against the Israeli population. Nasrallah was again compelled to stop his education and assume the responsibility of conducting resistance against the invaders. He was never able to attain his ultimate goal of passing the third stage of schooling to become a jurisprudent and a mujtahid.[445]

The Iranian leadership shrewdly exploited the upheaval in southern Lebanon and the deplorable social conditions of the Shi'ite there as fertile ground for exporting its revolutionary system to an Arab country. It

443 Jaber, op. cit., p. 54.
444 Ahmad, op. cit., pp. 19, 20.
445 Ibid.

set out an ambitious plan of a million dollars in financial aid, military training and equipment through Syria. Hezbollah, with Iran's help, embarked on constructing a wide range of social welfare infrastructure in the south. Tens of schools, mainly with Islamic curricula, modern hospitals, paved roads and job opportunities were made available, which established Hezbollah's status not only as a freedom fighter but as a humanitarian institution. A noteworthy point is that Hezbollah leadership, with the recommendation of Imam Khomeini, availed all these facilities to the Muslims as well as Christians. The party boasted that, although its social welfare system was initiated to accommodate the needs of the Shi'ites, it was also accessible to other religions and sects.[446]

Between 1982 and 2000, Hezbollah engaged in major combative confrontations against Israel, which boosted the party's status as a powerful military and strategic entity in the Middle East. All other movements' resistance activities, including those of the Amal Party, were rather ineffective and were eclipsed by Hezbollah's vigorous attacks.

Buttressed by the forceful Iranian and Syrian support, the most damaging onslaughts against the Israeli occupation were carried out by Hezbollah fighters who, as time passed, were becoming bolder, gaining more accuracy, learning better planning and acquiring more sophisticated skills.[447]

Hezbollah was conducting two-pronged attacks, one against the Israeli forces and one against an Israeli-created security zone adjacent to the Lebanese borders. The security zone was commanded by Major Sa'ad Haddad, a Maronite Christian Lebanese officer who defected from the Lebanese army to become an ally of Israel. He founded the Christian militia, the South Lebanese Army (SLA), which was situated in the security zone to collaborate with the Israeli forces.[448] Following Haddad's death in 1984, General Antoine Lahad, another Lebanese Maronite officer who defected from Lebanon's army, took over the command of SLA and continued the fight against Hezbollah.

Hezbollah's deadliest attack against the Israeli occupation forces was carried out on November 11, 1982, by Ahmad Qassir, a

446 Jaber, op. cit., pp. 146-148.
447 Ahmad, op. cit., pp. 8-10.
448 Jaber, op. cit., p. 13.

seventeen-year-old boy who drove a bomb-laden car into Israeli headquarters, killing 141 soldiers and officials. The attack caught the Israelis so by surprise that they initially did not know it happened, and they initially denied that it was a planned assault. Ahmad Qassir's attack was followed by a succession of suicide attacks by very young men and women members of Hezbollah.[449]

Israel's torturous occupation lasted for more than two decades and rendered Hezbollah's hard-line policy attractive to a wide range of Arab Muslims. The party's fearless tactics and constant brazen attacks became a source of pride to Lebanese Shi'ites, Sunnis and Christians, and a large number of volunteers joined the party to take part in the combat against the enemy and to seek martyrdom.

The 1990s witnessed major combative confrontations between Hezbollah and Israel, which precipitated new historical and strategic events in the Middle East. The Israeli government staged two major military attempts—"Operation Accountability"[450] in July 1993, and "Operation Grapes of Wrath"[451] in April 1996—to crush Hezbollah and the Lebanese resistance, but they both failed to accomplish their goal. In fact, the stiff resistance by the Lebanese against the formidable Israeli army catapulted Hezbollah to new heights of international status and boosted Hassan Nasrallah's political status. In response to Israel's Operation Accountability attack in July 1993, which was the severest since the war of 1982, Nasrallah called the leaders of the resistance together for a meeting to deal with the situation. As a result of that meeting, they all decided to adopt the following plan:

1. Wage an immediate attack against Israeli location.
2. Urge the Lebanese citizens not to leave their villages and stand fast against the Israeli onslaught, and the party would protect them.
3. Relentlessly continue bombardment of Israeli north settlements without cessation.[452]

449 Ibid., pp. 75-76.
450 Noe, op. cit., p. 100.
451 Norton, op. cit., p. 84.
452 Ahmad, op. cit., pp. 134, 135.

The main goals of the vigorous Israeli military Operation Accountability campaign were to burn the lands, force the people to migrate, pressure the Lebanese government to stop the resistance activities, break the will of the resistance, and eliminate it from the lands adjacent to the Israeli borders. To achieve these goals, Israel waged 1,300 air raids and hurled 30,000 missiles against Lebanon.[453]

Hassan Nasrallah was able to take the initiative in combatting the Israeli campaign. He united the resistance front and boosted the morale of the villagers, while maintaining relentless missile attacks against the northern Israeli settlements, forcing those occupants to flee to the south. Six days later, by July 31, 140 Lebanese civilians were killed, and nearly a quarter of a million Shi'ite refugees streamed into downtown Beirut. Yet, Israel admitted that the operation failed to accomplish its goal of squashing Hezbollah's resistance. Instead of agitating popular hatred against Hezbollah, as Israel expected, the Lebanese called for more vigorous support for the resistance.[454]

The significant development that resulted from the 1993 military campaign carnage was an unwritten agreement that obligated both Hezbollah and Israel not to attack each other's civilian points. While this understanding between the two warring sides lasted for a time, the tit-for-tat confrontations between the resistance and IDF continued.

Israeli Prime Minister Yitzhaq Rabin vowed to carry on his attacks until the Shi'ite guerrillas were wiped out and Hezbollah's fighters were eliminated. Nasrallah, on the other hand, defiantly pledged to intensify his attacks against Israel's "security zone" and its northern settlements. Hezbollah's determination and steadfastness gained increasing government and popular support. Between 1993 and 1996, during the unwritten "understanding" commitment, Hezbollah claimed that Israel breached the truce and attacked Lebanese targets 231 times. Both UN and Western diplomatic sources in Lebanon confirmed Hezbollah's allegations.[455] In retaliation, Hezbollah intensified its attacks against Israeli soldiers and SLA militias. In the first months of 1996, Hezbollah killed and injured a number of Israelis, which provoked Israel to respond

453 Ibid.
454 Jaber, op. cit., p. 178.
455 Ibid, p. 173.

with heavy bombardment.

The reciprocal hostilities culminated on April 11, 1996, in Israel's termination of the 1993 agreement via an all-out onslaught against several parts of Lebanon, which resulted in several massacres. This "Grapes of Wrath" campaign lasted for sixteen days. It was another ferocious attempt by Israel to uproot the fighters of Hezbollah from southern Lebanon to retrieve the northern parts of the Jewish state. However, the conflagration ended in a military fiasco for Israel and extremely damaged Prime Minister Shimon Perez, who had promised his people to eradicate, once and for all, what he described as "Hezbollah terrorists." Hezbollah fired back salvos of rockets into northern Israel to remind the government of the provision of the 1993 understanding. The message was loud and clear—if Lebanese civilians and villages were to be hit, then Israeli settlements and settlers would suffer consequences.[456] More of a blow to Israel was the fact that Perez and the IDF were forced to admit that the resistance was not going to quit, and Hezbollah possessed enough military power to bombard Israel indefinitely.[457]

The operation ended in another unwritten understanding obligating the two enemies to refrain from targeting civilians. However, the military strife never abated. For the rest of the 1990s, Iran and Syria kept reinforcing Hezbollah capabilities while Israel endured a costly war of attrition in human life and financial health.[458]

In 1999, former Chief of Staff General Ehud Barak was elected prime minister of Israel, defeating incumbent Prime Minister Benjamin Netanyahu. One of the main campaign promises by Barak was that he would withdraw the Israeli forces from Lebanon within one year after assuming office.

Before departing from his office, during the period of transferring authority, Netanyahu gave orders to the IDF to demolish the Lebanese infrastructure to force Hezbollah to stop attacking the settlements. For three months, Hezbollah reacted to Netanyahu's proposal by waging a total of 1,525 operations, piercing what was thought to be impenetrable fortification. One of Hezbollah's members, Anwar Mahmoud,

456 Ibid, p. 174.
457 Noe, op. cit., pp. 144, 145.
458 Ahmad, op. cit., pp. 94-97.

was able to carry out a suicide mission against an Israeli military convoy in the heart of the occupied zone, and inflicted substantial damage. That operation was to coerce Ehud Barak to implement his promise of withdrawal in June of 2001.[459]

In May 2000, Israel's unilateral withdrawal from Lebanon began. Fears spread that Lebanon would be overtaken by chaotic violence, including the slaughter of collaborators and bloodshed. Hassan Nasrallah hastened to issue statements assuring that Hezbollah was fully prepared for the aftermath of the absence of the Israeli forces.

The final withdrawal came on May 24, 2000, when the last Israeli soldier left Lebanon, abandoning large amounts of military equipment and ammunition, which were confiscated by Hezbollah fighters. It was a time of overwhelming celebration in all of Lebanon, but especially by the Shi'ite in the south. Displaced residents flocked back into the south to repossess their homes and villages. In the rest of the country there were very few incidents of violence and a remarkable degree of calm.

SLA militia fled to Israel with their families, and those who remained were tried for collaboration and received appropriate sentences.[460]

HEZBOLLAH INTERNATIONAL

The 1990s encounters by the Lebanese against Israel precipitated profound historical, military and strategic consequences. Iran successfully established a well-entrenched foothold in an Arab country, to which it exported its Shi'ite political system of *Wilayat al-Faqih*. Hezbollah's successful confrontations against the formidable IDF became a prelude to the party's recognition as a cross-border military and political entity in the Middle East.

However, the war that catapulted Hezbollah to its zenith to become Hezbollah International came as a result of the relentless and prolonged attacks by its fighters, which forced the IDF to withdraw in 2000 from south Lebanon unilaterally, unconditionally and in full defeat, while Hezbollah's weapons were more powerful than ever and

459 Ibid, p. 146.
460 Norton, op. cit., pp. 88-90.

capable of reaching any point inside Israel.[461]

Hezbollah's international status was recognized when Hassan Nasrallah appeared on the widely watched American television news program *60 Minutes*. He conveyed his ideologies to the U.S. and Western media in general, asserting that the American invasion of Iraq would precipitate the birth of numerous armed groups that would attack the USA and the Western world. Commenting on Nasrallah's radical statement, Democratic Senator Bob Graham of Florida, a presidential aspirant, responded to *60 Minutes* reporter Ed Bradley's questions, maintaining that Hezbollah would sooner or later attack the United States just as al-Qaeda had done. Graham also asserted that Hezbollah has a global network of radical Islamic supporters with enough operatives to pose terrorist threats in the U.S.[462]

Back at the Middle East battlefield, the mutual hostilities between Hezbollah and Israel continued. Responding to daily Israeli provocations such as raids, abduction of citizens from their homes, air and ground violations,[463] Hezbollah retaliated on July 12, 2006, by carrying out a dramatic operation intended to authenticate the party's advanced combat capabilities while seeking popular support from the Arab world. The tactical accuracy of the operation was stunning. Hezbollah's fighters ambushed a motorized Israeli patrol in north Israel, captured two soldiers, and killed three others.[464]

The next day, July 13, Israel promptly reacted by unleashing massive air, sea and land assaults against Lebanon. Nasrallah admitted that he did not expect such a voluminous onslaught but he scurried to rally his military assets and stated, "You want an open war, and we are heading for an open war. We are ready for it."[465] His missile volleys damaged targets deep inside Israel, hit its maritime fleet and destroyed a number of armory vehicles. The war lasted for thirty-four days (July 12 to August 14), with a high number of civilian and military casualties.

Both claimed victory, but it was rather a draw. In Israel, the war

461 Ibid.
462 Noe, op. cit., pp. 287, 288.
463 Ibid, p. 381.
464 Ibid.
465 Norton, op. cit., p. 136.

was considered a fiasco. Hezbollah boasted that its much smaller forces successfully confronted the most powerful army in the Middle East for such a long time, inflicting substantial damage to it. Nasrallah became a hero for the entire Arab-Muslim world as the leader who taught Israel the severest lesson since the 1973 Arab-Israel "Yom Kippur" war, when the Arab armies scored a substantial military success. Hezbollah claimed that its fighters had shattered the myth of the undefeatable army alleged by Israel's commanders and accentuated by the Western mass media.[466]

Hezbollah fighters are invariably being trained by Iranian highly ranked officers and funded by Tehran, and have gained wide experience to use the most sophisticated weaponry to confront a modern army. Hundreds of Hezbollah fighters have died in Syria since 2011, while supporting its president, Bashar al-Assad, in the civil war against his adversaries, but the party members are not demoralized because they firmly believe that the fighters who are killed in combat are martyrs who will live with God in paradise.

Since its birth in the early 1980s, Hezbollah has metamorphosed from a Lebanese local party into an international military and ideological power to be reckoned with. In July 2016, ten years after the war against Israel in 2006, the party boasted a much mightier military capability than in 2006, claiming to possess hundreds of thousands of more accurate weapons with larger warheads capable of reaching all over Israel, including Jerusalem and Tel Aviv.

Commemorating the same 2006 event, Israeli commanders in Tel Aviv asserted that "Hezbollah is not a group or movement. It is an army, a big terrorist army."[467]

Thousands of Hezbollah fighters, hardened by several years of combat in the Syrian battlefield and its confrontations with Israel, are active in different parts of the Middle East. They are fighting side by side with the Iranian and Russian armies to support the Syrian regime, supporting Iraq's pro-Iranian Shi'ite government. Today, the party is also backing the pro-Iranian Shi'ite Houthi rebels fighting against the Yemeni

466 Zaki, su'oo wa taraju'a lmashru' al-suhuni, op. cit., pp. 443-448.
467 Booth, op. cit., p. A10.

government, which is supported by the Sunni Saudi Arabian government. The Saudi government in 2015 became involved in Yemen's civil war to back its government against the Houthi rebels who espouse Iran's Shi'ite expansionism.[468]

However, these far-reaching activities agitated doubts across the Islamic world as they revealed that Nasrallah is motivated by deep sectarianism. By stating his staunch loyalty to Iran and his firm belief in the theocratic system of Wilayat al-Faqih, Nasrallah lost much of the popular adulation he and his party previously enjoyed in Lebanon. After being regarded as a loyal leader fighting against Israel's menace, Nasrallah and his party have been reconsidered by some Arab countries as a non-patriotic, terrorist organization promoting the expansionist aggression of a hostile country—Iran.[469]

Regardless of the controversies, it is a stark historical fact that Hezbollah has become a powerful, integral part of the anti-secular, anti-nationalist, theocratic thesis of Khomeinism in the Middle East and the Islamic world.

468 Ibid.

469 Noe, op. cit., p. 406.

Chapter 9

Modern Islamic Turkey and the Downfall of Secular Kemalism

Historical Background

One of the earliest oppositions that Kemal Ataturk faced was the revolution of Shaykh Said, the Islamic leader who, in 1925, rebelled against the Turkish government's secular Westernization policy. Since that upheaval, the state directed its utmost efforts to confront any sort of opposition. However, even the subsequent execution of Shaykh Said did not end the conflict between secular and religious movements; numerous Islamic mutinies erupted, but they were not organized and were brutally crushed.

After Kemal Ataturk's death in 1938, the National Assembly (Parliament) voted his closest friend and protégé, First Lieutenant General Ismet Inonu Pasha, as the country's president and the leader of the Republican People Party (RPP). Inonu closely followed Ataturk's steps and the Constitution of 1924, pursuing the secular tradition and the aforementioned six principles of Kemalism.[470]

Although Mustafa Kemal was never able to eradicate Islam from his modernizing republic, no serious challenge to his secular regime occurred until after World War II. After the United Nations (UN) was established in 1945, a number of the RPP members requested that

470 Cleveland, op. cit., p. 185.

certain rights enshrined in the UN charter be included in Turkey's domestic laws, including the freedom of religion. The request was refused by the Inonu government. In response to the government's refusal, the Democratic Party was founded in 1946 by two prominent Islamic-inclined politicians, Celal Bayar and Adnan Menderes. Their activities would later result in essential political changes in Turkey.[471]

The new Democratic Party showed its first signs of popular strength in the election of 1946. Although the Democrats won only 65 out of 465 seats in the national assembly, the fact that an opposition party was present indicated a significant development in the Turkish political system. During the following few years, the Democratic Party frequently contravened the government's polity in the assembly and constantly confronted the representatives of the RPP in heated debates. The Democrats also hastened to spread their political presence by establishing branches all over the country.[472]

By the 1950s, the multi-party system of Turkey was dominated by the Democratic Party, as it constituted the majority of the general assembly. Its founders and leaders were President Celel Bayar and Prime Minister Adnan Menderes. Both were upper-class, highly educated gentlemen. Bayar (1882–1961) was a banker and veteran government employee, while Menderes (1899–1961) was a lawyer who descended from wealthy landowners. Neither man had any military background. The nature of the political elite started changing after 1950. The trend of being ruled by government bureaucrats and military veterans-turned-politicians shifted; the national assembly now included a large number of civilian professionals and business people. Many historians believe that the Democratic Party gained popularity because a vast part of the masses desired to change the Ataturk legacy of secularism.[473]

The first sign of policy change undertaken by the new government was evidenced when, as soon as the Democratic Party's victory was announced to the public, the forbidden call for prayer (*adhan*) in Arabic was heard for the first time in decades from the mosques in several regions of the country. Other anti-Kemalism measures quickly

471 Herman, op. cit., p. 39.
472 Cleveland, op. cit., p. 278.
473 Herman, op. cit., p. 39.

followed. Religious institutions were reintroduced to Muslim students in elementary schools, unless parents requested exemption. The number of schools for training Muslim prayer leaders was increased, and a large amount of government funds was earmarked for the repair of neglected mosques and to build some five thousand new ones. There was also significant overproduction of publications of books and journals dealing with religious subjects, in addition to renewed recognition of traditional Islamic rituals such as fasting during the holy month of Ramadhan and the pilgrimage to Mecca.[474]

A noteworthy point here is that the new policy was more in response to the wide religious desire among the religious people rather than a decrease of Kemalism. They kept claiming to adhere to secularism. Yet, Adnan Menderes was prone to bolster Turkey's position with the world in general and, boldly, with the Islamic countries in particular. In 1952, Turkey requested and was granted membership in the North Atlantic Treaty Organization (NATO). In 1955, and supported by the United States, Turkey entered into the Baghdad Pact with Great Britain and a number of predominantly Islamic countries, including Iraq, Pakistan and Iran.[475] Turkey's economic cooperation with the Islamic countries began to grow quickly.

The system of the Democratic Party government typified a synthetic period in which Bayar and Menderes revived religion to cater to popular demands, while emphasizing the retention of secularism to assuage the military and the Kemalist supporters. However, a synthetic period might evolve either towards the old thesis, or towards the new antithesis. Adnan Menderes' activities aroused deep consternation among the pro-Kemalist military, and in the early morning of May 27, 1960, the Turkish army, under the command of General Cemal Gursel, seized control of Istanbul and Ankara. All high official leadership of the government, including President Bayar and Prime Minister Menderes, were arrested. The main purpose of the coup was to stop the process of Islamization and preserve Turkish modernizing nationalism. In 1961, Prime Minister Menderes was hanged after courts passed an

474 Cleveland, op. cit., p. 279.
475 Zaki, Prosperity of Iraq Under the Royal Regime, op. cit., p. 364.

execution sentence against him.[476] Thus the secular Kemalist thesis was re-established in Turkey, while Islamism withdrew into temporary ebb.

From the 1960s through the 1980s, Turkey suffered continuous instability. Several military coups occurred, followed by the election of civil government rulers. The parties in power kept shifting until the election in 1983, when a new political organization, the Motherland Party, founded and led by Turgut Özal (1927–1993), an engineer and expert economist, came to power. Although the Motherland Party was composed of a disharmonized combination of Islamic revivalists and secular liberals, Özal was influential enough to form a majority government, curtail the military domination, steer his system towards a neo-liberal political economic policy and entrust politics in the hands of civilians.[477] Özal became prime minister (1983–1989) and the eighth president of the republic, from 1989 until his death in 1993. During that time, Turkey's politics were dominated by centrist or right-of-center politics. This trend continued and, as a result of Özal's liberal policy, the conservative popular mentality was changed. In 1993, Dr. Tansu Ciller, an economist, was elected as the first female prime minister of the predominantly Muslim Republic of Turkey.[478] With its free market policy, Tansu Ciller's True Path Party was able to provide for economic prosperity of the upper class. Yet, whereas the pro-business True Path government gratified those on top, the lower classes and large peasantry were attracted towards the Islamic-oriented parties.

After enduring periods of setbacks, the Islamic parties achieved a dramatic comeback in the 1990s. The roots of this success could be traced back to the politics pursued in 1980 during one of the military-controlled periods before and during the first term of Turgut Özal's rule. The military junta resorted to despotic practices to counter the surge in communist and socialist movements steadily increasing among educated groups.

In 1982, an elected constitutional committee headed by Professor Orhan Aldikacti outlined a first draft for a new constitution. Power was concentrated in the executive authority, and restrictions were imposed

476 Zurcher, op. cit., p. 307.
477 Cleveland, op. cit., p. 285.
478 Zurcher, op. cit., pp. 388-389.

on the freedom of the press, freedom of unions, and the rights of liberty of individuals. By and large, the harsh measures were directed against such movements as the ultra-leftist *Devrimci Sol* (the Revolutionary People's Liberation Party), the militant *Milliyet Harkat Partesi* (the Nationalist Movement Party), and the revolutionary Kurdistan Workers Party (PKK), among others.[479]

The military also perceived that encouraging religious feelings would counter the leftist ideologies. The military high command introduced compulsory courses on religion in the state-run schools. It also augmented the network of religious schools that trained students to practice basic ulema functions such as leading prayers and delivering speeches in mosques. These religious schools provided educational opportunities and future jobs for the youth of the lower classes, and by early 1990, the schools became so appealing that enrollment in them reached almost three hundred thousand students.[480]

Meanwhile, the military miscalculated, as the Islamic movements grew quickly out of control and filled the political vacuum left by the devastated leftist movements. The largest and best-organized of the Muslim parties was the Refah Party, or Welfare Party, led by Professor Necmettin Erbakan (1926–2011), an engineer and university professor.

The political course of Professor Erbakan began when he became president of the Union of Chambers of Commerce and Industry and boosted his status as an Islamic political leader and an advocate of small business. After being elected to the National Assembly in 1969, Erbakan, with few followers, founded the *Milli Nizam Partisi* (MNP), the National Order Party (NOP), which was based on Islamic fundamentalism, in 1970.[481] The party was closed by the government in 1971 and re-emerged under the name of the *Milli Selamet Partisi* (MSP), the National Salvation Party (NSP) in 1973. In the same year, the MSP joined the government's coalition of Bulent Ecevita RPP, and Erbakan assumed the position of vice-premier and minister of state.

In 1977, after serving in JP, the National Front Cabinet of the liberal Suleyman Demirel, Erbakan denounced the JP and Demiril for

479 Ibid, pp. 280, 281.
480 Cleveland, op. cit., p. 528.
481 Fisher, op. cit., p. 494.

being stooges of the Freemasons and the Zionists, which are enemies of Islam.[482] He then banned them from political life in 1980 and returned to lead the Islamic Welfare Party in the late 1980s.

The continuous growth of religious feelings increased the popular support for the Islamic Welfare Party. It culminated in the 1995 election of the National Assembly in which the party received 21 percent of the popular vote, more than any other party. In July 1996, Erbakan became the first Islamist prime minister of Turkey since the downfall of the Ottoman Empire. However, the army, which considered itself the protector of Ataturk's legacy, was provoked by the growing religious influence of Erbakan and his party. In 1997, the High Military Command forced Erbakan to resign, his party was banned by the Constitutional Court, and several leaders, including Erbakan, were forbidden from political activities for several years.[483]

Despite banning Islamic parties and persecuting religious movements, the Turkish High Military Command was never able to limit the spread of Islamic-oriented political affiliation. Support for religious politicians invariably kept growing. While concentrating on promoting modernization and secularism, and oppressing popular religious feelings, the Military High Command overlooked a critical matter of protecting the constitutionally defined concept of the democratic nature of the Turkish Republic. Despotism, political instability, unemployment and economic hardship, and disillusion with all major political parties enticed the people to seek possible salvation in religion.[484]

The Islamic Welfare Party drew its strength from dissatisfied rural residents who adhered to Muslim customs and whose interests had been neglected by the ruling elite for a long time. They were the migrants from the villages into the cities, seeking jobs and a better life for their children, and they were particularly supportive of the Islamic Welfare Party's message. Mr. Tayyip Erdogan, Recep's father, was one of these poor people who lived in the dilapidated working-class district in Istanbul.

482 Zurcher, op. cit., p. 257.

483 Tinal, Nadhim, The Democratic Change in Turkey, LArdric (al-Mahrusah Center for Publishing, Journal Services and Information, 2012), pp. 98, 99.

484 Cleveland, op. cit., p. 527.

Into this religious milieu, Recep Tayyip Erdogan was born, in 1954. As an outspoken youth, he became involved in politics while a university student, and gained popular recognition as a prominent football player. Deeply pious and an Islamic mystic, he joined the Islamic Welfare Party, and in 1994, at the mature age of forty, he was elected the first Islamic mayor of Istanbul in the republic's history. With Necmettin Erbakan as prime minister and Recep Tayyip Erdogan as mayor of the capital, Istanbul, the Kemalist Turkish Republic was experiencing social change of historical magnitude.[485]

Erdogan established his reputation as an average servant of the people. As a mayor who took a strong stance against criminals, he proved to be a good administrator who kept the city clean and safe. He improved transportation, installed new water lines, planted trees to beautify Istanbul, and opened his doors for the people to directly convey their complaints to him. Erdogan became reputable as an ethical and just administrator. He was also known for his keen religious practices, as he promoted an Islamic agenda. He banned alcohol from city buildings and planned to build several mosques in several sections of the city. On one occasion he told a Western visitor:

> Our view of religion is different from yours. According to you, religion only counts in the places where you pray. Our religion is a way of life. I have no time at all, not one minute, without Islam.[486]

Erdogan was a strong advocate of *salafi* (traditional) Islamic family values, encouraging prolific birth rates, and encouraging women, including his wife, to wear the Islamic head scarf and to be satisfied to stay as housewives. Amazingly, many young, educated women in different parts of Turkey favorably responded to Erdogan's calls and began to follow the Islamic tradition.

To accentuate his Islamic devotion, Erdogan enforced the revival

485 Lashnits, Tom, Recep Tayyip Erdogan: Major World Leaders (Philadelphia: Chelsea House Publishers, 2005), pp. 72, 73.

486 Ibid.

of Islamic events and practices. He made the anniversary of the 1453 conquest of Istanbul by the pious Islamic jurist Sultan Mehmet II a city holiday and an historical event to celebrate. He also followed an Islamic charity policy of serving free hot meals for the fasting poor people after sundown during the holy month of Ramadan, when Muslims are required to fast from dawn to dusk.

In January 1998, when the Turkish courts decided to close Erbakan's Islamic Welfare Party, citing evidence confirming its actions against the principles of the secular republic, several Islamic Welfare Party officials and mayors were subjected to police investigation. The authorities also went after Recep due to a fiery speech he gave that was considered in conflict with the secular government. He was convicted and jailed because at a rally in Seirt City, Erdogan, amid enthusiastic applause, delivered the following militant Islamic poem:[487]

The mosques are our barracks
The domes are our helmets
The minarets are our bayonets
And the faithful are our soldiers

The poem shows the powerful influence of the salafi Muslim Brotherhood jihadist belief, set forth by Hassan al-Banna and al-Mawdudi, on Erdogan's political thinking and behavior.

After receiving his jail sentence, Erdogan instructed his supporters to organize a peaceful protest, while vowing to fight for his freedom and career. Thousands of people gathered outside Istanbul's city hall chanting the same jihadist poem for which Erdogan was jailed. The ardent popular support for Erdogan indicated the extent to which radical Islam had spread among the Turkish people.

Throughout the 1990s, the Islamic Welfare Party was never able to overwhelm the Turkish political arena, even though it kept gaining more popular support. The party remained either under the mercy of the secular Kemalist military, sometimes being banned and sometimes

487 Herman, River, Turkia: bayn al-dawlah al-deeniyah wa al-dawlah al-madaniyah, al-srra' al-thaqafi fi Turkia (Turkey: Between the Religious and Civil State; the Cultural Struggle in Turkey (al-Mahrusah Center for Publishing, Journal Service and Information, 2012), p. 135.

allowed, or it was compelled to enter in coalition with parties that had opposite ideologies in order to be able to participate in political activities and elections.

It was not until the beginning of the twenty-first century that political Islam achieved a sweeping success in Turkey when, in the fall of 2002, the Islamic Party and the Justice and Development Party (JDP), headed by Recep Tayyip Erdogan, won a stunning electoral victory, scoring 363 of 550 seats in the general assembly. The Republican People Party won 178 seats, and the independent candidate won nine seats.[488] Within a fortnight, Turkey's multiparty system was changed into a biparty system, as a prelude for the JPD to overwhelm the entire country.

The Turkish people found the JDP or AKP platform of solid welfare reform attractive, especially the announcement of its moderate Islamic policy.

The JDP had been in existence for only one year before it won a landslide election. In June 2001, the Turkish courts banned Erbakan's Virtue Party—as they had previously banned the Welfare Party—for anti-secular activities. Led by Erbakan, a group of older, more conservative Islamists founded a new party called *Saddat Partisi*, the Happiness Party. But Erdogan disagreed with Erbakan's lesser adherence to Islamic dogma, and in August 2001, he gathered new, more informed members of the old Virtue Party and, with Dr. Abdulla Gul, founded the Justice and Development Party.[489]

Abdulla Gul was born in 1949 in the small city of Kaysari. Similar to Erdogan, as a young student he advocated staunch Islamic values, and in 1980, he was arrested for his religious activities. He was able to pursue his studies until he obtained a Ph.D. in economic development, became a professor at Sekaria University, and achieved proficiency in the English language. Between 1983 and 1991, he worked as an economic expert at the Islamic Development Bank in Saudi Arabia. He joined the Rafah Party, and Prime Minister Necmettin Erbakan assigned him as minister of foreign affairs and the official spokesperson

488 Cleveland, op. cit., p. 532.
489 Zurcher, op. cit., p. 304.

of the Welfare Party. Afterward, he decided to join Erdogan in the leadership of the Justice and Development Party.

By choosing Dr. Abdulla Gul as a cohort, Erdogan bolstered the popularity of his newly born party and strengthened the Islamic current in the country. The two new leaders gave the people hope for a better future. Political surveys showed that more than 60 percent of Turkey's voters were dissatisfied with what was called the democratic system. People blamed the economic hardship, unemployment and social instability on the status quo, and they eagerly sought change. As one prominent Islamic leader in Istanbul stated: "We are crying out for change. The whole country wants a fresh start and we (the Islamists) can give it to them."[490]

Two weeks after the 2002 election, Erdogan nominated Abdulla Gul to the position of prime minister. On May 5, 2003, Erdogan was elected by the parliament as prime minister, while Gul was assigned minister of foreign affairs (2003–2007), after which he was elected president of the republic.[491]

The significance of Abdulla Gul's background is that a man with such a high educational level and multicultural exposure was expected to hold political beliefs similar to modern Western culture. Yet his staunch Islamic devotion indicates the profound and widespread influence of the Islamic dogma among all social classes, not only among the fatalistic lower-class, less educated people. While Gul represented the pious upper class, Erdogan exemplified the lower, less privileged classes. Both leaders reflected the beliefs of a large segment of the Turkish populace.

Abdulla Gul's background and the aforementioned background of Recep Tayyip Erdogan signify the main features of, and the transition to, the post-Kemalist secular era of the Republic of Turkey. Both leaders wanted to adjust their society to the requirements of modern times without abandoning their religious beliefs.

Upon his election to the position of prime minister in March 2003, Erdogan announced emphatically, "From now on nothing will

490 Lashnits, op. cit., pp. 89, 90.

491 Awsi, Hoshnik, The Time Bomb Between Erdogan and Gul, *Al-Khaleej*, No. 12688, February 13, 2014.

be the same in Turkey." He vowed to take action against corruption and make the government more transparent and accessible to the people. He promised to support democracy, freedom of religion and not force religious values on anyone. Both Erdogan and Gul stressed that they wanted to create a combination of a democratic Muslim government, somehow similar to an Islamic rendition of the Christian democratic countries of Europe. "We want to prove that a Muslim country could be democratic, transparent and compatible with the modern world,"[492] declared Abdulla Gul in a meeting with European leaders. Both Gul and Erdogan were pursuing the old Turkish objective to be admitted to the European Union.

Erdogan's approach towards Europe was to assure his opponents and calm their doubts about a rising Islamic theocracy. When he was reminded of his youthful strongly supportive Islamic statements and belligerent stands against Europe, he did not deny his old extreme views but explained his new attitudes by stating, "That was then, this is now." For example, he told voters, "We were anti-European; now we are pro-European. As for mixing religion and politics, Islam is a religion; democracy is a way of ruling. You can't compare the two. We just want to increase the happiness of the people."[493]

One of Erdogan's priorities was to improve the dire economic conditions he inherited from the preceding government. In November 2000, Turkey, under the rule of Prime Minister Bulent Ecevit, was suffering from a serious economic crisis. The government was in deep debt due to heavy borrowing from banks. The currency almost collapsed, there was widespread unemployment, the economy shrank by 9 percent and corruption was rampant.[494]

Erdogan and the JDP proved to be efficient organizers. The party established employment agencies to help people find jobs, opened an office in Istanbul, and made it available for people who had complaints about improper government services. The party also sponsored programs for helping the disabled and guidance for children. Immediately the people and the Turkish financial market gave Erdogan and the JDP

492 Lashnits, op. cit., p. 91.
493 Ibid.
494 Zurcher, op. cit., p. 315.

a strong vote of confidence. The value of the Turkish currency rose 4 percent, foreign agencies began to increase investments, and the stock market jumped 35 percent in the first week after the election.[495]

In the long run, the party built its reputation on the obvious economic success it achieved. Between 2002 and 2012, the economic growth reached 5.2 percent, with some temporary major jumps such as in 2010 when growth reached 9 percent, and while unemployment was reduced to lower than 5 percent. These domestic successes were accompanied by foreign investments of billions of dollars.[496]

In addition to these accomplishments, the poor classes, which had been neglected for decades, began to feel that they could take part in the political activities through the JDP government, which was open and transparent to the public. The government also provided the needy with generous amounts of food and other necessities such as free schools, free books and notebooks. Highways and transportation facilities were improved for commercial and tourism purposes. The government also built and distributed housing units for very affordable prices.[497] A nationwide poll indicated that about 70 percent of Turkish people supported Erdogan and his policy.

Erdogan and the JDP kept enforcing their religious inclination by building more mosques and religious schools for the Turkish youth. But their strategy also involved avoiding antagonizing their adversaries. Erdogan wanted to gain support from as many electoral voters as he could. While he kept reiterating his strong belief in democracy and modernization, he touched a very serious and controversial social issue—the women's headscarf. Both Erdogan's and Gul's wives wore headscarves. To avoid criticism by the anti-religious people, neither woman joined their husbands on official business. To further underscore this matter, the Erdogans sent their two daughters—wearing headscarves—to study in the U.S.

The government canceled a law that had banned university students from wearing Islamic headscarves. Both leaders stated that the law, which had been in effect since the 1920s, violated the personal

495 Lashnits, op. cit., p. 97.
496 Al-Izzi, Ghassan, "Crucial Elections in Turkey," *al-Khaleej*, No. 13156, May 27, 2015.
497 Toral, op. cit., p. 113.

freedom of individuals.[498]

The issue of women's headscarves became one of the main sources of conflict between the Islamic government of JDP and the judiciary, which was one of the ardent supporters of Kemalism and secularism. The scarf, according to the secular elite, is a symbol of a lifestyle that does not concur with the modern principles of secularism, while the Islamist majority considers it as a religious requirement and the individual's personal right.

In fact, civil courts have constantly been dealing with this social dilemma. Back in 1999, a woman and her two young daughters were imprisoned for seven months because they participated in a peaceful demonstration protesting banning scarves at the universities. The three women were accused of sedition and attempting to overthrow the secular government.

After the JDP removal of legal restrictions on women's scarves, a poll confirmed that 70 percent of the Turks stated that women should be allowed to wear scarves to government offices, public schools or anywhere in the country.[499]

After assuring his successful domestic policy, Erdogan turned his efforts towards Turkey's foreign policy. He embarked on a trip to Europe, visiting several countries to accentuate his moderate views and the benefits the European Union would get by admitting his democratic country. But his reception was lukewarm, and his critics referred to human rights abuses against minorities, the unstable government and lack of social progress.

Erdogan kept persisting with his efforts because he needed European foreign investments and loans; he needed Europe to become a large market for Turkish products. He explained to the European leaders that Turkey would become like a bridge between Christian Europe and the Muslim world, which would benefit both sides.[500] Turkey's attempts to join the EU continued.

Erdogan also sought to strengthen Turkey's relations with the Islamic world, the Arab countries, and especially with the theocratic

498 For details of the scarf controversy in Turkey, see Herman, op. cit., pp. 144-150.
499 Lashnits, op. cit., p. 100.
500 Ibid.

republic of Iran. But the relationship between Sunni Turkey and Shi'ite Iran, throughout the presidency of the fanatic Iranian President Dr. Mahmoud Ahmadinejad, was fraught with sectarian suspicion. The relations between the two Muslim countries began to improve after the moderate Dr. Hassan Rouhani was elected president of Iran in July 2013. Reciprocal visits took place between the foreign ministers of the two countries. Also, both foreign ministers, Dr. Mohammad Jayad Zarif of Iran and Dr. Mohammad Daoud Oglu of Turkey, were invited to Baghdad by Hoshyar Zebari, the foreign minister of Iraq, for a conference to coordinate their efforts to deal with problems of the region.[501]

Turkey's Prime Minister Recep Tayyip Erdogan made a very significant visit to Iran on January 29, 2014, to bolster the relations between Sunni Turkey and Shi'ite Iran in an attempt to reduce tensions between the two major Islamic factions. After the visit, Erdogan announced that the year 2014 would be a new birth for a new relationship with Iran, as both countries intended to boost their mutual commercial trade from $20 billion in 2013 to $30 billion by 2015. While Erdogan was visiting Tehran, the two countries announced the establishment of a Supreme Council for political and economic cooperation between the two peoples.[502]

The economic and political cooperation between the two countries kept growing to form an influential bloc. In 2017, they agreed to coordinate their efforts, under the guidance of Russia, to stop the several years-long bloody civil war in Syria.[503] The agreement signified the ascendance of Turkey and Iran's international status in the Middle East and worldwide.

Erdogan and the JDP government have had a peculiar relationship with the Republic of Egypt. The relations between the two predominantly Sunni Muslim countries were cordial. When Dr. Mohammad Morsi, the leader of the Muslim Brotherhood, was elected president of Egypt (June 2012–July 2013) and the Brotherhood controlled the

501 Zaidan, Nasser, "Erdogan's Significant Visit," *al-Khaleej*, No. 12679, Feb. 4, 2014.

502 Al-Rimawi, Mohammad, "Iranian-Turkish Cooperation: In Spite of Everything," *Al-Khaleej*, No. 12692, Feb. 17, 2014.

503 Report by *al-Khaleej*, No. 13765, Jan. 25, 2017.

parliament, Erdogan and his government rejoiced. During this period, Turkey and Egypt witnessed their closest relationship since the downfall of the Ottoman Empire. Erdogan hastened to further bolster his relation with the new government by welcoming members of the Brotherhood to several meetings he held in Ankara. But when President Morsi was ousted by a coup d'état in July 2013 and the Brotherhood was banned, Erdogan was infuriated. He denounced the coup and continued to hold meetings with the Brotherhood members.[504]

Erdogan's ardent support for the Brotherhood indicates the ideological identicalness between him, the JDP and the Islamic political movement of the Muslim Brotherhood. Erdogan's sympathetic attitude towards the banished Morsi and the Brotherhood provoked the wrath of the new Egyptian president, General Abdul Fattah-al-Sisi, and temporarily strained relations between the two countries.[505]

Meanwhile, a sharp disagreement occurred within the Islamic movement in Turkey that required Erdogan to concentrate on domestic affairs. The feud started when a bribery corruption scandal involving Erdogan and his son Bilal was exposed by the mass media, which provoked the resentment of Fethullah Gulen, the extremely pious Islamic leader and a close comrade of Erdogan.[506]

Recep Tayyip Erdogan and Fethullah Gulen were close friends and they both cooperated to promote their movement and guide the believers toward what they called an Islamic democratic system.

Gulen, a mystic Muslim, preached modernization of Islam and emphasized that Islam was not against democracy. He cited the early Islamic history of the period of Prophet Mohammad and his four successors, the Rashideen, the guided caliphs (632–661 AD) whose political system, Gulen claimed, was based on a social contract, that the government should be open for the people and willing to discuss and deal with the requirements of life. With these ideas and his appealing charisma, Gulen was able to rally a large number of supporters to his

504 Walad Abah, Sayid, The Arabs and the Myth of the Turkish Model, *al-Ittihad*, Abu Dhabi Aug. 30, 2012.

505 Abdul Aziz, Hashim, Egypt and Erdogan's Dreams, *al-Khaleej*, No. 13153, May 24, 2015.

506 Mazancigel, Ali, Gulen's Movement and the Modernization of Turkey, *Le Mond Diplomatique*, Nov. 2, 2014.

movement, which he called "Hizmet," meaning "serving."[507]

Gulen's Islamic modernizing movement kept growing very quickly in the 1990s. He claimed that his movement, Hizmet, was not political, but one that aimed to promote education. He was able to build a large network of elementary schools and high schools through which he promoted his calls to adopt Western technology and democracy, along with Islamic ethics. His network spread to some other Islamic countries, and it owned mass media such as the newspaper, *Zaman* (*Time*), and a television channel.[508] As a result of his diversified activities, Gulen developed a widespread reputation and became a powerful political leader.

During the general wave of suppression of Islamic currents in the 1990s, Gulen was accused of inciting religious hatred, which compelled him to take refuge in the United States in 1999. But his exile did not diminish his powerful influence or stop him from leading his movement in Turkey.[509]

From 2002 to 2011, Erdogan shrewdly exploited the powerful position of Gulen's movement to eliminate the control of armed forces and the secularists from the government and the judiciary, and to replace them with individuals of Muslim faith.[510]

Erdogan, the ever-ambitious prime minister, eagerly aspired to win the presidency by depending on his powerful religious conservative supporters. He was aware that his constituencies were basically composed of the pious rural residents who constituted the majority of the population. They were the segment which benefited from Erdogan's economic reform and supported his Islamic devotion. They considered Erdogan as their protector against the secularist elite who, if they returned to power, would close the mosques, persecute them and ban religious education, as they had done before. These concerns pushed the common people to ignore Erdogan's corruption scandals and vote for the JDP.[511]

---

507 Zurcher, op. cit., p. 291.
508 Herman, op. cit., pp. 166-170.
509 Zurcher, op. cit., p. 291.
510 Kazancigel, op. cit.
511 Faisal Jallul, Erdogan's Triumph, *al-Khaleej*, No. 12736, April 2, 2014.

Finally the long political course of Erdogan culminated on August 28, 2014, as he secured his place in history as Turkey's first popularly elected president.[512]

To reassure his followers, on several occasions Erdogan announced that Turkey is an Islamic country. He attacked the secularized Republican Party, accusing it of violating the spiritual values of the people's majority by closing the gates of the mosques and turning them into museums and animal stables. He vowed to reopen schools for imams and religious teachers and make them available for the youths to learn their religion. Further, on one occasion he surprised the world by announcing that women are not equal to men. On November 24, 2014, speaking at a summit in Istanbul on justice for women, Erdogan declared that biological differences between women and men meant they could not serve the same functions in life.[513] To justify his opinion, he said, "Our religion has defined a position for women in society—motherhood." He went on to elaborate that women and men could not be treated equally because it is against human nature. "Physiques of men and women are different. A mother's body is created to breastfeed her baby, while a man's is not equipped for that."[514]

Erdogan drew the wrath of the seculars and the feminists as he accused the women's liberation movement of being anti-motherhood. He urged the women of Turkey to have three children, and to oppose abortion and use of birth control pills. Secularists accused Erdogan of seeking to limit the civil liberties of women.[515]

Due to his ardent adherence to the Islamic dogma, encouragement of wearing the Islamic traditional scarf, and his belief in a different social status for women, the people began to wonder whether Erdogan and his JDP government would force women out of the workplace and schools, and compel them to stay home, similar to what the Islamists did in Afghanistan. These concerns prevailed in spite of Erdogan's continuous reiteration that his Islamic system also espouses democracy and modernization.

512 Mohammad Noor al-Din, "Erdogan and Turkey's Option," *al-Khaleej*, Aug. 14, 2014.

513 *The National* (Abu Dhabi), Nov. 25, 2014.

514 *Al-Khaleej*, No. 12973, Nov. 25, 2014.

515 *The National* (Abu Dhabi), Nov. 25, 2014.

The other vital issue that aroused doubts was Erdogan's persistent efforts to amend the constitution and change the parliamentary system of the government to a presidential system, which would concentrate power in the office of the president, eliminate the office of the prime minister, and reduce the power of the parliament. The secularist parties and even some Islamist movements like Gulen's Hizmet opposed the change of plans for fear that President Erdogan would assume absolute despotic authority and impose his decisions without any opposition.[516]

Corruption, uncertainties, sharp disagreements and brutal oppression caused political and economic crises. And on July 15, 2016, the Turkish people woke up to the news that the army had marched on a number of major cities and executed a coup d'état to topple the government of JDP and to oust President Erdogan.[517]

Erdogan hastened to call, by his cell phone, on the pious believers to come out and confront the "infidels." In a spectacular scene, a throng of tens of thousands of unarmed civilians stormed the tanks and armored vehicles and aborted the coup. By the next day, the coup was crushed, and the state-run agency reported that hundreds of soldiers had abandoned their weapons and surrendered to the government authorities.

That evening, President Erdogan dramatically stood on top of a bus outside his house, triumphant after squashing the military attempt by what he called a renegade faction of the military. He told his followers, "We only bow to God."[518]

Erdogan blamed the military rebellion on Gulen, even though he lived in exile hundreds of miles away in Pennsylvania, in the U.S. The authorities moved forcefully to purge Gulen's widespread network of supporters from state offices. The government issued decrees that expanded its powers under an emergency law, by which hundreds of government employees, along with undesirable academics, were purged. The nationwide clampdown by the JDP Islamic government on the

516 Mohammad Abdul Qadir Khalil, Erdogan: The President with Absolute Authority, *al-Khaleej*, No. 13759, Jan. 18, 2017.

517 Channels: CNN, BBC World News, BBC Arabic.

518 Tim Arango, Cylan Viginsu, Erdogan: Triumph After Coup Attempt, but Turkey's Fate Unknown, *The New York Times*, July 17, 2016.

opposition and secular opinions after the failed rebellion has since raised concerns about Turkey's moving toward authoritarianism.[519]

The prompt and widely popular response to President Erdogan's call for confronting the military coup d'état underscores the deep and broad spread of popular affiliation with the Islamic system of JDP. It also proves that secular Kemalism, after ruling for more than eight decades, did not penetrate the general mentality of the Turks. Even the generations that were born and raised amid the period of Kemalism remained impervious to the superficial Western aspects of behavior, such as some women without scarves smoking and drinking in public, or engaging in Western dancing with men in nightclubs. Erdogan's call for readopting the Islamic identity resonated quite favorably among a substantial portion of the Turks, which emboldened him to seek more political powers. It also encouraged other members of the JDP to demand further measures to renounce Kemalist secularism. The chairman of the parliament, Ismael Kahraman, defiantly announced that the several previous constitutions had designated Turkey as a secular country. This specification was adopted to convince the Western world to accept Turkey as part of the European continent. Yet, since the JDP was able to remove the military secular hegemony after a popular referendum was held in 2010 that supported Erdogan, the government began to undermine secularism and boost the Islamic tradition. Hence it was time for the government to respond to the people's desire and enact a new constitution based on Islamic Shari'ah.[520]

Kahraman's statement reflected the people's psychological preparation to undertake more steps towards Islamism. But the Republican People Party, which is the backbone of the secular movement, harshly responded to Kahraman's statement, demanding his resignation. The chairman of the RPP, Kemal Kilicdaroglu, stated that secularism is the safety valve of the social and political stability of the country. He also brought the attention of the JDP to the bloodshed in the Middle East caused by religious and factional conflicts.[521]

A stark historical reality is that the remarkable success of Erdogan's

519 *The Washington Post*, Turkey Detains Editor as Crackdown Expands, Nov. 1, 2016.
520 Mohammad Noorildeen, Turkey Turns Against Secularism, *al-Khaleej*, No. 13500, May 5, 2016.
521 Ibid.

Justice and Development Party in 2002 to control the parliament and the presidency marks the first major triumph of the Islamic ideology in the Middle East in the twenty-first century. It also marks the deep recession of the secular movement in its birth country, Turkey, and the advancement of the Islamic ideology set forth by Ayatollah Khomeini's revolution in Iran in 1979.

Yet, secularism in Turkey is far from dead. The secularist minority is lurking throughout the country—especially in urban areas—similar to some other parts of the Middle East, waiting for the right time and circumstances to make a political comeback.

As of January 2017, the JDP controls 317 seats in the parliament, while its adversaries, the Kemalist National Republican Party, have only 133 seats, and the Kurdish Democratic Party has 58 seats. All non-Islamic parties are attempting to form a coalition to confront President Erdogan's ambitions to assume absolute political authority.[522] But the sweeping popular support for President Erdogan and his party indicates that the Islamic rule will control Turkey, at least for the foreseeable future.

522 Mohammad Abdul Qadir-Khalil, Erdogan: A President with Absolute Authority, *al-Khaleej*, No. 13759, Jan. 18, 2017.

Chapter 10

THE ISLAMIC STATE IN IRAQ AND SYRIA (ISIS) OR, IN ARABIC, DAWLAT AL-ISLAM FI AL-IRAQ WA AL-SHAM (DAESH)

THE OTHER DRAMATIC development in the twenty-first century in the Middle East and the Islamic world, after the downfall of secular Kemalism, is the emerging and swift expansion of an ultra-fanatic Islamic organization in Iraq and Syria. It appeared in 2014 under the leadership of a man whose pseudonym is Abu Bakr al-Baghdadi, who proclaimed a self-styled Islamic caliphate.[523] His real name is Ibrahim Awwad al-Samarrai. Because he announced himself the first caliph of the Islamic world since the Ottoman caliphate was abolished in the 1920s, al-Samarrai compared himself with Abu Bakr al-Siddiq, the first caliph who ruled the Muslims after the death of Prophet Mohammad. Thus, al-Samarrai took the nom de guerre Abu Bakr.[524]

His life story is shrouded with mystery and with sparse details. He was reportedly born in 1971 to a poor Sunni Arab family in the Iraqi historic city of Samarra, located just north of Baghdad. There are equally deep conundrums and uncertainties about the origin of this ultra-fanatic religious organization which has committed, in the name of religion, heinous savagery and crimes against men, women,

523 *New York Magazine*, July 26, 2015, p. 33.

524 Jessica Stern, J.M. Berger, ISIS: The State of Terror (London: William Collins. An imprint of Harper Collins Publisher 2015), p. 33.

elders and children, slaughtering them like sheep before the eyes of terrified television viewers around the world. All opinions regarding the birth circumstances of this organization, which has terrorized unknown numbers of people, are speculative. Some writers speculate it is the offspring of al-Qaeda. What we know about ISIS today is that it emerged from the mind of Abu Musah al-Zarqawi, the Jordanian terrorist who brought a particularly brutal and sectarian approach to his understanding of jihad.[525] Al-Zarqawi is one of the leaders of al-Qaeda who deeply influenced al-Baghdadi.

In his early twenties, al-Zarqawi joined Tablighi Jamaat, an Islamist revivalist organization that preached the merits of cleaning oneself from life misdeeds. Tablighi Jamaat aims to create better Muslims through spiritual jihad, which means good deeds, contemplation and to create a just social order.[526]

Joining the Tablighi Jamaat, which means "Society for Spreading Faith," a Sunni Islamic missionary organization led Zarqawi to meet Sheikh Abu Muhammad al-Maqdisi, one of the organizers of a Salafi jihadist whose doctrine is based on the belief that any government that does not strictly follow the Islamic Shari'ah is an infidel regime that deserves to be violently overthrown.

Maqdisi would become Zarqawi's spiritual mentor and brotherly friend. After spending some time in Afghanistan, both men returned to Jordan; they were involved in organized terrorist attacks and they were imprisoned. For Zarqawi, prison was tantamount to an educational school where he met comrades and learned more about Salafi Islam. Zarqawi managed to escape from prison to Pakistan, then to Afghanistan, where he met Osama Bin Laden.[527]

When the Americans and their allies invaded Afghanistan after September 11, 2001, Zarqawi fought to defend al-Qaeda and the Taliban. Wounded in battle, in 2002, he fled to Iran and from there to northern Iraq, where he joined Ansar al-Islam (Supporter of Islam), a Kurdish jihadist group. After waging numerous terrorist attacks, Zarqawi joined al-Qaeda in Iraq (AQI), the jihadist movement under

525 Ibid, p. 13.
526 Esposito, op. cit., p. 38.
527 *Al-Khaleej*, No. 12936, Sunday, October 14, 2014.

the leadership of Osama Bin Laden.[528]

In June 2006, Abu Musab al-Zarqawi was killed as a result of an air raid by the U.S. air force. Al-Qaeda announced Zarqawi as a martyr and he was mourned by all its branches. One of al-Qaeda's leaders, Dr. Ayman al-Zawahiri, eulogized Zarqawi and used his martyrdom to call for AQI to establish an Islamic state in Iraq. Within a few months, a coalition of jihadist rebels known as the Mujahideen Shura Council declared the founding of the Islamic State of Iraq (ISI). It was headed by Abu Omar al-Baghdadi, a little-known Salafi figure, who was killed in 2010. ISI leadership was then assigned to Ibrahim Awwad Ali al-Badri al-Samarrai, better known as Abu Bakr al-Baghdadi.[529]

Some pundits assume that Abu Bakr al-Baghdadi and his organization were created by the United States, similar to the foundation of al-Qaeda and support for Bin Laden, to fight the anti-Israeli, pro-Iran Alawite government of Syria and to confront the expansionist policy of Iran. Others presume that ISIS is a spontaneously born Sunni fanatic organization in response to Sunni oppression and Iran's Shi'ite growth of power in the Middle East, especially in Iraq.[530] Some thinkers claim that ISIS was created, financed, and its wounded fighters are treated by Israel's hospitals to counter its stubborn enemy, the nationalist Ba'ath Party government of Syria under the leadership of the al-Assad family.

The latest opinion is that ISIS was born as a result of the so-called "Arab Spring," the popular rebellions that took place in certain Arab countries. It started in Tunisia in December 2010, spread to Egypt and throughout the countries of the Arab league and beyond.[531] As a result, rulers were deposed in Tunisia, Egypt (twice), Libya and Yemen. There was political upheaval in most of the other countries. Religious militants capitalized on the weakness of their governments and utilized the bitter feelings of the Sunni disenfranchisement that have become keener since the arrival of the prejudicial Shi'ite government of Prime

528 Patrick Cockburn, The Rise of Islamic State: ISIS and the New Sunni Revolution (New York: VERSO 2015), p. 9.

529 Stern, op. cit., p. 34.

530 Mazin Shindib (DAESH: mahiyyatahu, nash'atahu, irhabahu, ahdafahu, istratijeeyatahu) DAESH: Quality, Birth, Terrorism, Objectives and Strategy (Beirut: Arab Scientific Publishers, Inc. 2014), p. 107

531 Stern, op. cit., p. 39.

Minister Nuri al-Maliki after the departure of the American troops from Iraq in 2011. Thus, it is logical to assume that ISIS is the legitimate child of the Arab Spring.[532]

ISIS gained great power when numerous highly trained Sunni former Saddamist Ba'athist military ranks joined ISIS to seek employment and to fight the prejudicial Shi'ite government, which was founded by the American occupation authority after it invaded Iraq, deposed President Saddam Hussein, and implemented the policy of "de-Baathification," i.e., the eradication of the Ba'ath Party.[533]

When Abu Bakr al-Baghdadi started his leadership, the Islamic State of Iraq (ISI) had become powerful enough to wage its holy war. In 2012, amid growing Sunni hostile reactions against the prejudicial Shi'ite government of Prime Minister Nuri al-Maliki, al-Baghdadi boldly and defiantly announced a movement to "break down the walls," by which he promised to free his alleged insurgent jihadist comrades from their prisons.[534]

Using clandestine means to contact the prisoners in advance, ISI fulfilled Baghdadi's promise. The insurgents attacked eight prisons with weapons. They freed hundreds of prisoners, many of whom were senior leaders of ISI, or experienced ex-military officers who, after they were freed, joined the organization.

Late in the same year, Baghdadi announced the expansion of the Islamic State in Iraq (ISI) to become the Islamic State in Iraq and Syria (ISIS).

In a swift attack in January 2014, ISIS took over Fallujah (a town just forty miles west of Baghdad that had made history when it was beleaguered and invaded by the U.S. Marines ten years earlier), and the Americans suffered thousands of casualties in the takeover.

On June 6, 2014, ISIS fighters began their attacks on Mosul, the second-largest city in Iraq and a very important economic hub with its commercial centers and rich oil fields. Four days later, the city fell under the control of ISIS. The enormous amounts of funds and riches that the organization usurped are unknown. It was a surprising

532 Ibid.

533 Robin Moore, Hunting Down Saddam: The Inside Story of the Search and Capture (New York: St. Martin Press 2004), pp. 4, 5, 254, 269.

534 Stern, op. cit., p. 39.

military success by a small force of approximately 1,300 fighters against a 60,000-strong force that included a powerfully equipped army and police force.[535]

> Oh my Umma [nation] a new dawn has emerged, so witness the clear victory the Islamic state has been established by the blood of the truthful. No one will ever stand between the mujahideen and their people in Iraq after this day.[536]

Thus chanted the jihadist fighters of ISIS.

When two veteran members of parliament were asked why Iraq's one-million-strong security forces had been so inept against the jihadists, the answers were: "This is the harvest of total corruption. People pay money to join the army so they get a salary." Whereas the strength of the fundamentalist movement is derived from their belief that there is something inevitable and divinely inspired about its capability to confront the superior army or the formidable U.S. air power at Kobani, Syria.

Victoriously flaunting their black ISIS flag and marching everywhere in the territories they occupied, the jihadists kept augmenting their powers in Iraq and Syria and preaching apocalyptic prophecy: "And so the flame we started in Iraq, and its heat will increase by the will of Allah until it burns the crusaders in Daliq."[537] (Daliq is a town in Syria that ISIS fighters believed would be the field of the final battle with the "crusaders.")

After controlling the eastern borders of Syria and bolstering its hold on the strategically important town of al-Raqqa, the jihadists expanded their control westward, enforcing their own Islamic dogma, killing and executing people in the city's main square, banning smoking and consumption or sales of alcohol and imposing *jiziah* (tax) on Christians, for protection, according to Islamic Shari'ah. Even though ISIS is focused in Iraq, it does not consider Syria and Iraq to be separated. The two countries are considered one battlefield and the caliphate had effaced the

535 Cockburn, op. cit., p. 11.
536 Stern, op. cit., p. 112.
537 Ibid.

post-colonial borders, i.e., the Sykes-Picot Agreement imposed in 1916 by England and France to divide the Arab world into small entities to prevent them from uniting to form one powerful Arab state.

By 2015, the caliphate territory under the control of ISIS stretched from Turkey's borders with Syria to Mosul and Fallujah in Iraq, an area roughly the size of the U.S. state of Indiana. The lands controlled by the ISIS caliphate encompassed almost two-thirds of Syria and one-third of Iraq.[538]

For the U.S., Britain and the Western world, the birth and fast growth of the Islamic caliphate was a catastrophic development. Whatever they expected from their invasion of Iraq and the unseating of the national government of Saddam Hussein in 2003 or their efforts to depose Bashar al-Assad in Syria since 2011, all of these schemes by the Western countries ended in a huge fiasco. They never envisaged the rebirth of an Islamic caliphate after it was abolished in 1924, or the creation of a jihadist state almost the size of Britain, spanning northern Iraq and Syria, run by an organization a hundred times larger and much better organized than the notorious al-Qaeda of Osama Bin Laden. The war on terror waged by America and its allies, which restricted civil liberties and cost hundreds of billions of dollars, ended in a disastrous failure.[539]

Due to the swift and spectacular victories of ISIS against larger and stronger armies of Iraq and Syria, al-Baghdadi claimed divine support and was able to attract thousands of young believers in jihad "in the path of God" to join ISIS.

In an interview over the Internet by the American journal *Foreign Policy*, one of the ISIS leaders with the pseudonym of Abu Ahmad revealed epochal information. The details of the interview were translated and prepared for the newspaper *Al-Khaleej* by Ammar Awdah.[540] After investigating and authenticating his top leadership position in ISIS, the journal disclosed that Abu Ahmad stated that ISIS was created "by a big lie." He claimed that no one knows who Abu-Bakr al-Baghdadi is, or where he got his authority from, as his claimed relationship with

538 See details and map in the *Economist*, April 11-17, 2015, pp. 34, 35.
539 Cockburn, op. cit., p. 38.
540 *Al-Khaleej*, No. 13616, August 29, 2016.

al-Qaeda leadership was never confirmed. Abu Ahmad's declaration further complicated the information about the mysterious identity of al-Baghdadi and the origin of his equally shadowy organization.

Abu Ahmad was born in a city in northern Syria into a traditional religious family, and as a fanatic young student, he joined the anti-Bashar al-Assad revolution. He attended and described the notorious meeting of what is known as *Majlis Shura al-Mujahideen* (the Consultation Assembly of the Religious Fighters) in the town of Kafr Hamrah, which was attended by al-Baghdadi and a number of the most dangerous terrorists in the world, such as Abu al-Atheer, abu al-Misri, commander of the Egyptian fighters, Omar al-Shishani, one of the most wanted terrorists who came to Syria from Russian Georgia, Abu al-Waleed al-Leebi, a jihadist who came from Libya, Abdulla al-Leebi, the commander of Battar battalion, and two members of al-Nusra Front terrorist group. Al-Nusra was controlling the town of al-Raqqa before an armed conflict erupted with ISIS and al-Nusra was forced out of the city, which became headquarters for ISIS in Syria.[541]

Abu Ahmad revealed more ominous information that ISIS defeated a Syrian military unit in Khan al-Aral, a town close to Aleppo, and collected numerous barrels of chemical weapons which were used against the Syrian army, also killing civilians. Then the leadership of ISIS accused the Syrian army of committing that heinous crime. Abu Ahmad quoted the infamous terrorist Abu al-Atheer, bragging about sending cars loaded with chemical weapons to attack several Syrian military camps located in different cities. The last assault claimed by Abu al-Atheer was when he sent two hundred cars and trucks loaded with chemical weapons to carry out an attack that caused carnage in the city of Kafr Jom.[542]

In his elaboration to the *Foreign Policy*, Abu Ahmad asserted that young people from different parts of the world have been joining ISIS. Some of them are true believers who want to take part in the jihad, some are adventurers seeking salaries, while he describes others as demented butchers who enjoy cutting and collecting human heads.

541 *Al-Khaleej*, No. 13138, May 9, 2015.
542 *Al-Khaleej*, No. 13616, August 29, 2016.

The International Centre for the Study of Radicalism (ICSR) sets forth a detailed report, quoted by *Al-Khaleej*, showing the numbers of jihadist volunteers and the countries from which they came to join ISIS.[543]

Countries	**Number of Jihadist Volunteers**
Tunisia	3,000
Saudi Arabia	2,500
Jordan	1,500
Morocco	1,500
Lebanon	900
Russia	800
France	700
Libya	600
Britain	500
Germany	400
Turkey	400
Egypt	360
Pakistan	330
Belgium	300
Australia	250
Algeria	200
Kazakhstan	150
Holland	150
Albania	140
Kosovo	120
Total	16,300

543 Ibid.

After controlling a large population and a broad territory, leadership of ISIS endeavored to create a government structure to manage their present and future military, financial and immigration affairs. Several researchers attempted to delve into the political system of the caliphate, but the organization has not disclosed these details due to its secretive nature. However, after strenuous efforts, the following information was obtained by some inquirers to describe the structure of the Islamic State:[544]

1. The caliph: His pseudonym is Abu Bakr al-Baghdadi. His real name is Ibrahim Awwad Ibrahim al-Badri. He prefers to be addressed as Caliph Ibrahim.
2. Assistants: Al-Baghdadi is assisted by Abu Muslim al-Turkmani, who is in charge of managing the affairs of the province of Iraq, while Ali al-Anbari manages the affairs of Syria.
3. The military commander: Omar al-Shishani, a red-headed and bearded man, is the highest military commander and he supervises all military operations.
4. The official spokesperson: His name is Abu Mohammad al-Adnani, who is one of the highest leaders. He announced several verbal messages, the most well-known of which was the announcement of the founding of the caliphate.
5. Majlis al-Shura: This consultation council consists of responsible and high-positioned leaders of the organization who provide advice for al-Baghdadi and implement his orders. The reports also indicate that ISIS has other councils, each of which specializes in certain duties such as military matters, security, finance and media.
6. The provinces: The Order divided the territories under its authority into provinces, some of which are Neinawa, Diala, Baghdad, Kirkuk, Dair al-Zor in Iraq, and al-Baraka, al-Hiskah and Aleppo in Syria. Additionally, they have the Euphrates province, which includes Albukamal (Syria) and al-Qa'im (Iraq). Each province has its local military and administrative systems.

544 *Al-Khaleej*, No. 12960, November 12, 2014.

Due to the extremely secretive nature of the leadership of ISIS, the above information is the most verifiable that the investigators were able to obtain and share.

To reach out and influence as many believers as possible, ISIS adopted a *nasheed* (anthem) that they repeatedly broadcast to the world. It is as follows:[545]

> Our state was established upon Islam and although it wages jihad against the enemies, it governs the affairs of the people. It looks after its flock with love and patience. It does so carefully, and thereby does not receive any censure. The Shari'ah of our Lord is right, by it we rise over the stars. By it, we live without humiliation, a life of peace and security.

Chanting this anthem repeatedly, ISIS in August 2014 marked the arrival of *Eid al-Fitr* (the feast of ending the fasting of the holy month of Ramadan). A spokesman announced the following call:

> I am calling on all Muslims living in the West, America, Europe, and everywhere else to come to make (hijra) emigration with your families to the land of "Khilafah." Here, you go for fighting and afterwards you come back to your families. And if you get killed, then you'll enter heaven, God willing, and Allah will take care of those you've left behind. So here, the Caliphate will take care of you.[546]

Thus a new theocracy based on terrorism, unlimited violence and bloodshed was born in the Middle East, and it kept growing militarily and economically. The collapse of the Iraqi army and their abandonment in Mosul provided the caliphate with enormous amounts of a sophisticated assortment of weapons, which augmented the organization's military prowess and the morale of its fighters. Also, controlling

545 Stern, op. cit., p. 75.
546 Ibid.

oil fields, banks, and agricultural products within the lands it occupies provided ISIS with substantial amounts of funds to sustain all its economic needs and purchase more destructive weapons.[547]

After seizing several oil fields and Iraq's largest dam, the Islamic State controlled another powerful weapon besides oil—agricultural products. Fighters of ISIS had controlled large areas in several of Iraq's most fertile provinces, where, according to the United Nations food agency, about 40 percent of the country's wheat is grown. The jihadists overran grain stores in government silos, ground the grains, and sold flour to the local markets to finance their brutal activities.[548]

ISIS sells a barrel of oil for $25-30 a day in comparison to the $100 market price, which provides the Islamic caliphate with more than $1.5 million daily by selling 66,000 barrels per day.[549]

With such exorbitant funds, ISIS is able to sustain its expenses, purchasing all the weapons and equipment it needs and paying handsome salaries to its fighters.

After some heinous attacks in Europe and the occupation of Mosul by ISIS, the world became alarmed about the threat of the spread of barbaric terror attacks all over the world. Then-President Barack Obama hastened to establish a military coalition force constituted of air forces and armies from several European countries to combat ISIS and other terrorist groups. The coalition attacks in support of the armies of Iraq, Syria, the Kurdish Peshmerga and the *Hashd al-Sha'bi* (popular mobilization) militias in Iraq began their systematic attacks against ISIS, al-Nusra and other terrorist groups.[550]

Throughout 2016, relentless attacks by the coalition air raids and the local pro-government fighters in Iraq and Syria checked the growth and expansion of ISIS, and it began to retreat.

In a public message, the group leaders acknowledged the terrorist organization's dwindling fortune on the battlefield while facing the possibilities of gradually losing its strongholds.

547 See Vikeen Shiterman, A Phantom State in the Middle East, *La Monde Diplomatique*, Nov. 26, 2014.

548 Maggi Ficks, Maha al-Dahhan, ISIS State in Wheat Seizure, *The National*, August 15, 2014.

549 See details and oil fields under ISIS control in *Al-Khaleej*, No. 12910, September 23, 2014.

550 *Al-Khaleej*, No. 13666, October 18, 2016.

Although the loss of physical sanctuaries would constitute a major setback to the Islamic State, sharply limiting its capability to raise funds, train new volunteers or plan to wage difficult terrorist attacks, the group's decentralized system protects it against its adversaries and it will remain dangerous for a while, according to terrorist experts. Michael Hayden, the retired Air Force general who headed the CIA from 2006 to 2009, asserts that while al-Qaeda's hierarchical system made it somewhat predictable, ISIS's highly decentralized nature makes it very unpredictable.[551]

General Hayden's statements were confirmed when ISIS waged a terrorist attack in Istanbul on the night of New Year's Eve, December 31, 2017, which killed thirty-nine people, and three days later in January a series of attacks hit Baghdad while France's President Francois Hollande was visiting the Iraqi government to coordinate their efforts to combat terrorism in the Middle East.[552]

However, due to the relentless air and land attacks, the Islamic caliphate no doubt is moribund. Before the end of 2016, it had substantially shrunk, and by March 2017, it was helplessly confined into a small part of Mosul, while the military coalition's assaults are killing tens of jihadists daily. The United States is already hoping and planning to establish a liberal-democratic system in Iraq and Syria during the post-ISIS era.

On April 7, 2017, CNN, BBC International and other worldwide international television channels announced that the United States' fleet in the Eastern Mediterranean Sea launched cruise missile attacks, inflicting severe damage to the Syrian military defense system. The bombardment of Syria indicates that U.S. President Donald Trump started a two-prong military operation: to expedite the downfall of the abominable Syrian dictatorial regime, while continuing the air strikes to eradicate the religious terrorist movements of ISIS and others in both Iraq and Syria. Obviously President Trump is attempting to remove all impediments standing against the United States' intentions to rebuild the Middle East on a liberal-democratic basis. Hence the latest episode of tumult is typical of conflict between different ideologies in the Middle East, which will continue for the foreseeable future.

551 John Wagner, ISIS readies for fall of caliphate, *Washington Post*, July 13, 2016.
552 *Al-Khaleej*, No. 13743, January 3, 2017.

Chapter 11

CONCLUSION

THIS STUDY IS based on the framework of the philosophy of Georg Wilhelm Hegel (1770–1831) and his perception of the dialectical conflict of opposite ideologies, which is the pivot of historical development. It also discusses Hegel's accentuation of the role of leadership figures who adopt and preach the ideology, which then becomes the cause of social solidarity and rallies the believers around the leader, who guides them toward accomplishing his and his followers' objectives.

The author of this book utilizes Hegel's philosophy to elaborate on the gory upheaval caused by the conflict of the religious and secular ideologies which precipitated profound social and political changes in the Middle East.

By scrutinizing the nature of modern history of the Middle East, a stark fact becomes obvious: both religious and secular ideologies are there to stay. They are both viable and active and neither of them is going to disappear, at least during the foreseeable future.

Each one of the previously discussed leaders studiously promoted the ideology he believed in while attempting to eradicate, or at least undermine, the opposite ideology. But they all failed. Kemal Ataturk spared no means to eliminate religion from his secular Republic of Turkey. Gamal Abdel Nasser used his prevalent charismatic personality to impose his nationalist-socialism on the conservative Sunni Egyptian people while pushing back the role of religion. Ayatollah Khomeini's overwhelming religious leadership swept the Middle East and turned

Iran into a full-fledged Shi'ite Islamic theocracy while brutalizing the secularists. Nevertheless, none of these leaders was able to fully eliminate the ideologies opposing his own. Secular Kemalism succumbed to the popularly elected pious leader Recep Tayyip Erdogan and his Islamic Justice and Development Party. The Muslim Brotherhood in Egypt made a powerful comeback years after Nasser's death, and they won a popular vote to the presidency. The secularists in Iran's theocracy are still active and hoping to assume power. President Erdogan exploited the coup d'état of 2016 to brutalize the secular and all other opponents. Thus, the Middle East remains a battlefield for dialectical conflict between religious and secular ideologies.

Hence, what the region needs is an effective and wise leadership that is able to synthesize both ideologies in order to stop the bloodshed and reconcile the violent animosity. Is such a proposal feasible? It was successfully achieved by King Faisal I, who ruled the kingdom of Iraq from 1921 to 1933 (see Chapter 2).

King Faisal personified the leader with the political acumen to integrate the diverse religious, factional and ethnic minorities to establish a modernizing country without antagonizing the clergy or the pious people. Being a descendant of Prophet Mohammad's Hashimite family, he was able to gain the loyalty of the powerful Shi'ite community, while he was able to rally the Sunnis behind him due to his Sunni family background.

Utilizing his charisma, the experience he gained from participating in World War I, the wisdom he acquired from dealing with the Great Powers, and his deep knowledge of the Arab cultures, Faisal was able to integrate the diverse components of the Iraqi population to create a comprehensive national identity of Iraq.

Using his respectable status and convincing logic, Faisal hastened to extricate Iraq from the archaic social and political institutions of the Ottoman theocracy and propel his country into the process of modernization. His main instrument was adopting a modern educational system, and he enlisted one of his close followers, the renowned Professor Sati' al-Husary, an ardent believer in secular Kemalism, who outlined a modern pedagogical curriculum akin to that of Great Britain. Within two decades, the number of elementary and secondary schools multiplied tenfold. The spread of schools augmented the size of the middle class, who were rather more broad-minded and tolerant of diversity than their rigid Ottoman parents. In the 1920s and '30s, Iraq witnessed the birth of political movements ranging from the left socialist through the liberal pro-Western to the ardent religious. Women's social and economic status improved as a result of the new regime's encouragement of girls' education. In the northern part of Iraq, where the most traditional and conservative social traditions existed, former Colonel Amin Zaki, a multilingual scholar, was assigned as the director and inspector of education of the Northern Province. Professor Amin Zaki built and spread modern schools within his administrative territory without alienating the traditions that have been practiced for centuries. Utilizing his fluent Kurdish and Turkish languages, Amin Zaki understood the almost impossible mission of explaining to the leaders of the Kurds, Turkman and even the most uninformed Yazidi community that modern education did not contravene their religious instructions. Thus, he succeeded in building a number of modern schools in several parts of the north, even in Senjar, the isolated, mountainous and most underdeveloped town of the Yazidis. A number of the northern minorities became members of the Iraqi parliament and were thereby exposed to liberal aspects of political life. Also, younger generations of Kurds, Turkman, Shi'ites and Sunnis graduated from high schools and colleges and were qualified for different careers.

In summary, the Middle East needs leadership that espouses the right educational system which would teach the benefits of a liberal-Democratic system that could coexist in harmony with the people's religious beliefs. The historical role of religion promoting morality and righteousness should not be ignored or neglected.

An appropriate leadership may have a constructive role to find a remedy for the ideological conflict in the Middle East. In the last century, King Faisal I of Iraq was able to combine secular and religious learning to modernize and advance his country. Presently there are widespread demands by the growing numbers of educated people to require their government to hold honest political elections and allow freedom of opinion and equality for all while keeping religion alive in the mosques and churches.

In the Hashemite Kingdom of Jordan, the late King Hussein Bin Talal (1952–1999) and his son Abdullah Bin al-Hussein (1999–) have been pursuing a social and political system akin to that of the Hashemite Kingdom of Iraq, created, ruled and advanced by their relative, the late King Faisal the First. Both Kings Hussein and Abdullah have been able to achieve socio-political progress without antagonizing the religious institutions. Both of them have attempted to gradually reduce the influence of the archaic tribal system, and focus on advancing democracy, secular education for males and females, social equality and modernization to propel their country in the twenty-first century.

In Egypt, President General Abdul Fattah al-Sisi is doing his best, in spite of Islamic terrorist attacks, to enforce a balance between religion and politics and to encourage women to seek the highest political, administrative and judicial positions. (See details in *Al-Khaleej*, No. 13828, March 29, 2017.) The Tunisian president, Beji Caid Essebsi, is following the course of President Sisi to reform his country. In Iran and Iraq, women are demanding more freedom and aspiring to run for political and social privileges.

To use similar historic conditions, Europe went through the same stages after the Enlightenment era and the tumultuous labor period of the French revolution. It was the period when Europe was reborn and became the haven of democracy living side by side with ardent Christianity.

So, it is not far-fetched to hope that the new Middle Eastern generations are witnessing a period of social development that will eventually lead to more tolerant and progressive conditions, and that the people in the Middle East will live under better political and social circumstances.

GLOSSARY

Aba'ah	A black robe Muslim women cover themselves with in public from head to foot. In Iran it is called *chador*. The garment is indicative of decency and adherence to tradition.
Abayah	*See* Aba'ah.
Ahkam	Ordinances derived from the Quran or the Sunnah (tradition).
Ahl al-Kitab	People of the scripture, or of the book. Also called *dhimi*. They are the Jews and Christians under the protection of Islam.
Ahmad	The praised one. Another name for Prophet Mohammad.
Ayatollah	Sign of God. It is the highest clergy position in the Shi'ite sect.
Bay'ah	Fealty, election, selection practiced by the Muslim community to choose their leaders after Prophet Mohammad's death.
Caliph	Successor. It is the title acquired by Muslim leaders who succeeded Prophet Mohammad's death.

DAESH	(Arabic). Dawlat al-Islam fi al-Iraqi wa al-sham. In English it is ISIS. A fanatic terrorist group that emerged in Iraq and Syria in 2014. It committed heinous acts of terrorism in several parts of the world.
Da'wah	Evangelical call for adoption of a religion.
Dhimi	*See* Ahl al-Kitab.
Eid	Muslims' feast. Muslims celebrate two feasts: the fitir eid, which comes after the holy month of Ramadan when they stop fasting, and the Adha eid, or feast of sacrifice commemorating Prophet Abraham's sacrifice of the lamb.
Faqih	A jurisprudent or jurist authorized to interpret and make decisions based on Shari'ah and tradition.
Fiqh	Jurisprudence, interpretation of Islamic code.
Hadith	Prophet Mohammad's statement or opinion.
Hajj	Annual pilgrimage by Muslims to Mekka. Hajj is required only once in a lifetime by Muslim males and females.
Hajji	(male; hajjiyah, female) A title acquired permanently by persons who had fulfilled the religious duty of pilgrimage.
Haram	Taboo; religiously forbidden behavior or food.
Hijab	Veil or face cover worn by Muslim women in public.
Hijrah	Immigration. Prophet Mohammad's flight in 622 from Mekka to Madinah, where he established the first Islamic theocratic state.

Hijri	The Islamic calendar that began with Prophet Mohammad's hijrah from Mekka to Madinah to escape persecution by the idol worshippers.
Hizb	Party.
Hezbollah	Party of God. A Shi'ite fundamentalist party whose main headquarters is located in Lebanon, and it is active in other parts of the Middle East.
Ibn Taymiyah	The ultra-fanatic Sunni medieval Sufi theologian (died in 1329) who belonged to the strict Hanbali school of jurisprudence. He inspired the Wahabi Ikhwan movement and present time al-Ikhwan al-Muslimun and Osama Bin Laden, the founder and mastermind of the al-Qaeda organization.
Al-Ikhwan al-Muslimun	The Muslim Brotherhood. A fanatic Sunni Islamic movement, born in Egypt in 1928 to confront the westernization and secular movements that were growing in the Middle East.
Imam	Religious leader. A title ascribed by the Shi'ite sect to Prophet Mohammad's cousin, Ali Bin Abi Talib and his descendants. Also a man who leads Muslims' daily prayers.
Islam	Full submission to God. The religion revealed to Prophet Mohammad.
ISIS	Islamic State in Iraq and Syria. See DAESH.
Jihad	Holy war against the enemies of Islam.
Jizyah	A tax levied by the Islamic State on non-Muslim "dhimmi" working men.

Kabah	The holiest, cubic-shaped shrine toward which Muslims worldwide direct their daily prayers. It is located in the Grand Mosque in Mekka. Muslims annually gather around Kabah to perform their hajj rituals.
Kafir	Atheist, non-believer or blasphemous.
Kemalism	The secular modernization philosophy of Mustafa Kemal Ataturk, who created and became the first president of the Republic of Turkey.
Khaleefah	*See* Caliph.
Kufr	Atheism and blaspheme.
Al-Mahdi al-Muntadhar	Meaning of the name "the waited for, divinely guided one." The Islamic perception of the Messiah who would come back from time to fill the earth with justice and prosperity.
Majlis Shura	Consultation council.
Mufti	A faqih authorized to give legal decisions based on Shari'ah or tradition of Prophet Mohammad.
Muharram	The first month of the Islamic calendar, during which the Shi'ite sect mourn to commemorate the martyrdom of Imam al-Hussein, the son of Ali Bin Abi Talib.
Mujahid	(pl. Mujahideen) Holy warrior.
Mujtahid	One qualified to give an intellectual interpretation of Islamic law.
Mullah	A cleric.

Mustakbir	(pl. Mustakbirin) The proud, powerful and persecutors of the weak.
Mustaza'f	(pl. Mustaz'afin) The weak, deprived and persecuted people.
Muslim	One who surrenders to God. A person who belongs to Islamic faith.
Ommah	Nation.
Qadi	An Islamic judge.
Salafi	One who follows the piety of the ancestors; i.e., the first Muslim generation.
Salah	Prayer. A Muslim person is required to pray five times per day.
Salat	*See* salah.
Shahid	(pl. Shuhada') Martyr, a person who dies for the sake of God.
Shari'ah	The Islamic code.
Shaykh	Tribal chief, elder, a man who belongs to a mystic order.
Shi'ah	Followers or party. The Islamic sect constituted of the people who follow and revere Ali Bin Abi Talib and his descendants. The Shi'ah believe that Ali was the first legitimate caliph to succeed Prophet Mohammad.
Sufi	Religious people belonging to mystic orders.
Sunni	The Muslim sect that follow the Quran and Prophet Mohammad's tradition.

Taqiah	Disguise or protection. A Shi'ite practice to disguise their rituals to protect themselves against persecution.
Taqwa	Piety.
Ulema	Religious knowledgeable men and clergy.
Ummah	*See* ommah.
Zakah	Annual tax deduction from income of Muslims to distribute as charity to the poor.
Zakat	*See* zakah.

INDEX

B

F

G

H

I

J

K

L

N

Q

R

S

T

CPSIA information can be obtained
at www.ICGtesting.com
Printed in the USA
LVHW08s1038080718
583075LV00001B/122/P

9 781478 796268